LIBRARY OF NEW TESTAMENT STUDIES
466

Formerly the Journal for the Study of the New Testament Supplement Series

Editor
Mark Goodacre

GENESIS IN THE NEW TESTAMENT

Edited by

MAARTEN J. J. MENKEN
STEVE MOYISE

B L O O M S B U R Y
LONDON • NEW DELHI • NEW YORK • SYDNEY

Bloomsbury T&T Clark
An imprint of Bloomsbury Publishing Plc

50 Bedford Square   1385 Broadway
London   New York
WC1B 3DP   NY 10018
UK   USA

www.bloomsbury.com

Bloomsbury is a registered trade mark of Bloomsbury Publishing Plc

First published 2012
Paperback edition first published 2014

British Library Cataloguing-in-Publication Data
A catalogue record for this book is available from the British Library.

ISBN: HB: 978-0-5675-6302-6
PB: 978-0-567-24698-1

Library of Congress Cataloging-in-Publication Data
A catalog record for this book is available from the Library of Congress.

Typeset by Free Range Book Design & Production

CONTENTS

ABBREVIATIONS

AB	Anchor Bible
ABD	D. N. Freedman (ed.), *The Anchor Bible Dictionary* (6 vols; New York: Doubleday, 1992)
AnBib	Analecta biblica
ASTI	*Annual of the Swedish Theological Institute*
AUSS	*Andrews University Seminary Studies*
BBR	*Bulletin for Biblical Research*
BDAG	W. Bauer, F. W. Danker, W. F. Arndt, and F. W. Gingrich, *Greek-English Lexicon of the New Testament and Other Early Christian Literature*, 3rd edn, Chicago, 1999
BDB	F. Brown, S. R. Driver and C. A. Briggs (eds), *A Hebrew and English Lexicon of the Old Testament* (Oxford: Clarendon, 1907)
BECNT	Baker Exegetical Commentary on the New Testament
BETL	Bibliotheca Ephemeridum Theologicarum Lovaniensium
Bib	*Biblica*
BIS	Biblical Interpretation Series
BKAT	Biblischer Kommentar: Altes Testament
BNTC	Black's New Testament Commentaries
BU	Biblische Untersuchungen
BZNW	Beihefte zur ZNW
CBQ	*Catholic Biblical Quarterly*
CBQMS	Catholic Biblical Quarterly, Monograph Series
CChrSL	Corpus Christianorum: Series Latina
ConBNT	Coniectanea Biblica, New Testament
CSCO	Corpus Scriptorum Christianorum Orientalium
CTR	*Criswell Theological Review*
DJD	Discoveries in the Judaean Desert
DSD	*Dead Sea Discoveries*
ECC	Eerdmans Critical Commentary
EKK	Evangelisch-katholischer Kommentar
ESEC	Emory Studies in Early Christianity
FAT	Forschungen zum Alten Testament
HDR	Harvard Dissertations in Religion
HTKNT	Herders theologischer Kommentar zum Neuen Testament
HTR	*Harvard Theological Studies*
IBS	*Irish Biblical Studies*

ICC	International Critical Commentary
JBL	*Journal of Biblical Literature*
JPS	Jewish Publication Society
JSHRZ	Jüdische Schriften aus hellenistisch-römischer Zeit
JSJSup	Journal for the Study of Judaism, Supplement Series
JSNT	*Journal for the Study of the New Testament*
JSNTSup	Journal for the Study of the New Testament, Supplement Series
JSOT	*Journal for the Study of the Old Testament*
JSOTSup	Journal for the Study of the Old Testament, Supplement Series
JSP	*Journal for the Study of the Pseudepigrapha*
JSPSup	Journal for the Study of the Pseudepigrapha, Supplement Series
JSSM	Journal of Semitic Studies, Monograph Series
KEK	Kritisch-exegetischer Kommentar
LBT	Latin Biblical Texts
LNTS	Library of New Testament Studies
LSJ	Liddell, Scott, Jones, *Greek-English Lexicon* (Oxford: Clarendon, 1968)
LSTS	Library of Second Temple Studies
NA^{27}	Nestle and Aland, *Novum Testamentum Graece* (Stuttgart: Deutsche Bibelgesellschaft, 27th edn, 1993)
NCBC	New Century Bible Commentary
Neot	*Neotestamentica*
NICNT	New International Commentary on the New Testament
NIGTC	New International Greek Testament Commentary
NovT	*Novum Testamentum*
NovTSup	Novum Testamentum, Supplements
NTL	New Testament Library
NTS	*New Testament Studies*
OTL	Old Testament Library
OTP	*Old Testament Pseudepigrapha* (ed. J. H. Charlesworth)
PRS	*Perspectives in Religious Studies*
RevQ	*Revue de Qumran*
SBL	Society of Biblical Literature
SBLDS	SBL Dissertation Series
SBLEJL	SBL Early Judaism and its Literature
SBLSCS	SBL Septuagint and Cognate Studies
SBLSP	SBL Seminar Papers
SNTA	Studiorum Novi Testamenti Auxilia
SNTSMS	Society for New Testament Studies Monograph Series
SP	Sacra pagina
SPB	Studia Postbiblica
ST	*Studia Theologica*

STDJ	Studies on the Texts of the Desert of Judah
SVTP	Studia in Veteris Testament Pseudepigrapha
TB	Theologische Bücherei
THKNT	Theologischer Handkommentar zum Neuen Testament
UBS[4]	United Bible Societies *Greek New Testament*, 4th edn
VT	*Vetus Testamentum*
VTSup	Vetus Testamentum, Supplements
WBC	Word Biblical Commentary
WTJ	*Westminster Theological Journal*
WUNT	Wissenschaftliche Untersuchungen zum Neuen Testament
ZNW	*Zeitschrift für die neutestamentliche Wissenschaft*

List of Contributors

James W. Aageson is Dean of Arts and Sciences and Professor of New Testament and Early Christianity at Concordia College, Moorhead, Minnesota (USA), and author of *Paul, the Pastoral Epistles, and the Early Church* (Hendrickson, 2008).

Steve P. Ahearne-Kroll is Associate Professor of New Testament at Methodist Theological School in Ohio (USA) and author of *The Psalms of Lament in Mark's Gospel: Jesus' Davidic Suffering* (Cambridge University Press, 2007).

David M. Allen is tutor in New Testament at the Queen's Foundation for Ecumenical Theological Education (UK) and author of *Deuteronomy and Exhortation in Hebrews: A Study in Narrative Re-presentation* (Mohr Siebeck, 2008).

Jeannine K. Brown is Professor of New Testament at Bethel Seminary (St Paul, Minnesota, USA) and author of *Scripture as Communication* (Baker Academic, 2007).

Susan Docherty is Principal Lecturer in Biblical Studies and Head of the Department of Theology at Newman University College Birmingham (UK) and author of *The Use of the Old Testament in Hebrews* (Mohr Siebeck, 2009).

David Lincicum is Leverhulme Early Career Fellow in Theology at the University of Oxford and Research Fellow at Mansfield College (UK) and author of *Paul and the Early Jewish Encounter with Deuteronomy* (Mohr Siebeck, 2010).

Peter Mallen is Pastor of Rosanna Uniting Church in Melbourne, Australia, Lay Educator for the Banyule Network of Uniting Churches and author of *The Reading and Transformation of Isaiah in Luke-Acts* (T&T Clark, 2008).

Maarten J. J. Menken is Professor of New Testament Exegesis at the Tilburg School of Theology, University of Tilburg (The Netherlands), and author of *1, 2 en 3 Johannes: Een praktische bijbelverklaring* (Kok, 2010).

Steve Moyise is Professor of New Testament at the University of Chichester (UK) and author of *Evoking Scripture: Seeing the Old Testament in the New* (T&T Clark, 2008).

Jacques T. A. G. M. van Ruiten is Professor of the Reception History of the Bible at the University of Groningen (The Netherlands) and author of *Abraham in the Book of Jubilees* (Brill, 2012).

INTRODUCTION

Even in our secularized time, many stories from the biblical book of Genesis are still fairly well known. Lots of people know, at least in broad outline, the narratives of God creating the world in seven days, moulding Adam from dust and making Eve out of one of his ribs, of Eve and Adam eating from the forbidden fruit and being driven out of paradise, of Cain killing his brother Abel, of Noah and the flood, of the tower of Babel, and so on. Many people consider these stories as myth (in the negative sense of this word), others as literal religious truth, still others try to arrive at a more sophisticated religious understanding of them. Through the ages, Jews and Christians have considered Genesis as an authoritative, divinely inspired text, the first book of the Torah or Pentateuch and thus of the entire Bible. The book spoke (in pre-scientific, religious language, of course) to them of the origin of the world and of humankind, it explained how evil came into the world, it related how God chose one individual, Abraham, and his family as the beginning of his people. Through its religious significance, Genesis has also had a considerable cultural and artistic impact. One only has to think of Rembrandt's well known painting of Jacob blessing the sons of Joseph, for example, or Haydn's oratorio *Die Schöpfung*.

The first generations of followers of Jesus read the Scriptures, the Christian Old Testament, as referring in various ways to their Lord and to themselves as a community. Genesis was a prominent part of Scripture and thus an important source for early Christian preaching and theology, not only in the early phase when most followers of Jesus were Jews, but also later when the Christian communities became predominantly Gentile. Approximately 30 verses of Genesis are quoted in the New Testament, along with numerous allusions and other references.[1] The quotations are drawn mainly from the creation accounts[2] and the stories of Abraham,[3] along with a few references to Isaac and other people such

---

1   Most scholars would agree that the number of quotations is not necessarily a reliable guide to the importance of a particular book (or section of a book) but it is worth noting that Psalms (c. 82) and Isaiah (c. 67) are at the top of the list (as they are at Qumran), with Genesis, Deuteronomy, Exodus and the Minor Prophets all in the 30–35 range.

2   Gen. 1:27; 2:2, 7, 24.

3   Gen. 12:1, 3; 14:17-20; 15:5, 6, 13-14; 17:5, 8, 10; 18:10, 14, 18; 21:10, 12; 22:16, 17, 18.

as Enoch and Jacob.[4] The Genesis materials in the New Testament are the topic of this book. We have been fortunate to gather a group of scholars, most of whom have written monographs on their particular topic, for this fifth volume in the series, *The New Testament and the Scriptures of Israel*.[5]

The first chapter concerns the use of Genesis in early Jewish literature, and serves as an outline of the background and the context of early Christian interpretation of Genesis. Jacques van Ruiten gives a survey of early Jewish documents dealing with Genesis that date from the last centuries before our era and from the time of Jesus and of the nascent Christian church. Although in that period there was no list of holy books accepted by all Jews as authoritative, the five books of Moses and especially Genesis were generally regarded as authoritative word of God. But Genesis had to be interpreted in order to become relevant to Jews around the turn of the era, and interpretation is what happens in rewritten versions of Genesis (*Jubilees, Genesis Apocryphon*), in retellings of the creation story (*Sibylline Oracles* 1, *2 Enoch*), and in the recycling of important figures from Genesis. Van Ruiten finally compares the biblical story of the sacrifice of Isaac in Gen. 22:1-19 with the rewritten version in *Jub.* 17:15–18:19.

Stephen Ahearne-Kroll argues that there a number of places in Mark where passages from Genesis have had a substantial impact. These include the quotations from Gen. 1:27 and 2:24 in Mk 10:6-8, the allusions to Genesis 22 in Mk 1:11; 9:7; 12:6, and the allusion to Gen. 49:11 in Mk 11:2-4. Scholars have found other allusions to Genesis as well, but these are either not very significant or not specific enough to be real allusions. The allusion to Genesis 22, the story of the 'binding of Isaac', consists primarily in the qualification of Jesus as 'my beloved son' (cf. Gen. 22:2, 12, 16), but when Mark as a whole is read in the light of this primary allusion, such aspects as God's testing of Jesus, Jesus' doing of God's will and the sacrificial character of his death gain depth. In the story of Jesus' entry into Jerusalem (Mk 11:1-11), both Zech. 9:9 and Gen. 49:11 have been influential, and help to present Jesus as a humble and peaceful Messiah.

There are in Matthew's Gospel only a few quotations from Genesis (Mt. 19:4-5; 22:24, all derived from Mark), but, as Jeannine Brown shows, Genesis was nevertheless an important Old Testament book to Matthew. The genealogy of Jesus (1:1-17) has been modelled on Genesis, it starts with Abraham, and several other important persons from Genesis

---

4   Isaac (21:10, 12; 22:16-17, 18; 26:4); Enoch (5:24), Esau and Jacob (25:23); Jacob (28:12; 47:31), Jacob and Joseph (48:4).

5   See *The Psalms in the New Testament* (2004), *Isaiah in the New Testament* (2005), *Deuteronomy in the New Testament* (LNTS 358; 2007), and *The Minor Prophets in the New Testament* (LNTS 377; 2009). All volumes have been edited by Steve Moyise and Maarten J.J. Menken, and have been published by T&T Clark.

are mentioned in it. The story of Cain and Abel serves in Matthew as a foil to Christian behaviour, and Abel almost functions as a 'type' of Jesus (23:35; Isaac possibly plays a similar role). Several persons and places from Genesis occur throughout the gospel in various contexts, such as announcements of coming judgment. The evangelist appears to associate many Genesis references with God's covenant with Israel, which Jesus now also opens to Gentiles. Matthew's relationship to Genesis is apparently more a question of references to persons, places and events than of verbal agreements.

Although there are only few quotations from Genesis in Luke-Acts (Acts 3:25; 7:3, 6-7), Luke's two books have, as Peter Mallen shows, been influenced significantly by Genesis, mainly in its LXX version. Luke presents Jesus as the fulfilment of God's promise to Abraham, and in this promise he emphasizes that first Israel and then also the Gentiles will be blessed through the seed of Abraham (Gen. 22:18, quoted in Acts 3:25), that is, through Jesus. The blessing implies healing, forgiveness of sins, and restoration to community. Physical descent from Abraham is not enough to inherit this blessing; people must also live like Abraham, otherwise they will face God's judgement, depicted in terms of the flood and the destruction of Sodom and Gomorrah. In Acts 7 and 13, we find speeches, of Stephen and Paul respectively, which contain a selective survey of the history of Israel. Genesis materials are prominent in the first part of Stephen's speech; they serve to show that God is faithful to his promises, and help to invite Luke's Gentile audience to consider themselves as part of Israel's history.

The role of Genesis in John's Gospel and in 1 John is discussed by Maarten Menken. There are no marked quotations in these New Testament writings; there is one unmarked quotation (from Gen. 28:12 in Jn 1:51), there are several allusions, and also several 'straightforward references', that is, direct references to names and events known from Genesis. This state of affairs suggests that Genesis is functioning more as a narrative than as a text in John and 1 John. The interest of the Johannine author focuses on the stories of creation and fall (Genesis 1–4) and the Abraham narratives. He uses them in the interest of his Christology: the Jesus event is a new creation, and Abraham is a supporter of Jesus. The same Genesis materials also function in his polemics: the opponents of Jesus and of the Johannine community are children not of Abraham or of God but of the devil. The quotation in Jn 1:51 serves to present Jesus as the place of God's presence.

As David Lincicum shows, Genesis must have been to Paul an important and foundational document. Paul quotes several times from it, and makes use of a series of basic narratives from Genesis: the stories of the creation of the world and of humanity, of the fall, of Abraham and his descendents. Paul refers to the Genesis materials in such a way that we have to assume that his mainly Gentile audience must have been familiar with the substance of this biblical book. He considers Adam as a 'type' of Christ: as the first Adam was from the earth, sinned and had to die, so the second Adam, Jesus, is from heaven and brings God's grace and resurrection (1 Corinthians 15 and Romans 5). Abraham is presented in Romans 4 and Galatians 3–4 as one who believed before being circumcised; therefore God's promise to him concerns all believers and he can be the father of all believers, not only Jews but Gentiles as well.

The Genesis materials in the Deutero-Pauline Epistles consist of references to the stories of creation and fall in Genesis 1–3. Gen. 1:26-27 is alluded to in Eph. 4:24 and Col. 3:10, there is a quotation from Gen. 2:24 in Eph. 5:31, and there are clusters of allusions or echoes in 1 Tim. 2:13-15 and 4:3-4. James Aageson discusses these materials. He points out that in the Deutero-Pauline Epistles Greco-Roman household ethics, scriptural arguments derived from the first chapters of Genesis, and Pauline tradition converge. In 1 Timothy, Genesis materials function in the author's definition of the position of women in church gatherings (2:13-15) and in the conflict with his opponents about their renunciation of marriage and of certain foods (4:3-4). In both instances, the author uses the Genesis materials not so much to voice general principles as to regulate particular community problems.

Susan Docherty deals with the use of Genesis in Hebrews. There are some quotations from Genesis in this document, as well as passages that come near to a quotation. In addition, there are several allusions. In all instances, the LXX is the biblical text of the *auctor ad Hebraeos*. Genesis is to him often a source of materials that have to support his primary Old Testament references (see, e.g., the use of Gen. 2:2 to interpret Ps. 95[94LXX]:11 in Heb. 4:4). His exegetical methods are strongly reminiscent of those of early Jewish exegetes: he links texts that have common words, he quotes selectively when he deems it necessary, he specifies ambiguous words, he considers biblical words as deliberately ruling out their opposites ('to live' in Hab. 2:4, cited in Heb. 10:38, means 'not to die', which is then exemplified in various characters from Genesis in Hebrews 11), he gives new referents to scriptural terms. Scripture is to him a coherent whole, immediately relevant for the community that he addresses.

Genesis in James, 1 and 2 Peter and Jude is the topic of David Allen's chapter. The four documents differ in many respects, but they agree in referring not so much to the text of Genesis as to its narrative and to traditional interpretations of it, for instance in the form of a 'Rewritten Bible' (the only formal quotation, from Gen. 15:6, is found in Jas 2:23). The incorporation of traditional interpretations of Genesis sometimes leads to results that seem to go beyond the obvious meaning of the text of Genesis: obedience and submissiveness to Abraham are ascribed to Sarah in 1 Pet. 3:6, Cain is supposed to be the personification of wickedness in Jude 11. James is interested in Abraham (2:18-26) and in the stories of creation and fall (3:5-9), 1 Peter in Sarah (3:6) and in the flood narrative (3:18-20), Jude in the fall of the angels, Sodom and Gomorrah, and Cain (6-7, 11), 2 Peter derives materials from Jude and adds the positive example of Lot (2:7-9). In all four epistles, Genesis materials are put in the service of parenetical interests.

In the final chapter, Steve Moyise shows how the Book of Revelation draws on Genesis. At the end of his book, John resumes topics from Genesis 3. The tree of life (Rev. 22:2), the serpent (20:2, 10), and death (21:4) derive from the story of the fall in Genesis 3, but paradise is restored and transformed: believers will have access to the tree of life, and the serpent and death will be destroyed. One could say that in the arrangement of biblical books in the Christian Bible there is an *inclusio* between the beginning of Genesis and the end of Revelation. Other, less prominent Genesis themes in Revelation, are Sodom and Gomorrah (Genesis 19, see Rev. 9:2; 11:8), and 'the Lion from the tribe of Judah' (Gen. 49:9, see Rev. 5:5). John does not draw directly from Genesis, but he develops the themes from Genesis by using other traditions, both biblical and non-biblical. This is most evidently the case with his use of Genesis 3.

Each one of the chapters is a study in its own right of the function of Genesis in one document or group of documents, and each author has his or her own approach and interest. In that sense, the volume may be considered to be representative of the multiformity of present-day biblical scholarship. Nevertheless, some general lines become visible. First of all, the book of Genesis is functioning in the New Testament documents more as a *narrative* than as a *text*. In this respect Genesis, largely consisting of stories, differs from prophetic or legal Old Testament books. In the latter case, precise wordings are important, in the former, actors and story lines primarily count. The narrative character of Genesis also explains why the book has strongly influenced the New Testament but is relatively rarely cited in it. Moreover, when quotations from Genesis occur, they are in many cases from words spoken by God as a character in the narrative. Secondly, insofar as a textual basis for quotations, allusions and other references can be made out, it mostly is – as one would expect – the LXX. However, since the predominant use of Genesis in the New Testament is narrative, it has to be acknowledged that there is not much material to substantiate this. Thirdly, the book of Genesis as used in the New Testament is an already interpreted book of Genesis. Traditions of interpretation had already attached themselves to Genesis before New Testament times, and the New Testament use of Genesis presupposes these traditions.

It is evident that the New Testament tradents and authors show a preference for certain portions from Genesis. Two of these portions deserve to be mentioned. The stories of creation and fall in Genesis 1–4 appear to have been very popular; it is perhaps not very surprising that a new movement within Judaism (as Christianity was) went back to the very beginning and the original order of creation. The Abraham narratives constitute another part of Genesis that has been intensively utilized in the New Testament. Not only was Abraham the one with whom the Jewish people began and a model believer in God, he could also be considered as the father of both Jewish and Gentile followers of Jesus because he already was a model believer before he was circumcised, a circumstance fully exploited by Paul. From an early Christian perspective, Abraham united in his person, so to speak, Jewish Christianity and Gentile Christianity. Continuing on this line, this early Christian view of Abraham may even inspire in the present a productive (and necessary) dialogue between the three Abrahamic religions.

Chapter 1

GENESIS IN EARLY JEWISH LITERATURE

Jacques T. A. G. M. van Ruiten

Introduction

In early Judaism, before the 1st century C.E., there was no single list
of books regarded as authoritative – as the actual word of God – by
all Jewish people.[1] The Bible as the canon of Sacred Scriptures did not
yet exist at the time of the composition of, for example, *Jubilees* or the
Genesis Apocryphon. Nevertheless, there is enough evidence to suggest
that in the last centuries before the Common Era, several books were
considered by Jewish groups as divinely inspired, that is, as the word of
God, and prescriptive for religious life. There is even evidence that there
were already collections of such books in an early form, though the exact
content of these collections is less clear. It is generally assumed that many
of the books that were later incorporated into the canon of the Hebrew
Bible were regarded as authoritative at an early stage, but this cannot be
said of all of the books collected. Moreover, there is evidence that some
books which were regarded as authoritative by certain groups were not
incorporated into the Hebrew Bible. Indeed, in some cases, the content of
the books themselves was not completely determined and there may have
been different texts taken from the same book. It would appear that there
was a great deal of freedom in the transmission of sacred texts, as can also
be seen in the redaction history of the biblical books.

However, at least some books were regarded as authoritative and as
setting the standards for religious life, notably the five books of Moses,
and, in particular, the book of Genesis. But the inspired immutable word
of God needed explanation. The authoritative texts seemed to contain
ambiguities and were subject to more than one understanding. When one
realizes that language and culture are subject to constant change, this is

---

1   J. C. VanderKam, 'Revealed Literature in Second Temple Period', in idem,
From Revelation to Canon: Studies in the Hebrew Bible and Second Temple Literature
(JSJSup, 62; Leiden: Brill, 2000), pp.1–30. J. C. VanderKam, 'The Wording of Biblical
Citations in some Rewritten Scriptures', in E. D. Herbert and E. Tov (eds), *The Bible as
Book: The Hebrew Bible and the Judaean Desert Discoveries* (London: British Library,
2002), pp.241–56.

understandable. It provoked a long and rich history of biblical interpretation in ancient Judaism.[2]

The Book of Genesis in Early Jewish Literature

The book of Genesis had an enormous impact on early Jewish literature. Important narrative characters from this biblical book give the name to entire works: *Life of Adam and Eve*; *Testament of Adam*; *Apocalypse of Adam*; *1* and *2 Enoch*; *Testament of Abraham*; *Apocalypse of Abraham*; *Joseph and Aseneth*; *Testaments of the Twelve Patriarchs*; *Prayer of Jacob*; *History of Joseph*. Sometimes, the whole book of Genesis is the starting-point of a complete new work or of a part of it. The original text of Genesis is still clearly recognizable in these works, although important elements are added or omitted. I refer to the book of *Jubilees* (Genesis 1 – Exodus 19), and Pseudo-Philo, *Liber Antiquitatum Biblicarum* (Genesis – 1 Samuel). In this respect, one may also refer to Flavius Josephus who makes extensive use of the book of Genesis (beside other biblical books) in his *Jewish Antiquities*. It also happens that certain passages from the book of Genesis form the base of parts of other works. For example, the story of paradise is the base for the first book of the *Sibylline Oracles*, *2 Enoch*, and the *Life of Adam and Eve*. The short account of Enoch in Gen. 5:21-24 formed the basis of an extensive Enoch literature. The mythical story about the sons of God having intercourse with the daughters of men in Gen. 6:1-4 appealed to the imagination of later Jewish writers, and many other works made use of Genesis by referring to it and by quoting shorter or extensive pieces.[3] Philo of Alexandria (ca. 20 B.C.E. – ca. 50 C.E.), for example, is an important witness to the Jewish exegetical traditions in early Judaism.[4] He was a Greek-speaking Egyptian Jew and author of a multi-volume series of commentaries on the Pentateuch, among which the commentaries on Genesis have a prominent place.[5] He used allegorical interpretation to find common ground between his own tradition and Hellenistic

2   J. L. Kugel, *The Bible as It Was* (Cambridge, Mass.: Harvard University Press, 1997), pp.1–49.
3   For a collection of early Jewish literature in translation, see J. H. Charlesworth (ed.), *Old Testament Pseudepigrapha, I–II* (London: Darton, Longman & Todd, 1983–5). See also the series *Jüdische Schriften aus hellenistisch-römischer Zeit* (Gütersloh: Mohn) and L. DiTommaso, *A Bibliography of Pseudepigrapha Research 1850–1999* (JSPSup, 39; Sheffield: Sheffield Academic Press, 2001).
4   See J. J. Collins and D. C. Harlow (eds), *The Eerdmans Dictionary of Early Judaism* (Grand Rapids: Eerdmans, 2010), pp.1063–80.
5   See, for example, *Questions and Answers on Genesis and Exodus*. In *The Allegorical Commentary* are included: *On the Cherubim*; *On the Sacrifices of Abel and Cain*; *On the Posterity and Exile of Cain*; *On the Giants*. In *The Exposition of the Laws* are included: *On the Creation of the World*; *On Abraham*; *On Joseph*.

philosophy. Although biblical stories recounted historical events, they also had an understanding by which Abraham, Jacob, and other biblical figures were understood to represent abstractions or spiritual realities whose truth applied to all times and places.[6]

In this chapter, I will begin by looking at two works that adapt large parts of Genesis and in which the original text is clearly recognizable; both date back to the 2nd century B.C.E. (*Jubilees*; *Genesis Apocryphon*). I will then look at two works which date from the 1st century C.E., in which the creation story (Genesis 1–3) can be identified (first book of the *Sibylline Oracles*; *2 Enoch*), although the linguistic parallels are not extensive. I will then briefly look at some works that are related to biblical figures from Genesis, before concluding with a more detailed study of the offering of Isaac in Gen. 22:1-19 and its use in the book of *Jubilees*.

Genesis Rewritten

The Book of Jubilees

The book of *Jubilees* was written somewhere in the 2nd century B.C.E., possibly preceding the foundation of the community of Qumran.[7] *Jubilees*, which is presented as a revelation received by Moses on Mount Sinai and mediated by the angel of the presence, actually consists of a rewriting and interpretation of the traditional narrative moving from the creation (Genesis 1) to the arrival of the children of Israel at Mount Sinai (Exodus 19).

In the first chapter of the book, the setting of the revelation is depicted: Moses is on Mount Sinai.[8] This is important for the understanding of the

---

6   Cf. Kugel, *The Bible as It Was*, p.579.
7   Fourteen Hebrew copies of the book of *Jubilees* were found in Qumran. The oldest fragment (4Q216) may be dated to 125–100 B.C.E. Some scholars opt for a pre-Hasmonean time, since the book does not mention the persecution and decrees of Antiochus IV. See, e.g. G. W. E. Nickelsburg, *Jewish Literature between the Bible and the Mishnah* (2nd ed.; Minneapolis: Fortress, 2005), pp.73–4; M. A. Knibb, *Jubilees and the Origins of the Qumran Community* (Inaugural Lecture; London: King's College, 1989). A few others argue for a date late in the second century because of the similarities with the Qumran texts. See, e.g. C. Werman, 'The Book of Jubilees and the Qumran Community: The Relationship between the Two', *Meghillot* 2 (2004), pp.37–55 [Hebrew]; M. Himmelfarb, *A Kingdom of Priests: Ancestry and Merit in Ancient Judaism* (Philadelphia: University of Pennsylvania Press, 2006), pp.80–3. According to VanderKam, *Jubilees* antedates the founding of the Qumran community, and exercised strong influence on it. See J. C. VanderKam, 'Recent Scholarship on the Book of *Jubilees*', *Currents in Biblical Research* 6 (2008), pp.405–31.
8   On the first chapter of *Jubilees*, see G. L. Davenport, *The Eschatology of the Book of Jubilees* (SPB, 20; Leiden: Brill, 1971), pp.19–31; B. Halpern-Amaru, 'Exile and Return in Jubilees', in J. M. Scott (ed.), *Exile: Old Testament, Jewish and Christian Conceptions* (JSJSup, 56; Leiden: Brill, 1997), pp.127–44; Knibb, *Jubilees*; B. Z. Wacholder,

whole. The book portrays itself as having a heavenly origin and, moreover, as being an authentic expression of the Torah of Moses. It associates the production of the new work with the setting of the old one (Sinai) and with the same author, Moses. The new composition provides the context for the interpretation of the older traditions and at the same time, it gains its authority through its interweaving of authoritative texts.[9]

The first chapter also introduces the angel of the presence,[10] who dictates the rest of the book to Moses, namely the primaeval history (*Jubilees* 2–10),[11] the history of the patriarchs Abraham, Isaac and Jacob (11–45),[12] the people's exile in Egypt, the exodus and the first part of their wandering in the desert, including their arrival at Mount Sinai (46–50).

Although the text of *Jubilees* is guided to a large extent by the biblical books of Genesis and Exodus as far as content and sequence are concerned, one should acknowledge that other sources and traditions are also incorporated into the book. Firstly, one can point to the addition of material originating from the Enochic traditions (*Jub.* 4:15-26; 5:1-12; 7:20-39; 10:1-17).[13] Some scholars opt for a common source for *1 Enoch, Jubilees* and some of the Qumran texts (the so-called *Book of Noah*).[14] Others even consider *Jubilees* to be an Enochic document in which the so-called Zadokite Torah (that is, Genesis and Exodus) was incorporated into and digested by the Enochic revelation.[15] However, most scholars do not go that far, but instead speak about the incorporation of other traditions within the rendering and explanation of the biblical text, or about a fusing together and reconciliation of different Jewish streams in the second century B.C.E. Secondly, one can also

'Jubilees as the Super Canon: Torah-Admonition versus Torah-Commandment', in M. Bernstein, F. García Martínez and J. Kampen (eds), *Legal Texts and Legal Issues* (FS J. M. Baumgarten; STDJ, 23; Leiden: Brill, 1997), pp.195–211; J. C. VanderKam, 'The Scriptural Setting of the Book of *Jubilees*', *DSD* 13 (2006), pp.61–72.

9   Cf. also H. Najman, *Seconding Sinai: The Development of Mosaic Discourse in Second Temple* (JSJSup, 77; Leiden: Brill 2003), p.46.

10   On the angel of the presence, see J. C. VanderKam, 'The Angel of the Presence in the Book of Jubilees', *DSD* 7 (2000), pp.378–93.

11   For a comparison of Genesis 1–11 and *Jubilees* 2–10, see J. T. A. G. M. van Ruiten, *Primaeval History Interpreted: The Rewriting of Genesis 1–11 in the Book of Jubilees* (JSJSup, 66; Leiden: Brill, 2000).

12   For a comparison of the Jacob story in Genesis and *Jubilees*, see J. C. Endres, *Biblical Interpretation in the Book of Jubilees* (CBQMS, 18; Washington: Catholic Biblical Association of America, 1987).

13   See, for example, J. C. VanderKam, *Enoch: A Man for All Generations* (Studies on the Personalities of the Old Testament; Columbia, S.C.: Univerity of South Carolina Press, 1995), pp.110–21; G. W. E. Nickelsburg, *1 Enoch: A Commentary on the Book of 1 Enoch, Chapters 1–36; 81–108* (Hermeneia; Minneapolis: Fortress, 2001), pp.71–6.

14   See, for example, F. García Martínez, *Qumran and Apocalyptic: Studies on the Aramaic Texts from Qumran* (STDJ, 9; Leiden: Brill, 1992), pp.1–44; M. E. Stone, 'The Book(s) Attributed to Noah', *DSD* 13 (2006), pp.4–23.

15   See G. Boccaccini, *Beyond the Essene Hypothesis: The Parting of the Ways between Qumran and Enochic Judaism* (Grand Rapids: Eerdmans, 1998), pp.86–98.

point to the influence of other works. It is likely that the author of *Jubilees* also knew and used the traditions upon which the *Aramaic Document of Levi* is based (see, for example, *Jubilees* 31–32).[16] One can also point to the influence of *4Q Visions of Amram* (see *Jubilees* 46).[17]

In a recently published work, Michael Segal advances the thesis that the book of *Jubilees* is not a uniform and homogeneous work, composed by one single author.[18] He points to internal contradictions, doublets, tensions and discrepancies, both in detail as well as with regard to the biblical stories in general. These contradictions are the result of the literary development of *Jubilees*. Rewritten biblical stories and extant exegetical texts were adopted and assimilated into the new composition. The tensions and contrasts within the book result, therefore, from the integration of this existing material into a new framework.[19]

The Genesis Apocryphon

The *Genesis Apocryphon* was one of the first manuscripts that in 1947 were discovered in Qumran. The scroll was in a very bad condition and it is was only possible to unroll and to take photographs of it in 1954.[20] The manuscript contains the remainders of 22 columns. The text was written in Aramaic shortly before or shortly after the beginning of the

---

16   See, for example, É. Puech, *Qumrân grotte 4.XXII: Textes araméens, 1: 4Q529–549* (DJD, XXXI; Oxford: Clarendon Press, 2001), pp.285–6; H. Drawnel, *An Aramaic Wisdom Text from Qumran: A New Interpretation of the Levi Document* (JSJSup, 86; Leiden: Brill, 2004), pp.63–75; J. C. Greenfield, M. E. Stone and E. Eshel, *The Aramaic Levi Document: Edition, Translation, Commentary* (SVTP, 19; Leiden: Brill, 2004), pp.19–22; R. A. Kugler, *From Patriarch to Priest: The Levi-Priestly Tradition from Aramaic Levi to Testament of Levi* (SBLEJL, 9; Atlanta: Scholars Press, 1996), p.138.

17   Cf. J. T. A. G. M. Van Ruiten, 'Between Jacob's Death and Moses' Birth: The Intertextual Relationship between Genesis 50:15, Exodus 1:14 and *Jubilees* 46:1–6', in A. Hilhorst, E. Puech and E. J. C. Tigchelaar (eds), *Flores Florentino: Dead Sea Scrolls and Other Early Jewish Studies* (FS F. García Martínez; JSJSup, 122; Leiden: Brill, 2007), pp.467–89.

18   M. Segal, *The Book of* Jubilees: *Rewritten Bible, Redaction, Ideology and Theology* (JSJSup, 117; Leiden: Brill, 2007). Earlier Davenport (*Eschatology*) argued that *Jubilees* is a composite work, consisting of an original text and two subsequent revisions of it. Wiesenberg argued that chronological inconsistencies point to the activity of more than one writer. See E. Wiesenberg, 'The Jubilee of Jubilees', *RevQ* 3 (1961), pp.3–40.

19   Segal, *Book of* Jubilees, 29. According to Segal, a redactor adopted already existing rewritten stories and incorporated them into his book, but he added new material as well, mainly in the chronological framework and the law passages. The redactional strand is consistent in style, language and theological view, whereas adopted stories are not consistent in these respects. In this way, Segal is able to distinguish between a crystallized editorial layer and the sources included therein.

20   J. T. Milik, *Apocalypse of Lamech* (DJD, I; Oxford: Clarendon, 1955), pp.86–7 + pl.XVII; N. Avigad and Y. Yadin, *A Genesis Apocryphon: A Scroll from the Wilderness of Judaea* (Jerusalem, 1956); J. A. Fitzmyer, *The Genesis Apocryphon of Qumran Cave 1 (1Q20): A Commentary* (3rd ed.; BibOr, 18/B: Rome: Pontificio Istituto Biblico, 2004).

Common Era. Only one copy of this work is known and it is possible that it is the autograph,[21] but this is far from sure.[22] In this case, the original work can be dated before the end of the 1st century B.C.E. The work could have been written in Qumran,[23] but many authors opt for an origin outside Qumran.[24] The writer of the manuscript used a kind of ink that affected the leather, and which made unreadable the largest part of the text. The state of the manuscript deteriorated in later times but advanced techniques with infrared have lead to some unexpected results.[25] The official edition of the text in the DJD series (by M. Bernstein and E. Eshel) is still waiting.[26]

The *Genesis Apocryphon* seems to consist of two clearly distinguished parts. The most extensive part (column 1 until the middle of column 21) is written in the first person and consists of three autobiographic stories of Lamek, Noah and Abram. It retells the biblical text of Genesis 6–13 in the same order with many extensive additions. We are not sure whether the first chapters of Genesis were also included in the scroll, because the beginning of the manuscript is missing. From the middle of column 21 the style is very different. The story shifts to the third person and is very close to the biblical text of Genesis 14 and the beginning of Genesis 15 and has hardly any addition. We do not know how far the reformulation of Genesis lasted, since the last columns of the scroll are lost. Possibly it continued with the story of Genesis 15 or even beyond it but we cannot be certain where it ended.

The author of the *Genesis Apocryphon* used beside the biblical text also other sources. The story of Lamech has a clear parallel in *1 Enoch* 106–107. It is possible that the *Genesis Apocryphon* used the text of *1 Enoch* as a

---

21   See, e.g. S. White Crawford, *Rewriting Scripture in Second Temple Times* (Studies in the Dead Sea Scrolls and Related Literature; Grand Rapids: Eerdmans, 2008), p.106.

22   See, e.g. D. K. Falk, *The Parabiblical Texts: Strategies for Extending the Scriptures among the Dead Sea Scrolls* (LSTS, 63; London: T&T Clark, 2007), pp.28–9.

23   White Crawford, *Rewriting Scripture*, p.107.

24   Falk, *Parabiblical Texts*, ibidem.

25   J. C. Greenfield and E. Qimron, 'The *Genesis Apocryphon* Col. XII', in T. Muraoka (ed.), *Studies in Qumran Aramaic* (Abr-Nahrain Supplements, 3; Leuven: Peeters, 1992), pp.70–7; M. Morgenstern, E. Qimron and D. Sivan, 'The Hitherto Unpublished Columns of the *Genesis Apocryphon*', *Abr-Nahrain* 23 (1995), pp.30–54; M. Lundberg and B. Zuckerman, 'New Aramaic Fragments from Qumran Cave One', *CALNews* 12 (1996), pp.1–5; B. Zuckerman and M. Lundberg, 'Ancient Texts and Modern Technology: The West Semitic Research Project of the University of California', *AJS Perspectives* (Fall/Winter 2002), pp.13–15. Most recently: D. A. Machiela, *The Dead Sea* Genesis Apocryphon: *A New Text and Translation with Introduction and Special Treatment of Columns 13–17* (STDJ, 79; Leiden: Brill, 2009).

26   E. Qimron, 'Towards a New Edition of the *Genesis Apocryphon*', *JSP* 10 (1992), pp.11–18; idem, 'Toward a New Edition of 1Q "*Genesis Apocryphon*"', in D. W. Parry and E. Ulrich (eds), *The Provo International Conference on the Dead Sea Scrolls. Technological Innovations, New Texts, & Reformulated Issues* (STDJ, 30; Leiden: Brill, 1999), pp.106–9.

source,[27] but it is also possible that both texts go back to a common source.[28] The story of Noah has many similarities with the book of *Jubilees*. Many researchers opt for a dependency of the *Genesis Apocryphon* on *Jubilees*[29] but others argue for a common source for the common elements in both texts.[30]

The Creation Story Retold

The First Book of the Sibylline Oracles

The first two books of the *Sibylline Oracles* can be considered as a Jewish oracle with a Christian redaction.[31] The original Jewish oracle can probably be dated at about the turn of the era.[32] The first part of the first book (vv. 5-64) is a poetic rewriting of Genesis 1–3. It precedes the description of the continuation of the history, which is divided into ten generations. Seven of them are described in the first book. The text of *Sib. Or.* 1:5-64 retells the story of the creation quite freely, although the general structure of the passage follows the structure of Genesis 1–3 quite closely.

The first part (5-21) of *Sib. Or.* 1:5-64 is concerned with the creation of the world until the creation of man, and forms a parallel to the first account of the creation in Genesis (Gen. 1:1–2:4a); the second part (22-37) is concerned with the creation of man and woman, and forms a parallel to the second account of creation (Gen. 2:4b-25); and, finally, the third part (38-64) is concerned with the life in the garden, and the rejection away from it, and runs parallel to the story of the garden of Eden in Genesis 3. As far as the general structure is concerned, it is striking that the first account of the creation of man is rearranged and integrated in the second account, although it is only one element of it (the notion of the image of God) that is put in the actual account. In the Sibylline Oracles the creation of man and woman is set apart from the rest of the creation. Moreover, the description of the creation of man and woman runs very much parallel with the description in Genesis as far as the sequence of the events is concerned. With regard to the actual

---

27   Fitzmyer, *Genesis Apocryphon*, pp.139–40; White Crawford, *Rewriting Scripture*, pp.108–9.

28   See G. W. E. Nickelsburg, 'Patriarchs Who Worry About their Wives: A Haggadic Tendency in the *Genesis Apocryphon*', in M. E. Stone and E. G. Chazon (eds), *Biblical Perspectives: Early Use and Interpretation of the Bible in Light of the Dead Sea Scrolls* (STDJ, 28; Leiden: Brill, 1998), pp.137–58 (esp. 143) (republished in: J. Neusner and A. J. Avery-Peck [eds], *George W. E. Nickelsburg in Perspective: An Ongoing Dialogue of Learning*, Vol. 1 [JSJSup, 80; Leiden: Brill, 2003], pp.177–99).

29   See, e.g. Falk, *Parabiblical Texts*, pp.42–80.

30   García Martínez, *Qumran and Apocalyptic*, p.40. Others suggest that the *Genesis Apocryphon* was a source for *1 Enoch* and *Jubilees*; cf. Avigad and Yadin, *Genesis Apocryphon*, p.38.

31   See J. J. Collins, 'Sibylline Oracles', in *OTP* I, pp.317–472, esp. 330.

32   Collins, 'Sibylline Oracles', pp.331–2.

wording, both texts differ substantially. What is more, the creation is valued as something positive. Eve is not created so that sin and death might come to Adam or to humankind. Eve is created as a partner equal to Adam. Although later in the story she is the one who persuades Adam to eat from the fruit of the tree of knowledge, it is the serpent who is seen as primarily responsible. He is in fact the only who is to be cursed, whereas the curse on Adam and Eve is considerably lightened because it is connected with the blessing of God. In connection with the positive evaluation of the creation of Adam, the prohibition to eat from the tree of knowledge (Gen. 2:16-17) is also rearranged, and forms the direct introduction to the story of the temptation and transgression. Finally, sexuality is disconnected from the creation of Adam and Eve. Before the eating from the tree of knowledge, they seem to have a sort of Platonic relationship. Only after this does sexuality enter their life.

Slavonic Apocalypse of Enoch

The *second book of Enoch* is also called the *Slavonic Apocalypse of Enoch* and was written probably in the 1st century C.E., originally possibly in Greek, but was passed down only in the Slavonic language.[33] It is possibly of Hellenistic Jewish origin, because time and again the author tries to mediate between the Jewish tradition and Hellenistic philosophy.[34] The work can be considered as an amplification of Gen. 5:21-32. It describes events from the life of Enoch until the coming of the flood. The first part describes the ascension of Enoch to heaven and is followed by the revelation of God, which can be divided in three parts: (1) the history preceding the first week of creation (24–27); (2) the first week of creation (28–32); (3) the eschatological conclusion (33–36).

The most striking element in the rewriting is that the whole story of Genesis 2–3 is integrated into the description of the sixth day of creation. On this day Adam and Eve were created (both outside the garden), they were placed in the garden of Eden and on this very day they were driven away from the garden. Eve was created so that death might come to Adam, although it is also stated that both life and death are part of his nature (*2 En.* 30:10c). All elements in the text of Genesis that refer to a marital relation between the first man and woman are omitted altogether. The first sexual

---

33   F. I. Andersen, '2 (Slavonic Apocalypse of) Enoch', *OTP I*, pp.91–213, esp. 94–7; C. Böttrich, *Das slavische Henochbuch* (JSHRZ, V.7; Gütersloh: Mohn, 1995), pp.807–13. For the complicated textual transmission of the text, see Andersen, '2 Enoch', pp.92–4; Böttrich, *Henochbuch*, pp.788–99.

34   For the Alexandrine Hellenistic Jewish background of 2 Enoch, see Böttrich, *Henochbuch*, p.811. Some have pleaded for an Iranian provenance of the work. See, e.g. D. Winston, 'The Iranian Component in the Bible, Apocrypha, and in Qumran. A Review of the Evidence', *History of Religions 5* (1966), pp.183–216, esp. 196–9; M. Philonenko, 'La cosmogonie du "Livre des secrets d'Hénoch"', in *Religions en Egypte Hellénistique et Romaine: Colloque de Strasbourg 16–18 mai 1967* (Paris: Presses universitaires de France, 1969), pp.109–16.

relationship took place between Eve and Satan, who entered Paradise as a demon (*2 En.* 31:6: 'In such a form he entered paradise and corrupted Eve'). The point of the story of the creation of Eve is that she has brought death to Adam: 'so that death might come to him by his wife' (*2 En.* 30:17). And death comes by sin, as it is said in *2 En.* 30:16e: 'After sin there is nothing for it but death.'

Biblical Figures Recycled: Adam, Abraham, Jacob and Joseph

Important narrative characters in Genesis are namegivers of entire works. In relation to Adam, one can point to the *Testament of Adam*.[35] Although this work lacks the narrative framework of the genre of a testament and is of uncertain provenance (it seems to be Christian in origin), it does use older Jewish traditions that date back to the beginning of the Common Era. The first two parts are an elaboration of Genesis 1–3. There is also the gnostic *Apocalypse of Adam*, found in Nag Hammadi (Egypt). It contains a secret revelation told by Adam to his son Seth. The book paraphrases large parts of the book of Genesis.

Some works are connected to the patriarch Abraham. The *Testament of Abraham* is a short story about the events preceding Abraham's death.[36] Despite repeated attempts of the archangel Michael, Abraham refuses to die. Therefore, Michael takes Abraham with him on a journey through this world and the coming world. After their return, Abraham dies through the cunning and guile of Michael. Thereupon, Michael takes Abraham's soul into heaven, while Isaac buries his body. The work exists in two Greek recensions but was probably originally written in Hebrew or Aramaic in the second part of the 1st century C.E. The *Apocalypse of Abraham* is a story about Abraham's conversion from idolatry.[37] After Abraham's offering (compare Genesis 15), he is transferred to the seventh heaven. God's throne, the heavens, the universe, and the future of his line until the last judgement are revealed to him. The apocalypse is known to us only in a Slavonic translation. It probably goes back via a Greek stage to a Hebrew original from the beginning of the 2nd century C.E.

In connection with Jacob, one can mention the *Ladder of Jacob*, a disgression on the dream of Jacob at Bethel (Gen. 28:11-22).[38] After the

---

35   Cf. e.g. S. E. Robinson, 'Testament of Adam: A New Translation and Introduction', in *OTP I*, pp.989–95.

36   E. P. Sanders, 'Testament of Abraham: A New Translation and Introduction', in *OTP I*, pp.871–904.

37   Cf., e.g. R. Rubinkiewicz, 'Apocalypse of Abraham: A New Translation and Introduction', in *OTP I*, pp.681–705.

38   For a detailed study of this work, see J. L. Kugel, *The Ladder of Jacob: Ancient Interpretations of the Biblical Story of Jacob and his Children* (Princeton: Princeton University Press, 2006).

description of the dream, Jacob wakes up and the archangel Sariel explains the dream. The ladder represents the history of the world and of Israel. The twelve stairs are the periods in which the times can be devided. The faces are the kings of the wicked nations who will threaten Jacob's descendants during different periods. In the end they will be punished. The work has come down as part of a larger Slavonic work, and underwent several redactions. Possibly, it goes back to an original Greek text, written in the 1st century C.E. by a Jew.

Apart from the novel *Joseph and Aseneth*, only fragments of works in relation to Joseph remained.[39] The *History of Joseph* is an originally Jewish work, written in Greek, before the 4th century C.E., and can be characterized as a kind of midrash on Gen. 41:39–42:36. The *Prayer of Joseph* possibly dates from the 1st century C.E. and is linked with Jacob's blessing to Joseph's sons in Genesis 48.[40] The central motif of the text, however, is Jacob's wrestling with the angel in Gen. 32:22-33.

The Binding of Isaac (Gen. 22:1-19 and Jub. 17:15–18:19)

In the remainder of this chapter, I will focus on the offering of Isaac (Gen. 22:1-19) and its use in *Jubilees*. It is clear that the story itself is rewritten quite literally in *Jub.* 18:1-17. The most striking deviation is the fact that the rewriting is preceded by an introduction (*Jub.* 17:15-18) and followed by a halakic addition (*Jub.* 18:18-19).

The Introduction to the Binding (Jub. 17:15-18)

Genesis leaves the reader with the question of why God had to test Abraham in such a cruel way. Moreover, for the ancient reader it might have been a problem that God did not know the result of the test in advance. In the introduction (*Jub.* 17:15-18), the author of *Jubilees* makes clear that it is not God who takes the initiative but the prince of Mastema. *Jubilees* keeps evil away from God, who is completely good.[41] According to *Jubilees*, the test was not to show to God that Abraham is God-fearing but to demonstrate his loyalty to others (cf. *Jub.* 18:16: 'I have made known to everyone that you are faithful to me in everything that I have told you'). Moreover, Abraham has already been tested six times (Abraham's land, the famine, the wealth of kings, his wife when she was taken forcibly, circumcision, Ishmael and his

39   For a study of *Joseph and Aseneth*, see, e.g. G. Bohak, *Joseph and Aseneth and the Jewish Temple in Heliopolis* (Atlanta: Scholars Press, 1996); C. Burchard, *Joseph und Aseneth* (Leiden: Brill, 2003); S. Docherty, 'Joseph and Aseneth: Rewritten Bible or Narrative Expansion?' *JSJ* 35 (2004), pp.27–48.

40   Cf. D. C. Harlow, 'Joseph, Prayer of', in J. J. Collins and D. C. Harlow (eds), *The Eerdmans Dictionary of Early Judaism* (Grand Rapids: Eerdmans, 2010), pp.824–5.

41   Cf. Segal, *Book of* Jubilees, p.190.

servant girl Hagar when he sent them away),[42] God knows that Abraham is faithful to him (*Jub.* 17:17-18). The introduction runs as follows:

Jub. 17:15-18

15a	During the seventh week, in the first year, during the first month – on the twelfth of this month – in this jubilee,
15b	there were words in heaven regarding Abraham,
15c	that he was faithful in everything that he told him,
15d	that the Lord loved him,
15e	and (that) in every difficulty he was faithful.
16a	Then prince Mastema came
16b	and said before God:
16c	'Abraham does indeed love his son Isaac
16d	and finds him more pleasing than anyone else.
16e	Tell him to offer him as a sacrifice on an altar.
16f	Then you will see whether he performs this order
16g	and will know whether he is faithful in everything through which you test him.'
17a	Now the Lord was aware that Abraham was faithful in every difficulty which he had told him.
17b	For he had tested him through his land and the famine;
17c	he had tested him through the wealth of kings;
17d	he had tested him again through his wife when she was taken forcibly,
17e	and through circumcision;
17f	and he had tested him through Ishmael and his servant girl Hagar when he sent them away.
18a	In everything through which he tested him he was found faithful.
18b	He himself did not grow impatient,
18c	nor was he slow to act;
18d	for he was faithful
18e	and one who loved the Lord.

---

42   S. Sandmel, *Philo's Place in Judaism: A Study of Conceptions of Abraham in Jewish Literature* (New York: Ktav, 1971), p.44, n.129, speaks about six trials in *Jub.* 17:17. See also L. A. Huizenga, 'The Battle for Isaac: Exploring the Composition and Function of the *Aqedah* in the Book of *Jubilees*', *JSP* 13 (2002), pp.33–59 (esp. 38); J. Kugel, 'On the Interpolations in the Book of *Jubilees*', *RevQ* 94 (2009), pp.215–72 (esp. 263–4). One can also come to seven, if Ishmael and Hagar are seen as two separate trials. So Kugel, *The Bible as It Was*, p.168; J. C. VanderKam, *Book of Jubilees* (Guides to Apocrypha and Pseudepigrapha; Sheffield: Sheffield Academic Press, 2001), p.54; F. García Martínez, 'The Sacrifice of Isaac in 4Q225', in E. Noort and E. Tigchelaar (eds), *The Sacrifice of Isaac: The Aqedah (Genesis 22) and Its Interpretations* (Themes in Biblical Narrative, 4; Leiden: Brill, 2002), pp.44–57 (esp. 49).

One can consider the introduction as an addition to the text of Gen. 22:1-19. It first places the *Aqedah* within the overall chronological framework of the book. According to the author of *Jubilees*, the binding of Isaac takes place during the seventh week, in the first year of the forty-first jubilee (cf. *Jub.* 17:15a), which is 2003 *a.m.* Isaac was born in 1988 *a.m.* (cf. *Jub.* 16:15; 17:1), and should have been fifteen years at the time of the binding. The test started on the twelfth of the first month (*Jub.* 17:15a).

It is very well possible that there is a clue in the biblical text for this introduction, i.e. the very first sentence of Gen. 22:1: ויהי אחר הדברים האלה. This formula occurs in the book of Genesis outside Gen. 22:1 in Gen. 39:7; 40:1, and in slightly different form also in Gen. 15:1; 22:20; 48:1.[43] The formula provides the connection with the preceding passage.[44] The author of *Jubilees* has taken over the formula only in *Jub.* 14:1 (= Gen. 15:1): 'After these things', and in *Jub.* 39:14 (= Gen. 40:1): 'In those days'.[45] It is possible that the author of *Jubilees* interpreted the formula of Gen. 22:1 as referring to something that happens before Abraham is put to a test, though he could not find this in the text of Genesis. By way of a midrash, he then suggests that something in the heavens caused the test. More precisely, it seems as if he interpreted דברים (LXX: ῥήματα) as 'words'. The phrase 'there were words (*qalat*) in heaven regarding Abraham' (*Jub.* 17:15b), seems to reflect the opening phrase of Gen. 22:1.[46] Prince Mastema raises objections with regard to Abraham. Although he is a model of good behaviour, you can only know if he is really faithful when you ask him to offer his son Isaac, claims the prince. God complies with prince Mastema's request, though he knows it is not really necessary. The test is being executed in the first place for Mastema (*Jub.* 18:9, 12), but also for others (*Jub.* 18:16).

43　　　Outside the book of Genesis, see 1 Kgs 17:17; 21:1. In slightly different form, see Josh. 24:29; Est. 2:1; 3:1; 7:1. The function of the formula seems to be to fit the individual events into the entire story. So, e.g. C. Westermann, *Genesis 12–36* (BKAT, 1.2; 4th edn; Neukirchen-Vluyn: Neukirchener Verlag, 1999), p.433; H.-D. Neef, *Die Prüfung Abrahams: Eine exegetisch-theologische Studie zu Gen 22,1-19* (Arbeiten zur Theologie, 90; Stuttgart: Calwer, 1998), p.51.

44　　　Cf. H. Seebass, *Genesis II: Vätergeschichte I (11,27-22,24)* (Neukirchen-Vluyn: Neukirchener Verlag, 1997), p.203.

45　　　The passages in which Gen. 22:20 and 48:1 occur are not taken over in *Jubilees*. Gen. 39:7 is rewritten in *Jub.* 39:5, but *Jubilees* does not have an equivalent for 'It happened after these things'.

46　　　Since the heavenly 'words' (*Jub.* 17:15b) reflect the 'words' of Gen. 22:1a, the plural reading seems to be preferred. See M. Kister, 'Observations on Aspects of Exegesis, Tradition, and Theology in Midrash, Pseudepigrapha, and Other Jewish Writings', in J. Reeves (ed.), *Tracing Threads: Studies in the Vitality of Jewish Pseudepigrapha* (SBLEJL, 6; Atlanta: Scholars Press, 1994), pp.1–34 (esp. 10); J. C. VanderKam, 'The Aqedah, Jubilees and Pseudojubilees', in C. A. Evans and S. Talmon (eds), *The Quest for Context and Meaning: Studies in Biblical Intertextuality* (FS J. A. Sanders; BIS, 28; Leiden: Brill, 1997), pp.241–62 (esp. 249).

Jub. 17:15-18 forms the beginning of a history of interpretation of Gen. 22:1. A comparable interpretation occurs in *4Q225*,[47] *L.A.B.* 32:1-4; *b. Sanh.* 89b and *Gen. Rab.* 55:4.[48] These texts describe the events that precede the binding of Isaac, which are the direct cause for the test of Abraham. From several sides, doubts are cast upon the true loyalty of Abraham. In *Jub.* 17:15-18 and *4Q225* it is prince Mastema who doubts; according to him, Abraham is not willing to offer his only son.[49] In *L.A.B.* 32:1-4, it is recounted that all the angels were jealous of Abraham and that all the worshipping host envied him.[50] In *b. Sanh.* 89b, Satan puts forward objections. According to him, Abraham has prepared many feasts, but he had not even a turtledove or a young bird to sacrifice to God. In *Gen. Rab.* 55:4, objections against Abraham are put forward, first by Abraham himself, then by the ministering angels, and finally by the nations of the world. Although Abraham caused everyone to rejoice, he did not set aside a single bull or ram for God. Thus, in the course of the tradition, several instigators of the test of Abraham are mentioned, whereas the reasons why they object to Abraham are diverse. In *Jubilees* and *4Q225*, God meets the challenge of Mastema; in Pseudo-Philo he responds to the jealousy of the angels; in *b. Sanh.* 89b and *Gen. Rab.* 55:4 God is reacting to objections put forward by several sides. In all cases, God is the one who tests Abraham. The goal of the test is to show to others how faithful Abraham is to God.

The Story of the Binding (Gen. 22:1-19; Jub. 18:1-17)

The actual text of the trial of Abraham (*Jub.* 18:1-17) is a quite literal reproduction of Gen. 22:1b-19, apart from a few additions which are related to the introduction of Mastema (*Jub.* 18:9, 12, 16), motivated by the introduction of the story (*Jub.* 17:15-18):

47   For a study on 4Q225, which has many similarities with *Jub.* 17:15–18:19, see VanderKam, 'Aqedah', pp.241–61; R. Kugler and J. C. VanderKam, 'A Note on 4Q225 (*4QPseudo-Jubilees*)', *RevQ* 20 (2001), pp.110–15; García Martínez, 'The Sacrifice of Isaac', pp.44–57; R. Kugler, 'Hearing 4Q225: A Case Study in Reconstructing the Religious Imagination of the Qumran Community', *DSD* 10 (2003), pp.80–103; J. Kugel, 'Exegetical Notes on 4Q225 "Pseudo-Jubilees"', *DSD* 13 (2006), pp.73–98; B. Halpern-Amaru, 'A Note on Isaac as First-Born in *Jubilees* and Only Son in 4Q225', *DSD* 13 (2006), pp.127–33.

48   For the following, see Kister, 'Observations', pp.10–15; cf. also VanderKam, 'Aqedah', pp.249–50; García Martínez, 'The Sacrifice of Isaac', pp.49–51.

49   4Q225 9-10 reads: 'And the prince of Mastema came to God and accused Abraham with regard to Isaac.'

50   The envy might be caused by his being loved by God, or because he got a son from his barren wife.

9a	Then I stood in front of him, and in front of the prince of Mastema.
9b	The Lord said:
9c	'Tell him not to let his hand go down on the child,
9d	and not do anything to him
9e	because I know that he is one who fears the Lord.'
	....
12a	The prince of Mastema was put to shame.
	.....
16c	'... I have made known to everyone
16d	that you are faithful to me in everything that I have told you.
16e	Go in peace.'

When one compares Gen. 22:11-18 with *Jub.* 18:9-16, it is striking that whereas in Genesis the 'angel of Yhwh' twice calls to Abraham, he is not referred to explicitly in *Jubilees*. However, an angel does indeed play a part in *Jubilees*. In *Jub.* 18:9-11 the use of the 1st person singular refers to 'the angel of the presence', who is dictating the whole book of *Jubilees* to Moses (cf. *Jub.* 2:1).[51] In *Jub.* 18:14, the 1st person plural is used. The angel speaks directly (*Jub.* 18.10-11) or indirectly (*Jub.* 18:14: 'just as we had appeared in order to speak to him'). In contrast to Genesis, the angel of the presence explicitly receives the command to speak from God (*Jub.* 18:9: 'The Lord said: "Tell him ..."'). Moreover, God dictates literally (*Jub.* 18:9) what the angel later on says to Abraham (*Jub.* 18:11). In *Jub.* 18:14, it is explicitly stated that the angels speak to Abraham 'in the Lord's name'. In addition, in *Jub.* 18:15, the 3rd person singular is used ('He said') and this refers to God, not to the angels. In conclusion, on the one hand one can say that, more explicitly than in Genesis, God is held responsible for the content of what the angel says. On the other hand, it is clear that by putting the words of Gen. 22:12 into the mouth of the angel (*Jub.* 18:11), God is protected against the reproach that he is uninformed. He should have known beforehand how Abraham was going to behave. It is possible that the use of 'now' in *Jub.* 18:11 contributes to this interpretation, for this word does not occur in *Jub.* 18:9, where God is speaking.[52]

Most of the deviations in *Jub.* 18:1-17 with regard to MT Gen. 22:1-19 are of a text-critical nature. They run parallel to alternative readings of words and phrases in one or more ancient versions of Genesis. Therefore, they could be due to the fact that the author of *Jubilees* had a text of Genesis in front of him that was slightly different from MT. There are also quite a lot of small differences between *Jub.* 18:1-17 and MT Gen. 22:1-19, which are

51   Some Ethiopic manuscripts read *Jub* 18:10a: 'He called'; cf. J. C. VanderKam, *The Book of* Jubilees *II* (CSCO, 511; Scriptores Aethiopici, 88; Leuven: Peeters, 1989), p.106.
52   Apparently, the contradiction between *Jub.* 18:9a ('I stood in front of him, and in front of the prince of Mastema') and *Jub.* 18:10a ('I called to him from heaven') was not relevant for the author of *Jubilees*. It illustrates the tendency in this chapter to follow the biblical text as closely as possible.

not attested in ancient versions, and which do not fundamentally change the meaning of the text. Many of these small deviations, either text-critical or not, are discussed by VanderKam, and it is not necessary to go into all these differences here.[53] I restrict myself to the following.

Firstly, three times MT Gen. 22:1-19 contains the word 'your only one' (יחידך: Gen. 22:2, 12, 16), the first time completed with the phrase 'whom you love, Isaac' (Gen. 22:2: אשר אהבת את יצחק). In all these places, the LXX, Old Latin and EthGen read 'your beloved one' instead of 'your only one' and this reading possibly goes back to the form יחידך. Likewise, *Jub.* 18:2 (= Gen. 22:2) reads 'your beloved one'. In *Jub.* 18:11 (= Gen. 22:12) and in *Jub.* 18:15 (= Gen. 22:16), the reading is 'your first-born son', in the last case followed by the phrase 'whom you love', as is the case in Gen. 22:2 (= *Jub.* 18:2). The original Hebrew of *Jubilees* probably read בכורך, a reading not attested in any of the versions of Gen. 22:12, 16.[54]

Secondly, some of the differences have to do with the place of the offering. In his rendering of Gen. 22:2 ('the land of Moriah') with 'a high land' (*Jub.* 18:2), the author of *Jubilees* comes close to the reading of the Septuagint (τὴν ὑψηλήν).[55] This reading possibly goes back to a Hebrew *Vorlage* of Gen. 22:2, which did not have המריה but something like המרה.[56] However, it is also possible that the author of *Jubilees* deliberately changed his *Vorlage* because in *Jub.* 18:13, it becomes clear that the place where Abraham is going to offer his son is identified with Mount Zion. The identification of Moriah and Zion (Jerusalem) occurs also in 2 Chron. 3:1 ('... the house of Yhwh in Jerusalem on Mount Moriah, where Yhwh had appeared...'), and in rabbinic sources.[57] In three places where the text deals with the place of the sacrifice, *Jubilees* changes or omits the relative clause: *Jub.* 18:2 reads

53   VanderKam, *Book of* Jubilees *II*, pp.105–9. For a complete list of the differences, see J. C. VanderKam, *Textual and Historical Studies in the Book of Jubilees* (Missoula: Scholars Press, 1977), pp.150–98; cf. also J. C. VanderKam, '*Jubilees* and the Hebrew Texts of Genesis – Exodus', in idem, *From Revelation to Canon*, pp.448–61.

54   Note that the Latin text of *Jubilees* reads in 18:11: *primogenito* (= בכורך), and in 18:15: *unigenito* (= יחידך). In fact, neither the reading 'your only son' nor 'your first-born son' is adequate to describe Isaac who is not Abraham's first-born son. According to Segal, the use of the 'first-born son' in relation to Isaac might have been influenced by the parallelism between the *Aqedah* and Passover. See Segal, *Book of* Jubilees, pp.196–7.

55   Cf. also Old Latin and EthGen.

56   The versions differ quite a lot in their rendering of המריה. The Samaritan Pentateuch has המוראה, while the Peshitta reads '*mwrj*', reflecting האמרי. Symmachus reads τῆς ὀπτασίας, which might reflect a vocalization of the verb יראה in Gen. 22:14 as a passive form: 'will appear, be seen'. Cf. A. Salvesen, *Symmachus in the Pentateuch* (JSSM, 15; Manchester: University of Manchester, 1991), p.44. *Gen. Rab.* 55:7 gives several etymologies of the word המריה: הוראה ('teaching'), יראה ('fear'), מוריד ('bring down', i.e. the nations to Gehenna), ראוי of the correspondence of the Temple to the heavenly Temple, מור of the myrrh of the Temple and in Song of Songs 4:6. Cf. also Salvesen, *Symmachus*, p.44, n.177; M. M. Kasher, *Encyclopedia of Biblical Interpretation: Genesis III* (New York: American Biblical Encyclopedia Society, 1957), p.133.

57   E.g., *Gen. Rab.* 56:10; *b. Pes.* 88a; *b. Ber.* 62b.

'Offer him on one of the mountains which I will show you', which could perhaps be better translated with 'which I will *make known* to you', against the MT: 'which I will *tell* you' (Gen. 22:2: אשר אמר אל יך); *Jub.* 18:3 omits the relative clause of Gen. 22:3 (אשר אמר לו האלהים), whereas in *Jub.* 18:7, he interprets the 'place of which God had told him' (Gen. 22.9) with 'the mountain of the Lord', which can hardly mean anything other than Mount Zion. The author of *Jubilees* thus consistently interprets the place of the offering as Mount Zion and he might therefore have deliberately changed 'the land of Moriah' (Gen. 22:2) into 'a high land' (*Jub.* 18:2) and the changes the author makes with regard to the description of the place (*Jub.* 18:3, 7) serve the same goal.

The Halakic Addition

The relationship of the halakic addition at the end of the text (*Jub.* 18:18-19) with the preceding rewriting of Gen. 22:1-19 is somewhat unclear. It seeks to prove the patriarchal origin of a festival of seven days:

Jubilees 18:18-19

18a	He used to celebrate this festival joyfully for seven days during all the years.
18b	He named it the festival of the Lord in accord with the seven days during which he went and returned safely.
19a	This is the way it is ordained
19b	and written on the heavenly tablets regarding Israel and his descendants:
19c	(they are) to celebrate this festival for seven days with festal happiness.

Although *Jub.* 18:18-19 seeks to relate the origin of this festival to the journey of the binding of Isaac, one should be aware of the fact that there is no reference in the rewritten narrative for '*this* festival'. The last reference to a festival is in *Jub.* 16:20-31, where the festival of tabernacles (*Sukkot*) is described. Also this festival is called 'this festival' (*Jub.* 16:21), and 'a festival of the Lord' (*Jub.* 16:27). It is a festival of joy (*Jub.* 16:20, 27, 29, 31), and it lasts for 'seven days' (*Jub.* 16:22, 25). Moreover, this festival is written on the heavenly tablets (*Jub.* 16:29). This does not mean that the description of the unnamed festival in *Jub.* 18:18-19 refers to the festival of tabernacles.[58]

---

58   According to M. Testuz, *Les idées religieuses du Livre des Jubilés* (Geneva: Droz, 1960), pp.162–3, however, the travel of Abraham took place on the festival of tabernacles. See also A. Caquot in A. Dupont-Sommer and M. Philonenko (eds), *La Bible: Écrits intertestamentaires* (Paris: Gallimard, 1987), p.710. For the rejection of this opinion, see A. Jaubert, *La notion d'alliance dans le Judaïsme aux abords de l'ère chrétienne* (Paris: Seuil, 1963), p.90, n.5.

In the literary context, the joy of the festival of tabernacles is related with Abraham's and Sarah's joy (*Jub.* 16:19), and the date ('the seventh month') with the return of the angels (*Jub.* 16:16). In the preceding narrative of *Jub.* 18:18-19, there is no explicit mention of joy, whereas the binding takes place in the first month and not in the seventh.

According to most exegetes, the festival mentioned in *Jub.* 18:18-19 refers to the festival of the unleavened bread, which is related to Passover.[59] Apart from the festival of tabernacles, it is the only festival that lasts for seven days. Moreover, it takes place in the first month, and according to *Jubilees* itself, it is a joyful festival (*Jub.* 49:2, 22). Several exegetes have tried to strengthen the connection between *Jub.* 18:18-19 and the preceding narrative by considering the *Aqedah* as a prefiguration of Passover. According to Vermes, the saving virtue of the Passover lamb proceeded from the merits of the first lamb, i.e. Isaac, who offered himself upon the altar.[60] Huizenga stresses that 'the author has made the *Aqedah* an etiology of Passover: Isaac's near-sacrifice takes place at the precise calendrical time of the paschal ritual'.[61] It must be admitted that there are some similarities between the story of the binding of Isaac and the description of Passover in *Jubilees*.[62] Apart from the date (*Jub.* 49:1), one can also point to the important role of Prince Mastema both in the *Aqedah* and in the Passover (*Jub.* 48:2, 9, 12).[63] Halpern-Amaru points to the transformation of Isaac as 'only' and 'beloved son' (Gen. 22:2, 12, 16; cf. *Jub.* 18:2) into a 'first-born' son after he is no longer at risk (*Jub.* 18:11, 15). According to her, 'the author of *Jubilees* is creating a deliberate association between the rescued Isaac and the first-born sons of the Israelites who are saved from the tenth plague'.[64]

I think it is clear that *Jub.* 18:18-19 refers to the festival of unleavened bread. Moreover, there are some parallels between the story of the *Aqedah* and the Passover story. However, the connection of *Jub.* 18:18-19 with the preceding narrative is much looser than, for example, that of the festival of tabernacles with its context. There is no mention of joy in the narrative of the *Aqedah*, and no month is given in *Jub.* 18:18-19. Moreover, in the Bible (cf. Exod. 12:15-20; Lev. 23:6-8; Num. 28:16-25; Deut. 16:8) the festival

59   G. Vermes, 'Redemption and Genesis xxii – The Binding of Isaac and the Sacrifice of Jesus', in idem, *Scripture and Tradition: Haggadic Studies* (SPB, 4; 2nd ed. Leiden: Brill, 1973), pp.193–227 (esp. 215, n.3); Jaubert, *Notion*, p.90, n.5; VanderKam, 'Aqedah', p.247.

60   The tradition of the association of the *Aqedah* and Passover continued to play a part until the 2nd century C.E. See Vermes, 'Redemption', pp.215–16.

61   Huizenga, 'Battle for Isaac', p.33.

62   Segal quite strongly emphazises that the rewritten version of Gen. 22:1-19 in *Jubilees* considers the *Aqedah* as a foreshadowing of the Passover, on the basis of the date of the story, Isaac as firstborn, the occurrence of the sheep, and Mount Zion. See Segal, *Book of* Jubilees, pp.191–8.

63   VanderKam, 'Aqedah', p.248; Huizenga, 'Battle for Isaac', pp.45–6.

64   Halpern-Amaru, 'Note on Isaac', p.129; see also Segal, *Book of* Jubilees, pp.194–7.

of unleavened bread is from the 15th until the 21st of the first month.[65] This might indicate that according to the halakic addition, the dates of Abraham's travel took place from the 15th until the 21st. This is in contrast, however, with the preceding narrative, which speaks about the 12th of the first month as the date for the beginning of the trial (cf. *Jub.* 17:15), and there is no hint of any delay between the revelation to Abraham and the actual departure.[66] Apart from *Jub.* 17:15a, indicators of time can be found in 18:3a ('early in the morning'), 18:3e ('on the third day', or 'in three days'), and 18:18b ('seven days during which he went and returned safely'). It seems to be obvious that the challenge of Mastema and the commandment of Yhwh took place on the 12th of the first month, which is according to the calendar of *Jubilees* a Sunday. According to some, the departure of Abraham was on Monday, the 13th ('early in the morning'), whereas the arrival and the binding of Isaac should then have been on Wednesday the 15th. The return-trip started on the 16th and ended on the 18th, a Saturday.[67] In the light of the strict Sabbath observance, some find it problematic to imagine that Abraham would have travelled on a Sabbath day.[68] However, when one realizes that the author of *Jubilees* could have viewed the evening as the beginning of the day, it works out somewhat differently.[69] In this case the challenge of Mastema took place during the evening or night of the 12th of the first month, but 'early in the morning' (*Jub.* 18:3a) was still on the same day. The arrival at the mountain was, in this view, not on the 15th but on the 14th,[70] whereas the return-trip took place from the 15th until the 17th. The 18th could in this case be celebrated as a Sabbath. In this proposal, however, the trip lasted for only six days, which is in contrast with *Jub.* 18:18b ('... the seven days during which he went and returned safely'). Whether one reckons with a journey of seven (12th–18th of the first month) or six days (12th–17th of the first month), in both cases this does not match the biblical date of the festival of unleavened bread (15th–21th of the first month). One could argue that *Jub.* 18:18-19 does not say that the dates of the

---

65   Cf. VanderKam, 'Aqedah', p.248; J. Baumgarten, 'The Calendar of the Book of *Jubilees* and the Bible', in idem, *Studies in Qumran Law* (Leiden: Brill, 1977), pp.101–14 (esp. 103–4). Compare *Jub.* 49.1 ('Remember the commandments which the Lord gave you regarding the passover so that you may celebrate it at its time on the fourteenth of the first month, that you may sacrifice it before evening, and so that they may eat it at night on the evening of the fifteenth from the time of sunset').

66   Cf. Segal, *Book of Jubilees*, pp.200–1.

67   This is more or less the opinion of Le Déaut, although according to him, Abraham departed on the 12th. R. Le Déaut, *La nuit pascale: Essai sur la signification de la Pâque juive à partir du Targum d'Exode XII 42* (AnBib, 22; Rome: Institut biblique pontifical, 1963), pp.179–84; cf. A. Jaubert, 'Le calendrier des *Jubilés* et les jours liturgiques de la semaine', *VT* 7 (1957), pp.252–3.

68   VanderKam, 'Aqedah', p.246. See esp. *Jub.* 2:29-30.

69   J. Baumgarten, 'The Beginning of the Day in the Calendar of *Jubilees*', *JBL* 77 (1958), pp.355–60; VanderKam, 'Aqedah', pp.247–8.

70   G. Vermes, 'Redemption and Genesis xxii', p.215, n.3; Jaubert, *Notion*, p.90, n.5; VanderKam, 'Aqedah', p.247.

festival are the same as the days of the travel of Abraham. However, according to some, when the author wanted to connect the story of Isaac's binding with the festival of unleavened bread one would have expected an agreement in reference to the dates.[71] It does not seem that Abraham himself celebrated the festival from the 12th to the 18th in conformity with the dates of the story.[72] This understanding is a harmonization of the legal passage in the light of the narrative, but the solution is uncharacteristic for *Jubilees*.[73]

According to Segal and Kugel, the tension between the two parts of the text presupposes that they are of different provenance.[74] *Jubilees* 18:18-19 would be the work of an interpolator, who might have thought that the original author, who rewrote Gen. 22:1-19, intended to create a precedent for Passover. However, according to Kugel, the original author did not refer to Passover. In fact, it was not necessary to create a precedent for the Passover in patriarchal times, since it has been proclaimed before the Sinai events (Exodus 12; cf. *Jub.* 49).[75] Moreover, the date of the near-offering was not chosen because of the date of the offering of *pesah*, but he chose the 15th of the month, because it was a significant day for him.[76] The least one can say is that the author of the halakic passage connects the rewritten story with the festival of the unleavened bread, albeit in an imperfect way as far as the date is concerned. I doubt whether the conclusion that both parts are of different origins because of the different dates is correct. The preceding narrative of the festival of weeks puts the offering of Noah and the conclusion of the covenant on the first of the third month (*Jub.* 6:1). The festival of weeks is first dated merely 'in the third month' (*Jub.* 6:17, 20; cf. 6:11).[77] Later in the book, it is placed in the middle of this month (*Jub.* 15:1; 16:13; 44:4). With regard to the festival of tabernacles, no date is given, neither in the halakic addition, nor in the preceding narrative.[78]

71   So also Segal, *Book of Jubilees*, pp.198–9.

72   This is the opinion of J. van Goudoever, *Biblical Calendars* (2nd edn; Leiden: Brill, 1961), pp.68–9.

73   Segal, *Book of Jubilees*, p.199.

74   Segal, *Book of Jubilees*, pp.201–2; Kugel, 'On the Interpolations', pp.233–6. Segal, *Book of Jubilees*, p.201, prefers not to resolve this tension between the rewritten story and the halakic passage against the plain meaning of both passages. According to him, in the rewritten story the *Aqedah* is a foreshadowing of Passover, whereas the halakic passage refers to the festival of the unleavened bread. Both passages are from a different origin.

75   Kugel, 'On the Interpolations', p.235, n.27.

76   Kugel, 'On the Interpolations', p.235. He refers especially to Ravid for this observation. See L. Ravid, 'The Book of *Jubilees* and Its Calendar – A Reexamination', *DSD* 10 (2003), pp.371–94 (esp. 381).

77   An important reason for Kugel to presuppose that the festival mentioned in *Jub.* 6:17-22 is not the festival of weeks, but a festival of oaths, is the fact that the date of Noah's offering did not match with the festival of weeks. Only in a later stage were both festivals combined. See Kugel, 'On the Interpolations', pp.241–8.

78   In contrast to this, one can point of course to the day of antonement. Both in the halakic addition (*Jub.* 34:18) and in the preceding narrative (*Jub.* 34:10-17) the same date is given ('the tenth day of the seventh month').

Concluding remarks

Before the 1st century C.E., there was no single list of books regarded as authoritative by all Jewish people. Nevertheless there is enough evidence to suggest that at least some books were considered as divinely inspired. There appear to be collections of such books, although the exact contents of these collections and the exact form of these books is less clear. The five books of Moses were highly regarded and the object of interpretation and the book of Genesis had an enormous impact on early Jewish literature. In this contribution, I have pointed to works that completely rewrote the book of Genesis (e.g., *Jubilees*, *Genesis Apocryphon*), that were shaped by the creation story in the book of Genesis (first book of the *Sibylline Oracles*, *2 Enoch*), and were named after important narrative characters (Adam, Abraham, Jacob, Joseph). Lastly, I looked at the story of the offering of Isaac and the way it was used in the book of *Jubilees*. The story is reproduced fairly literally but was introduced and rounded off by a halakic addition. With regard to the halakic addition, I have tried to show that the author of the passage connects the rewritten story with the festival of unleavened bread, albeit in an imperfect way. However, this does not necessarily lead to the conclusion that both parts are of different origins.

Chapter 2

Genesis in Mark's Gospel

Stephen P. Ahearne-Kroll

Introduction

There are only two direct quotations from Genesis in Mark, both in chapter 10 (Gen. 1:27 in Mk 10:6 and Gen. 2:24 in Mk 10:7), so this chapter will flow differently than others in this book that have multiple quotations to discuss. The first section of this chapter will discuss these quotations, but it will also discuss allusions to Genesis 22 in Mk 1:11; 9:7; and 12:6; to Gen. 1:27 and 2:24 in Mk 10:6-8; and to Gen. 49:11 in Mk 11:2-4 that I have judged to have a substantial impact on the sections of Mark in which they appear. The second section will discuss allusions that have a less significant impact on Mark (Gen. 37:20 in Mk 12:7 and Gen. 39:6-20 in Mk 14:51-52), and the third section will briefly discuss allusions (sometimes faint) that I have judged to have little impact on Mark (Gen. 14:8 in Mk 5:7; Gen. 6:5 and 8:21 in Mk 7:19; Gen. 1:31 in Mk 7:37; Gen. 18:14 in Mk 10:27; and Gen. 38:8 in Mk 12:18-19). In each section, I will discuss the quotations and allusions in the order they appear in Mark. Finally, I will offer some synthesizing comments at the end of the chapter on the use of Genesis in Mark. The issues of textual affinities between Mark and the MT and LXX of Genesis will be discussed on a very limited basis since there are only two direct quotations of Genesis in Mark (both in the same passage). Allusions are difficult to confirm, even under the best of circumstances, so determining the textual relationship between Mark and Genesis in these cases usually leads to few probable conclusions.

Quotations and Major Allusions

Genesis 22 in Mk 1:11; 9:7; 12:6

The voice at Jesus' baptism declares to him, 'You are my beloved son; in you I delight'.[1] Most scholars point to Ps. 2:7 as the main referent of

---

1   Mk 1:11. All translations of the original languages are mine unless otherwise noted.

the first part of this declaration, but the lexical similarity between it and LXX Gen. 22:2, 12, and 16[2] makes it a likely reference, as well.[3] Both use ἀγαπητός and a possessive pronoun (μου in Mk 1:11 and σου in Gen. 22:2, 12, 16) as the qualifiers for υἱός. The same lexical similarity appears in Mk 9:7 and 12:6. The sacrificial overtones of Jesus' death later in the story (esp. Mk 10:41-45) could be understood to evoke Isaac's near sacrifice at God's behest (cf. 14:36). The lexical similarities and the thematic similarities of the sacrifice of the beloved son suggest that Genesis 22 should be read along with Mark's story of Jesus starting with the baptism.

Only some scholars would concede that Gen. 22:2, 12, and 16 shaped Mk 1:11 (and, subsequently, 9:7, 12:6, and perhaps 14:36), and even those that do offer this as a possibility rarely discuss the implications for Jesus' baptism and the story as a whole.[4] Matthew S. Rindge, however, offers one

---

2   All references to Genesis 22 will be to the LXX.

3   One need not choose between the two because more than one biblical reference may be held in tension by Mark and the audience. Holding multiple references in tension reflects the frequent ambiguity of Mark's story and adds to the depth of imagery used to portray Jesus in Mark. See E. Struthers Malbon, *Mark's Jesus: Characterization as Narrative Christology* (Waco, TX: Baylor University, 2009), p.190; and T. R. Hatina, 'Embedded Scripture Texts and the Plurality of Meaning: The Announcement of the "Voice from Heaven" in Mark 1.11 as a Case Study', in T. R. Hatina (ed.), *Biblical Interpretation in Early Christian Gospels: Volume I, The Gospel of Mark* (LNTS, 304; London: T&T Clark, 2006), pp.81–99.

4   J. Gnilka says, 'Eine Anlehnung an die Isaaktypologie ist schwerlich auszumachen' (*Das Evangelium nach Markus* [2 vols; EKK; Zürich: Benzinger, 1978], p.1.53). A. Yarbro Collins considers the evocation of Genesis 22 in Mk 1:11a, but then argues that Isa. 42:1, a verse that is 'actualized or fulfilled' in Mk 1:11b, inspired the expression ὁ ἀγαπητός (*Mark: A Commentary* [Hermeneia; Minneapolis, MN: Fortress, 2007], p.150). J. Marcus looks to the importance of Isaac's binding in rabbinic traditions and notes that these traditions might be extant in the first century. But then he opts for the eschatological trajectories of interpretation found in post-biblical Judaism regarding Psalm 2 and Isaiah 42 and subsequently drops consideration of Genesis 22 playing any significant role on the baptism of Jesus (*Mark 1–8* [AB, 27; New York: Doubleday, 2000], pp.162, 166–7). I. Brent Driggers says the allusion to Genesis 22 in Mk 1:11 'strikes an ominous tone' in the prologue to Mark, but he does not develop this idea other than to link it to the theological tension present in these first verses of the Gospel (*Following God through Mark: Theological Tension in the Second Gospel* [Louisville, KY: WJK Press, 2007], p.19). V. Taylor only mentions Gen. 22:2 as an echo in Mk 1:11 (*The Gospel According to St. Mark* [2d edn; Grand Rapids, MI: Baker Book House, 1966, repr. 1981], p.162). B. M. F. van Iersel simply comments that the reader is reminded of Abraham in Genesis 22 when reading Mk 1:11 (*Mark: A Reader Response Commentary* [trans. W. H. Bisscheroux; London: T&T Clark, 1998], p.101). Hatina says, 'If Mark and/or his audience associated the binding of Isaac with the baptism of Jesus it would probably not have been limited to the story as it is found in the MT or the LXX, for aside from the dictional parallel, there is very little theological or thematic resemblance' ('Embedded Scripture Texts', p.88). The rest of his analysis in 88–93 has an interesting treatment of the post-biblical interpretation history of the Aqedah to show the possibility that Mk 1:11 may have been interpreting the Aqedah either similarly to some contemporaries or through the filters of this interpretive

of the more extensive and convincing treatments of the connection between the Gospel as a whole and the Aqedah. After he establishes the lexical and thematic similarities described above, Rindge argues that the rest of the Gospel contains some suggestive allusions to Genesis 22, indicating an interest in depicting the story of the Markan Jesus as a reconfiguration of the Aqedah.[5] Rindge first points to (1) the testing (πειράζω) of Jesus, beginning at Mk 1:12, which recalls Gen. 22:1, ὁ θεὸς ἐπείραζεν τὸν Αβρααμ; and (2) Mark's use of σχίζω in 1:10 to describe the opening of the clouds for the descent of the Spirit, which recalls Abraham's splitting of the wood for the impending sacrifice of Isaac in Gen. 22:3. Rindge then points to the following intratextual relationships in the baptism scene and the death scene of Jesus in Mk 15:33-39: the use of σχίζω to describe the tearing of the sky at the baptism (1:10) and of the temple curtain at the death (15:38); the declarations by the voice at the baptism (1:11) and the centurion at the cross that Jesus is υἱὸς θεοῦ (15:39); and the voice (φωνή) at the baptism (1.10) and Jesus' cries from the cross (φωνή; 15:34, 37). This allows Rindge to link the allusions to Genesis 22 with the death scene in Mark. Rindge also notices that, like Genesis 22, Mark contains three references to the beloved son – 1:11; 9:7; and 12:6. There are also striking similarities between Genesis 22 and the scene at Gethsemane in Mark 14. For example, Jesus takes Peter, James, and John but leaves behind his disciples, while Abraham takes Isaac and leaves behind his servants. Isaac talks to his father (πατήρ) in Gen. 22:7 as does Jesus at Gethsemane (14:36).[6] Taking into account this chain of allusions to Genesis 22, Rindge argues that Mark, beginning with Jesus' baptism, reconfigures the story of the Aqedah to tell the story of Jesus. Mark links each reference to the impending death of Jesus, thereby presenting Jesus as an Isaac figure. The major difference between the Markan Jesus and Isaac is that God rescues Isaac before he is killed, whereas God does not rescue Jesus.

Rindge's argument is a complex one, and overall, it is convincing, even if some of the allusions he argues for are not certain. But once the lexical similarities between Gen. 22:2, 12, and 16 and Mk 1:11, 9:7, and 12:6 are established, then it is possible to read Mark in light of Genesis 22 as Rindge argues, and the implications for doing so are intriguing. For example, Rindge's argument for Mark's depiction of Jesus as an Isaac figure lends

---

tradition. Hatina's aim, however, is not to offer the implications of reference to the Aqedah for the overall narrative presentation of Jesus. Instead, his analysis offers part of his overall argument for plurality of meaning in Mark's use of Scripture. See also J. B. Gibson, *The Temptations of Jesus in Early Christianity* (London: T&T Clark, 2004), pp.71–8.

5   M. S. Rindge, 'Reconfiguring the Akedah and Recasting God: Lament and Divine Abandonment in Mark', forthcoming in *JBL*.

6   Philo's reading of Genesis 22 also has a close parallel to Mk 14:36. He has Abraham answer Isaac's question about the presence of the sacrifice with 'but know *all things are possible with God*' (πάντα δ' ἴσθι θεῷ δυνατά) (*Abr.* 175). See Rindge, 'Reconfiguring the Akedah'.

further depth to the sacrificial aspect of Jesus' crucifixion. There is another possible dimension to Mark's use of Genesis 22. In Genesis 22, there are three characters depicted in the drama – Abraham, Isaac, and God – whereas in Mark, there are really only two characters at play – Jesus and God. Jesus could be thought of as taking on the characteristics of *both* Abraham and Isaac because not only is Jesus the one offered up (like Isaac), he is also the one who is tested and offers up the beloved son, i.e. himself (like Abraham). The Gethsemane scene in Mark speaks to the ambiguity of whether God or Jesus is the Abrahamic figure in the story. There, it is Jesus who is tested and succumbs to the will of God – 'but not what I want, but what you [want]' (14:36) – not withholding himself from death seemingly at God's command. Whether Jesus or God takes on the role of Abraham, the point is that Mark arguably makes Jesus a sacrificial Isaac figure through the use of Genesis 22, and perhaps a faithful and obedient Abraham figure as well.

Gen. 1:27 and 2:24 in Mk 10:6-8

The only direct quotations from Genesis in Mark fall within Jesus' discussion with the Pharisees regarding divorce in 10:2-9. The Pharisees approach Jesus and ask whether a man is allowed to divorce a woman. Mark comments in v.2 that they did this in order to test Jesus. Jesus answers the question with a question, 'What does Moses command?' The Pharisees respond with an allusion to Deut. 24:1-4, which contains the only explicit directive about divorce in Scripture: a man is allowed to write a certificate of divorce and divorce his wife. Jesus then counters with his interpretation of Moses' directive (Moses allowed this because of 'your' hardness of heart [σκληρο–καρδίαν]) and his teaching that divorce does not fit God's original plan for humanity. Jesus does this by quoting Gen. 1:27 and 2:24 in the next two and a half verses, and affirming that marriage creates a relationship of unity rather than a partnership of two. Finally, he establishes this as God's doing, something which humans[7] should not undo.

The quotations from Gen. 1:27 and 2:24 likely both come from the LXX, although this is more clearly the case in the quotation from 2:24. The MT lacks any designation for 'the two', whereas the LXX has οἱ δύο as the subject of the end of 2:24 as it appears in Mk 10:8a.[8] In v.7, several

---

7   The word used here is ἄνθρωπος. Although this is the more gender-inclusive term for humanity, here it probably means 'man' because of the normal practice of a man securing a divorce from his wife. There is some evidence that Jewish women could seek a divorce from their husbands, but the process by which this happens is debated. What is at issue is whether a woman has the right to write a divorce certificate and present it to her husband, or whether the woman has the right to appeal to a court to convince her husband to divorce her. See D. Instone-Brewer, *Divorce and Remarriage in the Bible: The Social and Literary Context* (Grand Rapids, MI: Eerdmans, 2002), pp.85–90.

8   There is no reason to think that Mark was using a Hebrew source that also contained a phrase that would translate into 'the two' since the LXX matches exactly with what we have in Mk 10:8.

important manuscripts leave out καὶ προσκολληθήσεται πρὸς τὴν γυναῖκα αὐτοῦ from the quotation of Gen. 2:24.[9] This discrepancy was probably due to accidental scribal omission (skipping from the καί that starts this phrase to the καί that starts v.8), and so most scholars judge the phrase to be original to Mark.[10]

The use of these quotations by Mark's Jesus underlies the presentation of his teaching on divorce regulations in Judaism. While a full treatment of divorce practices in Judaism is beyond our scope, it is important to have a basic sense of these practices in order to situate Jesus' teaching within its greater context. Most important to our discussion is the fact that there is almost no evidence of opposition to divorce in Judaism during the first century C.E. What forces qualification of this statement is CD 4:19–5:2, whose meaning scholars debate. The text reads:

> The builders of the wall who go after Zaw – Zaw is the preacher of whom he said: 'Assuredly they will preach' [Mic 2:6] – are caught twice in fornication: by taking two wives in their lives, even though the principle of creation is 'male and female he created them' [Gen 1:27], and the ones who went in to the ark 'went in two by two into the ark' [Gen 7:9]. And about the prince it is written, 'He should not multiply wives to himself' [Deut 17:17].[11]

It is debated whether this passage prohibits polygamy or divorce. Adela Yarbro Collins argues clearly and convincingly against this passage prohibiting divorce by examining all the passages among the DSS that refer to divorce (CD 13:15-18 and 4Q271 frg. 3, lines 10-15) and concluding that the Damascus Document as a whole, and therefore CD 4:21, allows divorce and remarriage for a man only after the first wife is dead.[12] In any case, the thrust of the passage seems to be more focused on monogamy as the ideal, which is in line with 'the principle of creation' as articulated in Gen. 1:27.

The grounds on which one could divorce were more at issue in the first century than whether or not divorce was allowed. The Mishnah talks

---

9 ℵ B Ψ 892*. 2427 sy⁵. Verse 6 also has two major textual variants that do not change the significance of the quotation much. D W *pc* it ἄρσεν καὶ θῆλυ ἐποίησεν ὁ θεός, and A Θ Ψ *f*¹·¹³ *et al.* have ἄρσεν καὶ θῆλυ ἐποίησεν αὐτοὺς ὁ θεός.

10 See B. M. Metzger, *A Textual Commentary on the Greek New Testament* (2nd edn; Stuttgart: Deutsche Bibelgesellschaft, 1994), pp.88–9.

11 Text and translation from F. García Martínez and E. J. C. Tigchelaar (eds), *The Dead Sea Scrolls Study Edition* (2 vols; Leiden: Brill, 1997), p.1.556.

12 The most convincing part of the argument is the acceptance of divorce in CD 13:15–18, which requires a closer examination of CD 4:21. In the latter, 'all three scripture examples argue against polygamy, not against divorce' (Collins, *Mark*, 462; see pp.461–3 for the whole argument and the supporting secondary literature). J. A. Fitzmyer also argues that this passage talks of divorce and remarriage ('The Matthean Divorce Texts and Some New Palestinian Evidence', *TS* 37 [1976], pp.197–226). See also Marcus, *Mark 8–16* (AB, 27A; New Haven, CT: Yale University, 2009), p.708.

about the grounds of divorce debate among some of the great rabbis (*m. Gittin* 9:10). The debate centred around the interpretation of Deut. 24:1, which states that a husband could divorce his wife if he found 'something objectionable' (ערות דבר). 'Something objectionable' to the school of Shammai meant sexual misconduct on the woman's part, whereas the school of Hillel held that it could be anything, 'Even if she spoiled a dish for him', and Rabbi Aqiba held, 'Even if he found another more beautiful than she is'.[13] Instone-Brewer argues that the Pharisees' question to Jesus assumes a missing element referring to the grounds for divorce because divorce was such an accepted practice among Jews. In other words, no Jew would even think of debating the practice of divorce, so what the grounds for divorce were would most likely be assumed by the question. The parallel Matthean passage to Mk 10:2 (i.e. Mt. 19:3) makes explicit this assumption: 'Is it lawful for a man to divorce his wife *for any reason* (κατὰ πᾶσαν αἰτίαν)?'[14] If we can assume in the Pharisees' question in Mark what Matthew makes explicit, which seems reasonable, then Jesus' answer in Mk 10:6-8 is all the more unusual because he forbids divorce. *How* he answers concerns us most because his argument uses the double quotation from Genesis to justify his forbidding of divorce.

After the Pharisees ask their question in 10:2, Jesus asks them what Moses commanded, to which they answer by paraphrasing Deut. 24:1-4, the passage at the heart of first-century debate about the grounds for divorce. Jesus then trumps what Moses permits by appealing to the divine ideal as articulated in Gen. 1:27 and 2:24.[15] Craig A. Evans hyperbolically points to a problem of whether or not all of Scripture was equally authoritative to Jews in the first century by saying, 'The way Jesus sets one Scripture…against

---

13   See J. R. Donahue and D. J. Harrington, *The Gospel of Mark* (SP, 2; Collegeville, MN: Liturgical Press, 2002), p.296. See also Instone-Brewer, *Divorce and Remarriage*, pp.134–5, where he includes references to this debate in *y. Sota* 1.2, 16b, *Sifré Deut.* 269, Philo, *Spec. Leg.* 3:30 (2:304), and Josephus, *Ant.* 4:253.

14   Instone-Brewer, *Divorce and Remarriage*, pp.134–6. F. Moloney seems to miss this dimension of the discussion: 'They question him about the lawfulness of divorce (v.2b). There was some debate about this matter among the leading rabbinic schools of Hillel and Shammai, but this debate is not reflected in the Pharisees' questions. They ask for a judgment from Jesus on whether divorce should be allowed' (*The Gospel of Mark: A Commentary* [Peabody, MA: Hendrickson, 2002], p.193). Marcus says, 'It is odd that this question should be raised at all, since, as the Pharisees will immediately remind Jesus, the Law of Moses makes explicit provision for divorce…and therefore all of the major sects in the first century seem to have permitted it….It may be, therefore, that we should assume that Jesus' reputation for opposing divorce has preceded him and that the Pharisees want to get him in to trouble by forcing him to acknowledge this' (*Mark 8–16*, p.709).

15   Instone-Brewer notes that the linking of these passages is an example of the early rabbinic exegetical technique called *gezera shavah*. 'The two texts, Genesis 1:27 and 2:24, are linked so that a single conclusion can be drawn from them. The activity of God in the first text is inferred in the second text, and thus it is God who joins them together' (*Divorce and Remarriage*, p.137).

another...without resolving the tension is highly unusual, even unique'.[16] Instone-Brewer resolves this tension by claiming as original Matthew's version of the exchange between Jesus and the Pharisees, which has the Pharisees referring to Deut. 24:1-4 as a command, while Jesus refers to it as Moses' allowance for divorce.[17] After Joel Marcus points to some occasions where Jewish literature refers to an 'original version' of the Law (i.e. uncorrupted by tradition), he says, 'Despite these precedents, it is still a radical step for the Markan Jesus to imply that "halakah based upon Eden"...might *supersede* the halakah of Sinai'.[18]

Despite Evans' and Marcus' assertions that what Jesus does is terribly unusual, his actions fit quite well within the ongoing dialogue about the authority and nature of Scripture beginning within the Hebrew Bible and carrying on through early rabbinic texts. Steven Fraade outlines a segment of this larger debate, namely, the dialogue in early rabbinic Judaism about the role that Moses played in communicating the commands of God to Israel. Was Moses simply a passive conduit of the Torah from God to Israel, or was he more intellectually active in interpreting or even creating elements of the tradition? In other words, is the text a dictation directly from God, a creation of Moses who was in dialogue with God, or a little of both? These questions were debated in the Mekiltas, Tannaitic literature, Talmudic traditions, and later midrashic literature.[19] And these debates were not new since the biblical text itself is unclear about the role that Moses plays in communicating the Torah to Israel on Sinai.[20] In the context of this centuries-old debate, Jesus' statement in Mark can be thought of as privileging one text (Gen. 1:27 and 2:24) over another (Deut. 24:1-4) as more authoritative.[21]

---

16   C. A. Evans, *Mark 8:27–16:20* (WBC, 34B; Nashville, TN: Thomas R. Nelson, 2001), p.80.

17   Instone-Brewer, *Divorce and Remarriage*, pp.141–6.

18   Marcus, *Mark 8–16*, p.710. Malbon argues that the dynamic of contrasting the authority of certain texts is part of a pattern in Mark. With regard to our text, she says, 'When the Pharisees cite tradition, Jesus cites the commandment of God; when the Pharisees cite the commandment of God, Jesus cites an earlier commandment of God as primary!' (*Mark's Jesus*, p.156).

19   S. D. Fraade, 'Moses and the Commandments: Can Hermeneutics, History, and Rhetoric Be Disentangled?', in H. Najman and J. H. Newman (eds), *The Idea of Biblical Interpretation: Essays in Honor of James Kugel* (JSJSup, 83; Leiden: Brill, 2004), pp.399–422.

20   Among the many examples Fraade mentions, he includes the fact that in Deuteronomy, it is assumed that it is only the Ten Commandments that are communicated directly to the people at Mt Sinai. The rest was communicated by Moses only when the people reached the land of Moab and were getting ready to enter the Promised Land (cf. Deut. 5:19, 28; 6:1; 10:4). See Fraade, 'Moses and the Commandments', pp.399–400, n.2.

21   Donahue and Harrington say, 'The idea is that these texts override or "trump" Moses' concession to the hardness of heart in Deut 24:1-4'. I agree with this. However, the next statement is dubious, in my view: 'The basis for this idea is the concept of the "new creation" inaugurated in Jesus' ministry. Now God's original plan for men and women set forth in Genesis 1 and 2 can be actualized' (*Mark*, p.294). See also Moloney, *Mark*,

So, instead of answering the (assumed) question about the grounds for divorce, Jesus uses the double quotation from Genesis 1 and 2 to change the terms of the debate. For the Markan Jesus, it is more important to articulate the principles for monogamy than it is to debate the grounds for divorce as the Pharisees would like. Much as CD 4:21 uses Gen. 1:27 to articulate 'the principle of creation' (ויסוד הבריאה) as the basis for monogamy, Mark's Jesus uses the double quotation of Gen. 1:27 and 2:24 to express the divine intention for male and female, and thus he argues for the principle of monogamy as in line with divine intention.[22] This principle allows Jesus not only to forbid divorce but to equate it with adultery when his disciples ask him in private to elaborate on his teaching about divorce (Mk 10:10-12).

Gen. 49:11 in Mk 11:2-4

Mk 11:1-11 describes in great detail Jesus' entry into Jerusalem. Mark includes repeated references to a 'foal' (πῶλος and its pronouns are used twelve times), a detailed description of its location ('at a door outside on the street' [πρὸς θύραν ἔξω ἐπὶ τοῦ ἀμφόδου]) and condition ('tied up' [δεδεμένον] and 'upon which no person has ever sat' [ἐφ᾽ ὃν οὐδεὶς οὔπω ἀνθρώπων ἐκάθισεν]), and explicit instructions about what to do with it. The heavy focus on this animal and Jesus' unusual act of mounting it and riding it into the city[23] lead the reader to search for scriptural precedents to understand the animal's presence in the story.

---

p.194, for similar restoration language. Marcus has a similar argument, concluding, 'The continuation of the passage in 10.6a ("but from the beginning of the creation…") implies that this Mosaic provision was meant to prevail only for a limited time, until the dawning of the eschatological era that would restore the conditions of Eden' (*Mark 8–16*, p.710). Fraade's evidence for an ongoing debate within Judaism seems much more reasonable.

22   Mark's appeal to the primordial divine intention is similar to the way some Roman authors argue against divorce in the early Empire. M. R. D'Angelo offers a helpful discussion of Dionysius of Halicarnassus' attempt to appeal to the original ideal of the permanence of marriage from the mythological foundations of Rome (pp.72–3). She concludes, 'At best one might say that the treatment of marriage in the public debate supports the principle (central to the Roman legal discussions) that a stable marriage should not be disturbed, and its exegesis of Genesis excels the moral nostalgia of Dionysius of Halicarnassus's vision of an original, indissoluble Roman form of marriage. The teaching for the inner circle of the disciples revised that principle to equate remarriage after divorce with an infraction of the sixth commandment – and the Roman adultery law' ('Roman Imperial Family Values and the Gospel of Mark: The Divorce Sayings (Mark 10:2-12)' in S. P. Ahearne-Kroll, P. A. Holloway, and J. A. Kelhoffer (eds), *Women and Gender in Ancient Religions: Interdisciplinary Approaches* [WUNT, 263; Tübingen: Mohr Siebeck, 2010], p.77).

23   Collins says, 'The special arrangements described for obtaining a donkey imply that Jesus deliberately chose to ride into the city, rather than to walk' (*Mark*, p.518), and Moloney comments, 'It remains true that Jesus' gesture of riding into Jerusalem is irregular. Pilgrims normally walked into the city' (*Mark*, p.220, n.21).

The two most common Scripture passages that scholars appeal to as precedents for this episode are LXX Zech. 9:9 and LXX Gen. 49:11, both of which contain πῶλος.[24] Gen. 49:11 does not just mention a πῶλος, but the first half of the verse reads, 'Binding his foal to a vine | and his donkey's foal to a tendril' (δεσμεύων πρὸς ἄμπελον τὸν πῶλον αὐτοῦ | καὶ τῇ ἕλικι τὸν πῶλον τῆς ὄνου αὐτοῦ). So the similarities between this verse and Mk 11:2-11, and more specifically vv.2-4, include the reference to the πῶλος and its bound state. The relationship between Mk 11:1-11 and Zech. 9:9 is debated, but most scholars argue that Mark intended to tell the story of Jesus' entry into Jerusalem through the lens of Zech. 9:9 with Gen. 49:11 as additional background to depict Jesus as a royal messianic figure.[25]

The scene of the triumphal entry of Jesus into Jerusalem in Mk 11:1-25[26] certainly contains messianic images. Jesus riding on the foal to enter the

24   Most scholars focus on Zech. 9:9 as the key scriptural precedent for Jesus' act of riding into Jerusalem on a donkey. H. C. Kee is typical of those who include Gen. 49:11: 'There are indeed two unmistakable allusions to the Zechariah oracles at pivotal points in Mark. One is at 11:1-10, where Jesus is depicted as riding into Jerusalem on an ass – an obvious allusion to Zech. 9:9, which is made explicit in Matthew 21:5 (n.20: The incident also recalls Gen. 49:11, where the rising of the king from Judah is predicted)' (*Community of the New Age: Studies in Mark's Gospel* [Philadelphia: Westminster, 1977], p.111). See also M. E. Boring: 'Mark, unlike Matt. 21:4-5 and John 12:14-15, does not cite Zech. 9:9 or Gen. 49:11 specifically, though both are in the background, and both had already been interpreted messianically in first century Judaism' (*Mark: A Commentary* [NTL; Louisville: WJK, 2006], p.315).

25   Marcus' assessment is characteristic of the type of arguments scholars make: 'The royal implications of Jesus' entrance on a donkey would be deepened for those familiar with the scriptures, since the Markan description seems to echo two OT passages, Gen. 49:11 and Zech 9:9....These passages were both understood as messianic oracles in ancient Judaism...and the one from Zechariah has the same essential elements as Mark 11:1-11: the entry of the king, the messianic animal, and the jubilation of the people....The Genesis text is reflected in the otherwise superfluous note that the colt is tied (11:2, 4)' (*Mark*, p.778). But there are several major scholars who think that Mark had in mind neither Zech. 9:9 nor Gen. 49:11 in constructing his version of Jesus' entry into Jerusalem. Evans says, 'δεδεμένον, "tethered", may allude to Gen. 49:11' (*Mark 8:27–16:20*, p. 142), but the language is too common to press it. Moloney argues most strongly against the prevailing opinion: 'There is no trace of Zech 9 in the Markan episode, and we should not speculate that perhaps Mark had it in mind....Gnilka's reconstruction of a pre-Markan passage, on the basis of Zech 9:9 and Gen 49:10-11, is pure speculation,...Grundmann...uses Zech 9:9, Gen 49:10-11, and late rabbinic material to support his messianic interpretation of the passage' (*Gospel of Mark*, p.220, n.21).

26   Mk 11:1-25 describes a complex scene that happens over the course of two days, so strictly speaking, not all of the twenty-five verses describe Jesus' triumphal entry. However, as P. B. Duff has argued, Mark constructs the sequence of events in vv.1-25 in such a way that he combines Jesus' entry into Jerusalem and the temple with the cursing of the fig tree as a play on the typical literary scene of the triumphal entry of the Greco-Roman general or king into a newly conquered city. Therefore, the whole of vv.1-25 should be read as Jesus' triumphal entry into Jerusalem. See 'The March of the Divine Warrior and the Advent of the Greco-Roman King: Mark's Account of Jesus' Entry into Jerusalem', *JBL* 111 (1992), pp.55–71.

city alone should raise the eyebrow of the reader that Jesus is, at the very least, claiming a certain amount of authority for himself. The quotations of Ps. 118:25 and Ps. 148:1 in the crowd's royal acclamation in Mk 11:9-10, the use of κύριος as a self-designation for Jesus in Mk 11:3, and the act of entering into Jerusalem from the Mount of Olives all give the passage a strong messianic overtone, especially in the wake of Peter's declaration of Jesus as ὁ χριστός in 8:29. So even if the references to Zech. 9:9 and Gen. 49:11 are not explicit or unambiguously evoked, in the context of the way that Mark tells the story, one would not be off base to think these passages are alluded to purposefully by Mark. In this line of thinking, which represents the majority of scholars, it makes sense that Zech. 9:9 and Gen. 49:11 contribute to the royal messianic depiction of Jesus and nuance it significantly to show Jesus in a humble light rather than as a conquering, militaristic king.[27]

While there is nothing inherently wrong with the line of argument described above, it makes little attempt to interpret the use of Gen. 49:11 beyond its use as a prooftext for Jesus' messianic status or as part of a complex image of Jesus' messianship. Deborah Kraus, however, argues that Gen. 49:11, along with Zech. 9:9 and Ps. 118:25, form the scriptural framework for the construction of the story. They are not just background references to imbue the story with messianic significance, but the framework on which the story is built. Following Joseph Blenkinsopp, who describes the messianic interpretive history of the oracle in Gen. 49:8-11 within the Bible (namely, Zech. 9:9) and post-biblical Judaism,[28] Kraus argues for a creative interpretation of these passages by Mark:

> In light of the Genesis blessing, this protracted description of attaining the colt does more than merely set up the enactment [of] Zech 9:9. It takes Mark's audience back to an original image of blessing which the Zechariahan oracle associates with Davidic-dynastic power, and reverses it, more specifically, destroys it. By returning to the image of the colt bound to a vine, Mark shows that in Jerusalem the condition for abundant blessing no longer exists.[29]

Furthermore, she claims that Mark juxtaposes the public affirmation

---

27   Collins notes, 'He rides a donkey that evokes both the royal tradition of Gen. 49:11 and the humility (or the gentle and benign exercise of power) of Zech. 9:9' (*Mark*, p.518).

28   J. Blenkinsopp, 'The Oracle of Judah and the Messianic Entry', *JBL* 80 (1961), pp.55–64. See also Marcus, *Mark 8–16*, p.778: 'The two OT passages [Gen. 49:11 and Zech. 9:9] were traditionally related (see, e.g. their juxtaposition in *Gen. Rab.* 98.9), and it is likely that the Zecharian oracle was exegetically derived from the Genesis one.'

29   D. Kraus, 'The One Who Comes Unbinding the Blessing of Judah: Mark 11.1-10 as a Midrash on Genesis 49.11, Zechariah 9.9, and Psalm 118.25-26', in C. A. Evans and J. A. Sanders (eds), *Early Christian Interpretation of the Scriptures of Israel: Investigations and Proposals* (JSNTSup, 148/Studies in Scripture in Early Judaism and Christianity, 5; Sheffield: Sheffield Academic Press, 1996), pp.149–50.

about Jesus' coming Davidic kingship made by the crowds in Mk 11:8-10 with the 'private symbolic act [in vv.2-7] which erodes the very basis of the Zechariahan claims'.[30] So, Mark's use of Gen. 49:11 does not simply fill in the background of the presentation of Jesus' messiahship or add another image of royal messianism to the characterization of Jesus. Instead, it works ironically to undermine traditional notions of the state of blessing that Israel might perceive as a result of the presence of the Messiah in Jesus. Although not an airtight argument, it fits with Mark's narrative skill of building his narrative with creative interpretation of Scripture in mind.[31]

Less Significant Allusions

There are two recognizable allusions to Genesis that have a less significant impact on Mark's narrative; both come from the Joseph cycle in Genesis. The first shows up in Mk 12:7 in the midst of the parable of the wicked tenants. The resolution of the tenants to kill the beloved son uses the words δεῦτε ἀποκτείνωμεν αὐτόν, which are identical to those used by Joseph's brothers when plotting against him in LXX Gen. 37:20. Marcus argues for a further verbal connection between the two stories found in the tenants' desire to 'throw [the beloved son] out' of the vineyard (Mk 12:8) and Joseph's brothers wanting to 'throw him into a pit' (Gen. 37:20), but the verbs for throwing are different in the two verses (ἐκβάλλω in Mk 12:8 and ῥίπτω in Gen. 37:20).[32] Marcus goes on to compare the scene in Mark with the Joseph story to highlight the fact that, unlike Joseph, who forgives brothers, the lord of the vineyard doesn't forgive, destroys the tenants, and gives the vineyard to others.[33]

Only a few other scholars think that Gen. 37:20 has some influence on the parable in Mark, however. Along with Marcus, John Donahue and Daniel Harrington,[34] Joachim Gnilka,[35] Craig A. Evans,[36] Vincent Taylor,[37]

30   Kraus, 'The One Who Comes', p.150.
31   The more I study Mark's use of Scripture, the more it is clear, in places where we can demonstrate some purposeful use of Scripture by the author, how innovative the author is in utilizing creative interpretations of Scripture in narrating his story of Jesus.
32   Marcus, *Mark 8–16*, p.803.
33   Marcus, *Mark 8–16*, p.813.
34   Donahue and Harrington point to the possible Joseph typology, 'especially with regard to the theme of the two as innocent sufferers'. They go on to point to the 'more promising motif' of the jealousy that motivated Joseph's brothers as a type for the motivation of the tenants, who represent Jesus' opponents in Mk 12:1, 12 (*Mark*, p.339). Interestingly, Donahue's earlier work on this parable does not mention this typology (*The Gospel in Parable* [Fortress, 1988], pp.52–7).
35   Gnilka, *Das Evangelium nach Markus*, p.2.147.
36   Evans, *Mark 8:27–16:20*, p.236.
37   Taylor, *The Gospel According to St. Mark*, p.475.

and Rudolph Pesch[38] mention Gen. 37:20 as a possible background text to the story. Alexander Weihs gives an extensive treatment to the influence of the Joseph narrative on this parable and concludes that the verbal parallels between Gen. 37:30 and Mk 12:7 were probably traditional, and therefore inherited by Mark. So, Mark did not intentionally allude to the mode of Joseph's death in telling this story. But Weihs does argue that the motif of jealousy might play a role in understanding the death of Jesus in Mark,[39] which is something that Donahue and Harrington mention but do not develop.[40] Even if there is a typological relationship between the son in the parable – and, implicitly, Jesus – and Joseph, it does not seem to affect the parable or the understanding of Jesus' death alluded to within it in any significant way since the dominating intertext for the parable is Isaiah 5 rather than Genesis 37. Joseph's interaction with his brothers and his near death might add colour or contrast to the parable, but little else.[41]

The second recognizable allusion to Genesis appears in Mk 14:51-52, at the end of the scene of Jesus' arrest at Gethsemane. A young man escapes naked after leaving his garment behind as a result of the struggle with the armed mob. This is reminiscent of the scene in Gen. 39:6-20, that of Joseph in Potiphar's wife's room. After being pressured by her to have adulterous relations, Joseph escapes, leaving his garments in her hands. The LXX of Gen. 39:12 reads καταλιπὼν τὰ ἱμάτια αὐτοῦ ἐν ταῖς χερσὶν αὐτῆς ἔφυγεν. Compare Mk 14:52: ὁ δὲ καταλιπὼν τὴν σινδόνα γυμνὸς ἔφυγεν. The verbal similarities are underlined, with the dotted underline indicating a similarity in content but a verbal difference. One of the earliest commentators on Mark, commonly referred to as Pseudo-Jerome, recognized the parallel between these two passages in his seventh-century commentary,[42] so the tradition of linking these two passages goes back at least fourteen centuries, although the vast majority of commentators since then either do not recognize the allusion or do and simply note its presence without making sense of its meaning.[43]

38   R. Pesch, *Das Markusevangelium* (HTKNT, 2; Freiburg: Herder, 1976), p.2.219.

39   A. Weihs, 'Die Eifersucht der Winzer: zur Anspielung auf LXX Gen. 37,20 in der Parabel von der Tötung des Sohnes (Mk. 12,1-12)', *ETL* 76 (2000), pp.5–29.

40   Donahue and Harrington, *Mark*, p.339.

41   For a fine history of recent scholarship up through 1998, see K. R. Snodgrass, 'Recent Research on the Parable of the Wicked Tenants: An Assessment', *BBR* 8 (1998), pp.187–216. Curiously, Snodgrass does not mention the Joseph typology at all, except in a brief footnote referring to J. D. Levenson's book, *The Death and Resurrection of the Beloved Son*.

42   For the text and translation, see M. Cahill, ed., *Expositio Evangelii secundum Marcum* (CCSL, 82; Scriptores Celtigenae, pars 2; Turnhout: Brepols, 1997) and M. Cahill, *The First Commentary on Mark: An Annotated Translation* (New York/Oxford: Oxford University Press, 1998).

43   See Collins, *Mark*, 'Excursus: Scholarship on 14:51-52', pp.688–93 and Marcus, *Mark 8–16*, 'Appendix: The Youth Who Ran Away Naked', pp.1124–5, both of which contain excellent histories of scholarship, but neither of which witness to any serious discussion of the Joseph parallel, except for Waetjen's discussion.

Herman Waetjen, however, argues that this parallel is part of an extensive Joseph typology in Mark,[44] but this is doubtful, even if there are a few possible allusions to Joseph in Mark's Gospel.[45] As Marcus points out, the comparison between the two stories elicits a negative comparison rather than a positive one, since Joseph leaves for noble reasons and the young man flees to avoid capture by the soldiers, which is just the opposite of what Jesus does. Beyond that comparison, Marcus admits, 'There does, then, seem to be a verbal echo of the Joseph story, but it is difficult to know what to make of it'.[46] I agree.

Minor Allusions

This last section briefly examines some possible allusions to Genesis in Mark that have minimal impact on Mark. Some commentators are very anxious to find references to the Hebrew Bible or LXX in Mark, and so the list in this section could be much longer. The passages I have included represent the most likely of the minor allusions to Genesis in Mark.

Mk 5:7 falls within the story of the Gerasene demoniac. When the demoniac sees Jesus from a distance, he runs to Jesus, falls before him and cries out in a loud voice, 'What is it to me and you, Jesus son of God the Most High (υἱὲ τοῦ θεοῦ τοῦ ὑψίστου)? I adjure you by God, do not torture me!' LXX Gen. 14:18 calls Melchizedek 'priest of God Most High'. While the verbal connection between Mk 5:7 and Gen. 14:18 is clear, the epithet for the God of Israel, 'God Most High', is not limited to Gen. 14:18. 'God Most High', or some variation of it, can be found in the Psalms and Daniel, and the similar 'Lord Most High' is even more common. 'God Most High' is also the preferred epithet for God in *Joseph and Aseneth*. With so many other places this phrase shows up, not to mention the use of ὑψίστος as part of an epithet for other gods in the ancient world, namely Zeus, all that we can say with certainty is that Gen. 14:18 plays a small role in understanding the larger cultural landscape of this epithet for Jesus.

Similarly, Mk 7:19 may have some connection conceptually with Gen. 6:5 and 8:21, which talk about the evil inclinations of the heart of humans. Jesus' discussions of clean and unclean food and what really corrupts an individual in Mark 7 touches on this concept. But the concept of the evil inclination is not limited to Genesis, so the possible references to Gen. 6:5 and 8:21 can only form two pieces of a larger cultural context that would need to be explored in more depth.[47]

---

44   H. Waetjen, 'The Ending of Mark and the Gospel's Shift in Eschatology', *ASTI* 4 (1961), pp.117–20.

45   See Collins, *Mark*, pp.693–4, n.214 for a critique of Waetjen's argument. Evans also calls this typology 'doubtful' (*Mark 8:27–16:20*, p.428).

46   Marcus, *Mark 8–16*, p.995.

47   See Marcus, *Mark 8–16*, p.459–60.

The possible allusion to Gen. 1:31 in Mk 7:37 is more specific than the previous ones considered. This comes at the end of the passage narrating Jesus' healing of the deaf man by placing his fingers in the man's ears, spitting on his tongue, and reciting a prayer over him, which included the Aramaic command εφφαθα. The amazed crowd's response in v.37 is, 'He has done everything well (καλῶς πάντα πεποίηκεν); he makes the deaf to hear and the speechless to speak'. The LXX of Gen. 1:31 reads, 'And God saw all the things that he had made, and see, they were very good' (καὶ εἶδεν ὁ θεὸς τὰ πάντα, ὅσα ἐποίησεν, καὶ ἰδοὺ καλὰ λίαν). Although the verbal correspondence is not exact, there is enough to constitute at least a possible allusion by Mark.[48] This would be supported by the possible allusions to Gen. 1:31 by LXX Sir. 39:16 and LXX Qoh 3:11. Reading Mk 7:37 together with Gen. 1:31 does add a layer of meaning to the story deeper than that of the amazement of the crowds at Jesus' healing of the deaf man. It signals to the audience of Mark the relationship that Jesus' advent has to God's creative acts, in particular the ways that God is acting through Jesus to initiate an eschatological new creation.[49]

The next allusion to Genesis in Mark comes at 10:27, which is Jesus' response to those who object to his statement about the difficulty of the rich entering the kingdom of God (10:24-25). In 10:27, Jesus says, 'For humans it is impossible, but not for God; for all things are possible for God'. The idea of what is impossible for humans being possible for God is found in Gen. 18:14 with regard to the promise made to Abraham that Sarah, his barren, aged wife, would give birth to a son. But the power of God to transcend human possibility is prevalent in the Hebrew Bible and in extra-biblical literature, so, much like the passages already discussed, Gen. 18:14 cannot be considered the only, or even the major, referent for Mk 10:27. Instead, it is one passage among many that must be considered to understand the cultural context for this idea.

The final minor allusion to Genesis we will discuss comes at Mk 12:18-19 at the beginning of the debate with the Sadducees over the issue of levirate marriage and resurrection. The quotation that Mark contains regarding the regulations in the Law about levirate marriage is a conflation of Deut. 25:5-6 and Gen. 38:8, but the latter simply assumes what is in the former. In other words, the situation in Gen. 38:8 is simply an instance where levirate marriage customs come into play rather than the basis in the Law for the practice. The basis is found in Deut. 25:5-6, so that plays a much larger role

---

48   This allusion is widely accepted by commentators. See Moloney, *Gospel of Mark*, p.151, n.172 for references to most of the secondary literature. Marcus says, 'This Genesis verse was well remembered in later Judaism; it may already be echoed in Exod 2:2, where Moses' mother sees "that he is good"; later Rabbis, at any rate saw a Genesis allusion in this Exodus passage (see e.g. *Exod. Rab.* 1.20)' (*Mark 1–8*, p.475).

49   Collins, *Mark*, p.376. The theme of new creation in Isa. 35:5-6 is the passage that is most discussed as having influence on this verse and colouring the interpretation of the crowd's praise of Jesus.

in understanding the debate Jesus has with the Pharisees in Mark 12 than Gen. 38:8 does.

Conclusion

Our study has shown that, although there are places where passages from Genesis impact one's reading of Mark, Genesis is not a major interpretive lens through which the author of Mark constructs his story of Jesus. As I have argued elsewhere, it is important not to assume that the author's use of Scripture has an overriding pattern to it, or that he considers every passage of Scripture to be equally important for understanding the significance of Jesus. Instead, one must examine each scriptural reference in Mark on its own terms before attempting to discern a pattern of usage.[50] This interpretive strategy has been confirmed in this present study. While there are three places in Mark where Genesis does significantly affect the meaning of the passage in various ways, there seems to be no discernable pattern of usage of Genesis by the author of Mark across the story as a whole.

---

50   S. P. Ahearne-Kroll, *The Psalms of Lament in Mark's Passion: Jesus' Davidic Suffering* (SNTSMS, 142; Cambridge: Cambridge University Press, 2007), pp.1–39.

Chapter 3

GENESIS IN MATTHEW'S GOSPEL

Jeannine K. Brown

Introduction

The importance of the narratives and themes of Genesis within Jewish and Christian reflection needs no argument. Yet when it comes to weighing the influence of Genesis on the Gospel of Matthew, it certainly is the case that explicit Genesis citations and even fully agreed-upon allusions appear less frequently than to other Old Testament books, such as Isaiah and the Psalms. This situation does not, however, reflect the evangelist's disinterest in Genesis. Rather, Matthew refers fairly often to key persons, places, and events introduced in Genesis.[1] By doing so, the evangelist evokes foundational themes, paradigmatic stories, and characters that function as exemplars or foils.

Intertextuality is currently a burgeoning sub-discipline of New Testament studies. While space does not allow for a thorough hermeneutical discussion, brief methodological introductions are provided below that are relevant to the sections on textual allusions and persons/places. At the onset, two framing assumptions are offered.

First, I do not assume that Matthew must or does use Old Testament texts in the ways fully consonant with their Old Testament function and context. Matthew may cite or allude to an Old Testament text for a variety of purposes (e.g. Christological) not in view by the author of the Old Testament text. Nevertheless, I do not by default hold to a more traditional assumption that New Testament authors often use Old Testament texts without recourse to their contexts. In fact, a careful look at these Old Testament contexts may indicate significant interest in thematic or storied connections by Matthew.[2] In either case, by setting an Old Testament text in a new context, Matthew creates new significance via a new set of connections. In intertextuality, this phenomenon is referred to as 'transumption' – 'the way in which one text

---

1   References to 'Matthew' are a shorthand for the author of the first gospel and do not assume any particular stance on authorship.

2   R. Beaton, *Isaiah's Christ in Matthew's Gospel* (SNTSMS, 123; Cambridge: Cambridge University Press, 2002), e.g. pp.30–4. For example, each Old Testament citation in Matthew 2 derives from a literary context that highlights the theme of exile and restoration.

is taken up and changed by another text through an echo of the former'.[3] Therefore, it is not enough to identify a citation, allusion, or echo and delineate its formal connections to the precursor text. It is also important to determine the function of the precursor text in its new context.

Second, I follow Beaton in understanding Matthew's citations (and allusions) to be bi-referential;[4] that is, they link to both the story and discourse levels of the narrative.[5] While citations and allusions have a point of connection to the story that Matthew narrates, they also very often cohere with motifs woven throughout the narrative. For example, while the citation of Genesis 1:27 in Matthew 19 complements the story level focus on Jesus' controversies with the Pharisees (they cite Deuteronomy; Jesus brings them back to Genesis), this citation also contributes to Matthean themes of Jesus as consummate interpreter of the Law and the status reversal that is a part of God's kingdom (see below).

This chapter will discuss: (1) Mathew's textual affinities (e.g. LXX, MT); (2) explicit Genesis citations; (3) Genesis allusions or echoes; and (4) Genesis persons and places. The conclusion will offer some observations concerning Matthew's purposes in drawing upon Genesis.

Textual Affinities of Genesis Material in Matthew

The question of the biblical text used by Matthew for his Genesis quotations and allusions is complicated by the relative scarcity of full-blown citations from Genesis. To generalize from the three explicit citations is less than helpful.[6] And, although Gundry argues for a methodology that includes allusions as well as citations to determine the biblical text used by Matthew, the fact that Genesis allusions are infrequent in Matthew means that generalization remains difficult.[7] To mitigate this difficulty, textual analysis and comment will be included in the discussion of specific Genesis citations and pertinent allusions in sections II and III.

The following observations, however, address the three explicit Genesis citations (Gen. 1:27 and 2:24 in Mt. 19:4-5; and Gen. 38:8 in Mt. 22:24) in

---

3   K. D. Litwak, *Echoes of Scripture in Luke-Acts: Telling the History of God's People Intertextually* (JSNTSup, 282; New York: T&T Clark, 2005), p.52.

4   Beaton, *Isaiah's Christ*, p.5.

5   These are narrative-critical concepts that contribute to a heuristic model for understanding the features of any narrative. For a fuller description, see J. K. Brown, *Scripture as Communication: Introducing Biblical Hermeneutics* (Grand Rapids: Baker Academic, 2007), pp.157–63.

6   One of these (Mt. 22:24), Stendahl argues, is not a citation but an allusion that is of interest to textual questions given 'certain terminological details'. K. Stendahl, *The School of St. Matthew and its Use of the Old Testament* (Ramsey, N. J.: Sigler Press, 1991; orig. 1954), p.70.

7   R. H. Gundry, *The Use of the Old Testament in St. Matthew's Gospel with Special Reference to the Messianic Hope* (NovTSup, 28; Leiden: Brill, 1967), p.3.

Matthew. In each case, Matthew is using Mark as the primary textual basis for the Genesis quotation. At 19:5, Matthew adds to his Markan source the phrase καὶ κολληθήσεται τῇ γυναικὶ αὐτοῦ (absent from Mk 10:7), thereby aligning more closely, though not exactly, with the LXX (see note 10 below). A similar alignment is suggested at 22:24, where Matthew modifies Mark's λάβῃ (Mk 12:19) to ἐπιγαμβρεύσει (cf. γάμβρευσαι; Gen. 38:8). These changes in Genesis citations by Matthew support Stendahl's more general observation that 'a greater measure of agreement with the LXX may be observed in certain cases in Matthew' than in Mark.[8] Matthew, in these three cases, draws upon Mark's Septuagintal Genesis citations and retains their Septuagintal flavour, possibly aligning his renderings more closely with the LXX.

Genesis allusions in Matthew follow the LXX fairly closely in each case. The one example of a more complex source question arises with the potential allusion to Gen. 22:2 at Mt. 3:17 and 17:5. However, the possible textual connections to the LXX of Genesis are fairly straightforward in this case. It is the potential echo of Isa. 42:1 at 3:17 and 17:5 that is more complicated textually, with the likelihood of a Matthean rendering of a Semitic base text.[9]

Explicit Citations

There are few explicit citations of Genesis in Matthew upon which scholars routinely agree. Three such citations are identified in Matthew's treatment of divorce (19:3-9) and the controversy between Jesus and the Sadducees concerning resurrection (22:23-33).

Gen. 1:27 and 2:24 in Mt. 19:4-5

Matthew brings together citations from two Genesis texts already in his Markan source (Mk 10:6-7) in Mt. 19:4-5. In response to the Pharisees' question about legitimate reasons for divorce, Jesus cites Gen. 1:27 and 2:24.

> Have you not read that the one who made them at the beginning 'made them male and female', and said, 'For this reason a man shall leave his father and mother and be joined to his wife, and the two shall become one flesh'?
>
> (Mt. 19:4-5; NRSV)

οὐκ ἀνέγνωτε ὅτι ὁ κτίσας ἀπ᾽ ἀρχῆς ἄρσεν καὶ θῆλυ ἐποίησεν αὐτούς; καὶ εἶπεν, ῞Ενεκα τούτου καταλείψει ἄνθρωπος τὸν πατέρα καὶ τήν μητέρα καὶ κολληθήσεται τῇ γυναικὶ αὐτοῦ, καὶ ἔσονται οἱ δύο εἰς σάρκα μίαν.

---

8   Stendahl, *School of St. Matthew*, p.147; see also p.60. Menken, however, noting modifications in Matthew away from the LXX, concludes 'one cannot detect a systematic tendency on Matthew's part to assimilate quotations he finds in his sources to the LXX'. M. J. J. Menken, *Matthew's Bible: The Old Testament Text of the Evangelist* (BETL, 173; Leuven: Leuven University Press, 2004), p.281.

9   Gundry, *Old Testament*, pp.29–32.

The citation of both texts follows closely Mark's Septuagintal rendering of Gen. 1:27b and 2:24, including the presence of δύο ('two') from Gen. 2:24, which is not explicitly paralleled in the Hebrew (MT) though is attested by the Samaritan Pentateuch and some Targums.[10] Matthew introduces the first Genesis citation with ὁ κτίσας ἀπ' ἀρχῆς, a redaction of Mark's ἀπὸ δὲ ἀρχῆς κτίσεως.[11] This change emphasizes further God as creator and thus the intentional creation of the male and the female. In addition, this introductory Matthean phrase, which uses the verb κτίζω, may evoke the Hebrew verb used three times in Gen. 1:27 with God as subject (ברא: 'create'; the LXX renders this verb with the more general ποιέω).[12]

Gen. 1:27 and 2:24 are brought together in Mt. 19:4-5 to demonstrate the intention of God as creator of humanity for lifelong marriage or monogamy.[13] The use of this textual combination prepares for the next stage of the debate between Jesus and the Pharisees regarding allowances for divorce (19:7-9), in which Jesus emphasizes that divorce should not be granted 'except for sexual immorality' (19:9).[14]

Thematically, the use of the Genesis citations emphasizes that Jesus is the consummate teacher of the Law, a thoroughgoing Matthean motif (e.g. 5:17-46; 12:1-14; 15:1-20). In responding to the Pharisees' question about divorce, Jesus leads with Genesis and God's creational intentions. Although the Pharisees refer to Deut. 24:1-4 (Mt. 19:7), Matthew shows Jesus to be more than able to navigate the tension between Genesis and Deuteronomy. Jesus refers to the teaching on divorce in Deut. 24:1 as a concession to hardheartedness (19:8), with Genesis providing the foundational truth for

---

10   See Gundry, *Use of the Old Testament*, p.16; J. Nolland, *The Gospel of Matthew* (NIGTC; Grand Rapids: Eerdmans, 2005), pp.772–3. Modifications made to Mark include the use of the Attic form ἕνεκα instead of ἕνεκεν in Mark and the LXX and the addition of the clause καὶ κολληθήσεται τῇ γυναικὶ αὐτοῦ (found in the LXX [with προσκολληθήσεται πρός] and also present in some manuscripts of Mark, though likely secondary).

11   The Markan reference to creation parallels CD 4:21, which speaks of the 'foundation of creation' in concert with Gen. 1:27. Instone-Brewer considers this intertextual similarity as indication that Gen. 1:27 was a well-known proof for monogamy in first-century Judaism; D. Instone-Brewer, 'Jesus' Old Testament Basis for Monogamy', in S. Moyise (ed.), *The Old Testament in the New Testament* (JSNTSup, 189; Sheffield: Sheffield Academic Press, 2000), pp.75–105, here p.97.

12   This emphasis on creational intention is also assisted by the addition of καὶ εἶπεν in Mt. 19:5 between the two citations, which, for Farla, indicates that 'Gen. 2.24 is a pronouncement by God Himself in which He demonstrates the meaning of His creative deeds'. P. Farla, '"The two shall become one flesh": Gen. 1.27 and 2.24 in the New Testament Marriage Texts', in S. Draisma (ed.), *Intertextuality in Biblical Writings* (Kampen: Kok, 1989), pp.67–82, here p.71.

13   Instone-Brewer considers the primary context of Matthew's message to be one of polygamy; 'Monogamy', p.97.

14   Matthew is the only synoptic writer to provide an exception to the divorce logion (μὴ ἐπὶ πορνείᾳ, 19:9; cf. also 5:32).

understanding marriage.[15] Matthew's Jesus understands and teaches the Law rightly and calls his followers to a kingdom ethic in continuity with it.[16]

By elevating the Genesis text as the interpretive framework for the Deuteronomy instruction, Matthew also emphasizes the motif of status reversal, a theme that emerges clearly in this part of his gospel (18:1–20:34). As Carter has argued, 'Jesus' response contrasts [the marriage] relationship of mutuality and permanence with the Pharisees' concern to uphold male power and patriarchal structures in divorce'.[17] By citing Genesis in Matthew 19, Jesus legislates against more trivial reasons for divorce, thereby protecting women's interests and highlighting their value.[18]

Gen. 38:8 in Mt. 22:24

Gen. 38:8 makes its way into Mt. 22:24 by way of Mark's parallel account (Mk 12:19).[19] This particular reference to Genesis is complicated by its reception and refraction via Deut. 25:5 – the specific Torah regulation about levirate marriage derived from the story of Onan and Tamar in Gen. 38:8. Hagner considers the Matthean text 'a rather free quotation drawn from… Deut 25:5 and Gen 38:8'.[20]

> 'Teacher, Moses said, "If a man dies childless, his brother shall marry the widow, and raise up children for his brother."'
>
> (Mt. 22:24)

> … Μωϋσῆς εἶπεν· ἐάν τις ἀποθάνῃ μὴ ἔχων τέκνα, ἐπιγαμβρεύσει ὁ ἀδελφὸς αὐτοῦ τὴν γυναῖκα αὐτοῦ καὶ ἀναστήσει σπέρμα τῷ ἀδελφῷ αὐτοῦ
>
> (Mt. 22:24)

> …. γάμβρευσαι αὐτὴν καὶ ἀνάστησον σπέρμα τῷ ἀδελφῷ σου
>
> (Gen. 38:8)

---

15   Nolland, *Matthew*, p.771. Spencer emphasizes that Jesus is portrayed here as affirming the validity of both Genesis and Deuteronomy as 'creation prototype and wilderness proviso'. S. Spencer, 'Scripture, Hermeneutics, and Matthew's Jesus', *Interpretation* 64 (2010), pp.368–78, here p.377.

16   Farla, 'one flesh', pp.71–2. Davies and Allison indicate that through the use of Genesis 1–2 'the created order is a guide for the moral order'. W. D. Davies and D. C. Allison, *A Critical and Exegetical Commentary on the Gospel according to St. Matthew* (3 vols, ICC; Edinburgh: T&T Clark, 1988–97), III, p.10.

17   W. Carter, *Matthew and the Margins: A Sociopolitical and Religious Reading* (The Bible and Liberation Series; Maryknoll, N.Y.: Orbis, 2000), p.379.

18   J. K. Brown, *Disciples in Narrative Perspective: The Portrayal and Function of the Matthean Disciples* (Academia Biblica 9; Atlanta: Society of Biblical Literature, 2002), pp.79–80, 91–3.

19   Nolland (*Matthew*, p.903) surmises that Matthew has attended to and strengthened Mark's Genesis echoes here.

20   D. A. Hagner, *Matthew 14–28* (Dallas: Word, 1995), pp.640–1. Menken argues that the text of Matthew follows and redacts Mark without indication of Septuagintal influence. Menken, *Matthew's Bible*, pp.212–14.

The first half of Mt. 22:24 follows the shape (less so the vocabulary) of Deut. 25:5 (LXX). Common words include: ἐάν, ἀδελφός/οἱ, ἀποθάνῃ, and μή. Conceptually, the scenario of one brother dying without children (Matthew/Mark: τέκνα/ον; Deuteronomy LXX: σπέρμα) demonstrates that Deut. 25:5 is clearly in view in Mt. 22:24.[21]

The second half of Mt. 22:24 reflects Gen. 38:8 (via Mk 12:19) conceptually and lexically. Both texts share a form of the verb 'to marry' (Matthew: ἐπιγαμβρεύσει; Genesis: γάμβρευσαι)[22] and virtually the entire final clause: καὶ ἀναστήσει [Genesis: imperatival form] σπέρμα τῷ ἀδελφῷ [final pronoun].[23] This close connection to Genesis highlights the foundational story behind the Deuteronomy legislation that shapes the Sadducees' scenario. Although the question at 22:23 is not framed explicitly as a trap, it becomes clear from context (22:15, 35) as well as from the absurdity of the scenario itself that Matthew intends this pericope to be understood in concert with the surrounding tests of Jesus' authority and wisdom (22:15-46),[24] key themes in Matthew 21–22.

Important Genesis Allusions and Echoes

A spate of recent work within New Testament studies has offered a greater level of hermeneutical sophistication to the question of how to identify allusions or even 'echoes' of Old Testament texts. For example, Hays has offered seven criteria for determining plausible echoes of Old Testament texts in Paul, and others have applied and adapted Hays's methodological work to the Gospels.[25]

Of these seven, three criteria have garnered broad consensus and will be assumed in this discussion: (1) whether the precursor text was available to the author and audience of the New Testament text (availability); (2) the 'degree of explicit repetitions of words or syntactical patterns' (volume);[26]

---

21   In relation to Mark, 'Matthew has considerably simplified and abbreviated Mark's rather complex and long conditional clause' (Menken, *Matthew's Bible*, p.212).

22   Mark has λαμβάνω. While this seems to indicate that Matthew is using the LXX in addition to Mark, Menken suggests that Matthew uses 'a halachic term [ἐπιγαμ–βρεύσει] current in his environment' (*Matthew's Bible*, p.213).

23   Mark has the same final clause except with ἐξαναστήσῃ for ἀναστήσει.

24   F. D. Bruner, *Matthew: A Commentary* (Dallas: Word Press, 1990), pp.788–9.

25   R. B. Hays, *Echoes of Scripture in the Letters of Paul* [New Haven: Yale University Press, 1989). For these criteria applied to Luke-Acts, see Litwak, *Echoes of Scripture*. For application to John, see J. K. Brown, 'Creation's Renewal in the Gospel of John', *CBQ* 72 (2010), pp.275–90.

26   Hays, *Echoes*, p. 30. Litwak (*Echoes*, p.63) focuses on the first two of Hays's seven criteria as most helpful for identifying intertextual echoes. Another criterion Hays proposes – recurrence (whether there is repeated use of the precursor text by the specific New Testament author) – will be applicable to the question of the probability of Isaac evocations in Matthew (see below).

and (3) the alignment of the possible allusion or echo with the author's own rhetorical emphases (thematic coherence).

An additional insight in these methodological discussions is that conceptual (not only verbal) linkage is an important factor in determining the likelihood of an allusion or echo.[27] Identifying conceptual connections between texts will play a part in determining the possible echo of Genesis 4 in Mt. 5:21-25.[28]

Gen. 2:4 and 5:1 in Mt. 1:1

Commentators routinely trace the first two words of Matthew – βίβλος γενέσεως – to the identical phrase in both Gen. 2:4 and 5:1 (LXX) and argue for an intentional allusion here. The Greek phrase translates תולדת and ספר תולדת, in 2:4 and 5:1, respectively. The Hebrew word denotes a person's descendents, is often used with genealogies (e.g. Gen. 5:1; 10:1, 32; 11:10, 27; 25:12; 36:1, 9), and may be translated in such contexts with 'generations' or 'descendents'.[29]

The word γένεσις may be used to denote 'ancestry as point of origin', someone's birth, an account of someone's life, or 'persons of successive generations forming an ancestral line'.[30] The meaning of the term in Genesis 5:1 seems to be the latter denotation of generations or family lineage (in line with תולדת), since it is modified by ἀνθρώπων and introduces the genealogy of humanity which follows – from Adam to Noah (5:1-32). The precise function of γενέσεως at 2:4 is less clear because of its association with 'the heavens and the earth' (οὐρανοῦ καὶ γῆς) – a metaphorical use of γενέσεως. However, it is likely that the notion of 'origins' is in view at 2:4.[31]

The specific sense of γένεσις (with the genitive Ἰησοῦ Χριστοῦ) in Mt. 1:1 is debated, especially since it occurs again at 1:18 introducing the particulars of Jesus' birth (1:18-25). While rendering γένεσις as 'birth' at 1:18 is a good contextual choice, the use of γένεσις with the sense of 'birth' is less applicable at 1:1. For this reason, it is quite plausible that Matthew uses the term in a word play to frame the 'origins' of Jesus in two ways, first by introducing his lineage (1:1-17) and then by narrating the situation of his birth (1:18-25). For Matthew, the allusion to Gen. 2:4 and 5:1 highlights the connection between God's work at the beginning and God's work now in Jesus the Messiah.

---

27   P. Mallen, *The Reading and Transformation of Isaiah in Luke-Acts* (LNTS, 367; New York: T&T Clark, 2008), p.24.

28   D. C. Allison, Jr., 'Murder and Anger, Cain and Abel (Matt. 5:21–25)', in *Studies in Matthew: Interpretation Past and Present* (Grand Rapids: Baker, 2005), pp.65–78, here pp.69–70.

29   BDB, p.410.

30   BDAG, pp.192–3.

31   Nolland affirms that '[t]he predominant sense of γένεσις is, indisputably, "origin"'. J. Nolland, 'What Kind of Genesis Do We Have in Mt. 1.1', *NTS* 42 (1996), pp.463–71, here p.467.

A key interpretive issue is whether, by this allusion, Matthew intends to evoke a new creation motif.[32] While other New Testament writers draw upon this theme, Matthew's Gospel does not highlight new creation.[33] This argues against reading βίβλος γενέσεως as a clear allusion to new creation at 1:1.[34] Although evidence exists that γένεσις was used during the first century C.E. to refer to the first book of the Law ('Genesis'),[35] this does not necessitate that the βίβλος γενέσεως would have had only or even primarily this evocation, especially since this precise phrase at Gen. 2:4 and 5:1 in the LXX refers to 'a block of text *within* Genesis'.[36] Additionally, the recurrence of γένεσις at Mt. 1:18 indicates that, while Matthew 1 addresses Jesus' 'origins', the meta-theme of creation may not necessarily be prominent.[37] Instead, covenantal motifs are more resonant across this chapter, since the genealogy of 1:2-17 begins with Abraham (not Adam, as in Luke), includes key Gentile figures woven into God's covenant people, and emphasizes the exile as a threat to God's covenantal promises (1:11-12, 17).[38]

Genesis 4 in Matthew 5, 18, and 23

There are two, possibly three, allusions to the Cain and Abel narrative of Genesis 4; these occur in Matthew 5, 18, and 23. First, it is possible that the story of Cain and Abel from Gen. 4:1-16 is assumed at Mt. 5:21-25. Second, Matthew evokes Gen. 4:24 in Mt. 18:22 with the phrase

32   So Davies and Allison, *Matthew*, I, p.154; Carter, *Margins*, p.57; J. T. Pennington, 'Heaven, Earth, and a New Genesis: Theological Cosmology in Matthew', in J. T. Pennington and S. M. McDonough (eds), *Cosmology and New Testament Theology* (LNTS, 355; New York: T&T Clark, 2008), pp.28–44, here p.44; T. Hieke, 'Biblos Geneseos: Mt 1, 1 vom Buch Genesis her gelesen', in J. M. Auwers and H. J. de Jonge (eds), *The Biblical Canons* (BETL, 163; Leuven: Leuven University Press, 2003), pp.635–49; here pp.646–7.

33   For example, Paul explicitly uses the language of new creation – καινὴ κτίσις – at 2 Cor. 5:17 and Gal. 6:15. For the implicit theme of the renewal of creation in John's Gospel, see Brown, 'Creation's Renewal'.

34   Nolland, 'Kind of Genesis', pp.465–7.

35   Philo, who predates the Gospel of Matthew by a generation, refers to the first book of the Law as γένεσις (*Abr.* 1; *Post.* 127; *Aet.* 19). For Evans, this evidence coupled with the allusion to Gen. 2:4 and 5:1 at Mt. 1:1 suggests the following translation: 'The book of Genesis of Jesus Messiah, the son of David, the son of Abraham.' C. A. Evans, '"The Book of the Genesis of Jesus Christ": The Purpose of Matthew in Light of the Incipit', in T. R. Hatina (ed.), *Biblical Interpretation in Early Christian Gospels: Volume 2: The Gospel of Matthew* (LNTS, 310; New York: T&T Clark, 2008), pp.61–72, here p.67.

36   Nolland, 'Kind of Genesis', p.466 (author's emphasis).

37   Heckl argues that Matthew 1 evokes the biblical meta-theme of life lost–life regained from Gen. 5:1–6:4 (with eternal life lost introduced specially at 6:3); R. Heckl, 'Der biblische Begründungsrahmen für die Jungfrauengeburt bei Matthäus: Zur Rezeption von Gen 5,1-6,4 in Mt 1', *ZNW* 95 (2004), pp.161–80, here p.180.

38   See genealogy discussion below.

'seventy-seven times'. Third, Abel is explicitly mentioned in 23:35 as one whose righteous blood was shed.

Allison argues that Matthew alludes to the Cain and Abel story in the first 'antithesis', which addresses anger and murder.[39] Specifically, Matthew appears to draw upon the portrait of Cain bringing his (grain) offering before God (Gen. 4:3-5): 'So when you are offering your gift at the altar, if you remember that your brother or sister has something against you...' (Mt. 5:23). In addition to thematic and story connections of anger and murder, there are verbal ties between Matthew and the LXX: the language of bringing (φέρω) a gift (δῶρον)[40] and the repetition in both passages of ἀδελφός.[41] For Allison, an important indication of an allusion to Genesis 4 is the Matthean phrase ἐπὶ τὸ θυσιαστήριον ('at the altar'). This would have been an unusual way for Matthew to refer to a gift offered in the Jerusalem temple in the first century, since 'only priests were allowed at the altar'.[42] Although there is no altar explicitly mentioned in Genesis 4, the situation depicted fits the pre-temple picture of the story world of Genesis in which temporary altars are erected for specific purposes (e.g. Gen. 12:7).[43]

If there is an allusion to Genesis 4 in Mt. 5:21-25, its import is to provide additional paraenesis. The ἀδελφός (brother or sister) conceived in Jesus' example is no longer a generic individual; Cain's personage is evoked and functions as a striking foil to the ideal disciple Jesus describes in 5:17-48.[44] Allison also indicates a particular exegetical clarification gained through identification of the Cain evocation. The close connection Jesus makes between anger and murder as equally serious sins is clarified via the progression of events in Genesis 4. Anger leads to murder in the story of Cain and Abel.[45]

Matthew returns to Genesis 4 in 18:22, in the brief exchange between Jesus and Peter about forgiveness of one's ἀδελφός in the community of disciples. When asked by Peter how many times he ought to forgive an offending brother or sister, Jesus speaks of forgiving 'seventy-seven times'. This phrase renders ἑβδομηκοντάκις ἑπτά, which can refer to

39   Allison, 'Murder and Anger'; also T. Thatcher, 'Cain and Abel in Early Christian Memory: A Case Study in "The Use of the Old Testament in the New"', *CBQ* 72 (2010), pp.732–51.

40   In the LXX, δῶρον is used of Abel's gift (4:4); Cain's is called a θυσία (4:3). A single term is used in the MT for both Abel and Cain's offerings (מנחה). See n.49 below.

41   Allison, 'Murder and Anger', p.69.

42   Ibid., p.73.

43   Ibid., p.74.

44   Ibid., p.77. Allison states, 'one's revulsion for Cain spills over into an aversion for what Jesus condemns'. For the notion of Matthew's ideal disciple developed via Jesus' teaching as well as by means of character portrayals, see Brown, *Disciples*, pp.121–46.

45   Allison, 'Murder and Anger', p.76.

the number 77 or the equation 70 times 7.[46] This same phrase occurs in Gen. 4:24 (LXX), in the refrain of Lamech:

> For vengeance is taken seven times by Cain
> But by Lamech seventy-seven times (ἑβδομηκοντάκις ἑπτά; my translation) .

Although the allusion consists of only two words, the connection is clear thematically. The multiplied revenge that Lamech invokes for any who would harm him is reversed by Jesus' exhortation to multiplied forgiveness towards an offending brother or sister. In fact, it is likely that the phrase connotes unlimited forgiveness just as Lamech's words imply unlimited revenge.[47] The significance of this allusion rests in the reversal that Jesus insists should be a part of the covenant community reflecting God's kingdom and its values (18:1, 23). According to 18:22-23 and the following parable (18:23-35), 'lavish forgiveness toward one another in the Christian community...is not an option but an expectation of all those who set the kingdom as their priority'.[48]

Abel is portrayed in Mt. 23:35 (with parallel at Lk. 11:51) as the first martyr of the scriptural storyline, evoking Genesis 4 once again. Abel is described as righteous in Mt. 23:35, an expansion of the Genesis 4 narrative, which is less explicit concerning the relative merits of the offerings of Abel and Cain (4:3-5; MT). As Thatcher has noted, however, the LXX had already heightened the distinctions between their offerings by using a different word to describe each: θυσία ('sacrifice' or 'offering') for Cain's offering and δῶρον ('gift') for Abel's.[49] Correlated with this heightened emphasis in the LXX on the moral superiority of Abel, Matthew includes the descriptor ὁ δίκαιος.[50] This fits well the Matthean theme of righteousness (δικαιοσύνη, 3:15; 5:6, 10, 20; 6:1, 33; 21:32), as well as the specific use of the adjective to describe individuals who are righteous (Joseph in 1:19; Abel in 23:35; and Jesus in 27:19). In fact, the reference to the righteous Abel whose righteous blood (αἷμα δίκαιον, 23:35a) is spilled foreshadows Jesus, that righteous one

---

46   BDAG (p.269) indicates that, if the equation, it is a shortened form of ἑβδομηκοντάκις ἑπτάκις. More likely, the phrase refers to the number 77, as this is the clear referent of the Hebrew of Gen. 4:24: שִׁבְעִים וְשִׁבְעָה; A. J. Hultgren, *The Parables of Jesus: A Commentary* (Grand Rapids: Eerdmans, 2000), p.22.

47   D. Garland, *Reading Matthew: A Literary and Theological Commentary* (Macon, GA: Smyth & Helwys, 2001), p.194; W. Grundmann, *Das Evangelium nach Matthäus* (THKNT; Berlin: Evangelische Verlagsanstalt, 1986), p.421; Davies and Allison, *Matthew*, II, p.793.

48   Brown, *Disciples*, p.76.

49   Thatcher, 'Cain and Abel', p.734. In addition, the LXX changes significantly the wording of God's reply in 4:7, so that there is a negative evaluation of Cain's sacrifice in terms of how it was offered (p.734).

50   This appositional adjective is not present in Luke, so, assuming the two-source theory, Matthew seems to have added this descriptor to Q, which fits well his redactional emphases.

(δίκαιος, 27:19), whose righteous blood is betrayed (27:4, αἷμα ἀθῷον).[51] In the immediate context of Matthew 23, Abel and Zechariah son of Barachiah (2 Chron. 24:20) provide the beginning and end points for 'all the righteous blood shed on the earth' (23:35).[52] It is likely that these two personages are intended to refer to the canonical scope of martyrdom, since Genesis 4 and 2 Chronicles 24 sit at the outer parameters of the Hebrew canon.[53]

Possible Allusions to the Genesis Isaac Narratives

Allusions to the Isaac stories of Genesis are possible at a number of points in Matthew: Gen. 17:19 in Mt. 1:21 ('She will bear a son'); Gen. 22:2 in Mt. 3:17 and 17:5 ('This is my Son, the Beloved'); and Genesis 22 in Matthew 26.[54]

Huizenga argues that Matthew is quite deliberate in drawing on Isaac typology for his Christology.[55] In addition to suggesting an allusion to Isaac at 1:1 ('son of Abraham'; see below), Huizenga argues that an analogy between Isaac and Jesus is fostered by the significant linguistic and syntactical echoes of Gen. 17:19 (LXX) at Mt. 1:21:

τέξεται...υἱόν, καὶ καλέσεις τὸ ὄνομα αὐτοῦ Ισαακ

(Gen. 17:19a)

τέξεται...υἱόν, καὶ καλέσεις τὸ ὄνομα αὐτοῦ Ἰησοῦν

(Mt. 1:21a)

Huizenga also highlights the thematic connections between these parallel birth announcement narratives, including a divine figure announcing to a father the birth of a promised child to a mother outside of 'the natural boundaries of child-bearing status'.[56]

---

51   With ἀθῷος being a synonym of δίκαιος; see use of the two terms in Exod. 23:7 (LXX); BDAG, p.25.

52   For the conflation or confusion of two Zechariahs from Zech. 1:1 and 2 Chron. 24:20, see Nolland, *Matthew*, pp.946–7.

53   If the Hebrew canon at the time of Matthew concluded with Chronicles, as was later the case; see Nolland, *Matthew*, p.947.

54   Gen. 18:14 in Mt. 19:26 ('for God all things are possible') provides another possible allusion.

55   L. A. Huizenga, *The New Isaac: Tradition and Intertextuality in the Gospel of Matthew* (NovTSup, 131; Leiden: Brill, 2009); also P. Lefebvre, 'Le fils enchevêtré: Absalom, Isaac, Jésus', in *Double transmission du texte biblique* (Göttingen: Vandenhoeck und Ruprecht, 2001), pp.75–97; and Hieke, 'Biblos Geneseos', p.645. Crucial to Huizenga's argument is the premise that key elements of the Akedah – the story of the sacrifice of Isaac in Genesis 22, which then is picked up and expanded in Jewish traditions – were 'present in the cultural encyclopedia in which the Gospel of Matthew was produced and first received' (p.20). In my estimation, Huizenga successfully argues for this premise by analyzing precursor or contemporaneous texts, such as 4Q225, Judith, Philo, Pseudo-Philo, 4 Maccabees, and Josephus (*New Isaac*, pp.75–128).

56   Huizenga, *New Isaac*, pp.145.

Matthew's baptism and transfiguration accounts may reference the figure of Isaac from the Genesis story. The evangelist draws God's commendation of Jesus from one or more Old Testament texts: Gen. 22:2 (also 11-12, 15-16); Ps. 2:7; and/or Isa. 42:1. Though I consider Isa. 42:1 to be the primary allusive passage behind Mt. 3:17 and 17:5, it may be that more than one text is echoed here, as others have noted.[57] The linguistic connection between Matthew and Genesis 22 (LXX) consists in the phrase, 'my Son, the Beloved'.

ὁ υἱός μου ὁ ἀγαπητός
(Mt. 3:17; 17:5)

τὸν υἱόν σου τὸν ἀγαπητόν
(Gen. 22:2; parallel genitive phrase in 22:12, 16)

In determining whether Genesis 22 is evoked at Mt. 3:17 and 17:5, Huizenga draws upon the (Hays) criterion of volume to argue that previous allusions to Isaac and the Genesis stories about him lead the reader to hear another such reference here.[58] The volume criterion, however, also lends credibility to hearing Isa. 42:1 as significant at Mt. 3:17 and 17:5, since Matthew cites Isa. 42:1-4 in full at Mt. 12:18-21. While quite possibly one intended allusion, Genesis 22 is not the only or even primary evocation at Mt. 3:17 and 17:5.

Huizenga argues for a number of evocations of the Genesis Isaac narratives in Matthew's passion narrative. These include: (a) the overarching theme of Jesus' faithful obedience throughout his passion (as Isaac is portrayed as actively obedient in Jewish traditions on Genesis 22); (b) an echo of Gen. 22:5 at Mt. 26:36 in the unusual grammatical construction καθίσατε αὐτοῦ; and (c) the lexical ties for the instruments used in Isaac's sacrifice ('knife' [μάχαιρα] at Gen. 22:6, 10; 'wood' [ξύλα] at Gen. 22:3, 6, 7, 9) and those used by the crowd present at Jesus' arrest ('with swords and clubs' [μαχαιρῶν καὶ ξύλων] at Mt. 26:47, 55).

An Isaac Christology in Matthew would contribute to an understanding of the soteriological significance of Jesus' death. Based on the motif of Isaac's willing obedience in the Akedah traditions that presumably provides Matthew with an analogy for Jesus' willing obedience to the cross, Huizenga argues that a Christus Victor model is primary to Matthew's soteriology.[59]

57   E.g. Gundry, *Old Testament*, p.29. Huizenga himself speaks of Mt. 3:17b as 'polyvalent' and 'rich with poetic potential', although he argues against Isa. 42:1 or Ps. 2:7 as allusive backdrops. On the relationship between Isa. 42:1 and Mt. 3:17 and 17:5, see Beaton, *Isaiah's Christ*, pp.130–2.

58   Huizenga, *New Isaac*, p.167.

59   Ibid., pp.272–3.

Persons and Places

While explicit citations and even allusions to Genesis are not commonplace in Matthew, references to various persons and places introduced in Genesis contribute to a more robust set of interactions with that book. Certainly a number of Genesis personages are mentioned in the opening genealogy of Matthew. In fact, Nolland has argued that the genealogy itself is an intentional derivation of the annotated genealogies in Genesis.[60] Beyond the genealogy, references to other proper names from Genesis also seem to indicate that Matthew assumes his hearers know the Genesis stories. Beyond this knowledge, names may evoke key moments of the story of Israel, especially references to such central persons as Abraham and Noah.

Additionally, reference to key persons and events from the Old Testament may be used for a variety of purposes in New Testament texts, including paraenetic or apologetic ones. As such, the person or event evoked may not solely or primarily be linked to a particular Old Testament text; instead, it may be the composite figure, which resides in the collective memory of author and audience that is in view.[61] Such an expansive view of intertextuality is relevant to the discussion of key figures from Genesis in Matthew.

Abraham

Abraham is the most frequently referenced Genesis personage in Matthew. His name is given prominence in the gospel's opening title ('the son of Abraham', 1:1) and in the genealogy that follows, which begins with Abraham and leads to Jesus (1:2 and 17). The choice of Abraham as the starting point for Jesus' genealogy likely signals a covenantal framework for narrating the Jesus story.[62] Additionally, some commentators understand the reference to Abraham as evocative of his role as the ancestor of many nations (Gen. 17:4-5).[63]

Abraham is mentioned twice in 3:9, within John the Baptist's indictment of the Jerusalem leaders as they come to the Jordan where he is baptizing: 'Do not presume to say to yourselves, "We have Abraham as our ancestor"; for I tell you, God is able from these stones to raise up children to Abraham' (Mt. 3:9). The covenantal associations of Abraham's name are highlighted again, via John's critique of the presumption of participating in Israel's legacy

---

60   J. Nolland, 'Genealogical Annotation in Genesis as Background for the Matthean Genealogy of Jesus', *TB* 47 (1996), pp.115–22.

61   Thatcher, 'Cain and Abel', pp.749–50.

62   Note the more universal emphasis of Luke's genealogy traced back to Adam (Lk. 3:23-38).

63   R. T. France, *The Gospel of Matthew* (NICNT; Grand Rapids: Eerdmans, 2007), p.5; L. Nortjé, 'Die Abraham motief in Matteus 1–4', *Skrif en kerk* 19 (1998), pp.46–56; Hieke, 'Biblos Geneseos', p.645. Davies and Allison (*Matthew*, I, p.158) note that 'Abraham himself was a Gentile by birth, ... and he was sometimes portrayed as ... the first proselyte' in Jewish literature.

without commensurate repentance. An implicit focus on Gentile inclusion emerges here, given that Gentiles are the most obvious referent for the children of Abraham that God can raise up from stones.

The remaining references to Abraham occur in conjunction with the other patriarchs, Isaac and Jacob (8:11; 22:32). Again, it is likely that, at least in the first instance, covenantal associations are primary. In 8:11 Jesus marvels at the faith of a Gentile centurion, highlighting the reversal of expectation regarding who will participate in God's coming kingdom along with Abraham, Isaac, and Jacob. In 22:32, the three patriarchs are mentioned in the context of Jesus' teaching on final resurrection: it is the one who *is* the God of Abraham, Isaac, and Jacob who guarantees the future, resurrected life of the covenant faithful.

Genesis Persons in Matthew's Genealogy

The remaining names from Genesis in Matthew's genealogy (1:2-3) evoke story elements from Genesis. Isaac is first mentioned by the evangelist in the genealogy (1:2) but also in the phrase referencing the patriarchs, 'Abraham, Isaac, and Jacob' at 8:11 and 22:32. As discussed above, Isaac may also serve a Christological function in Matthew, if Huizenga is correct that Genesis 22 is the backdrop at key points in Matthew (3:17; 17:5; the passion narrative). Huizenga suggests, in fact, that 'son of Abraham' in Mt. 1:1 might bring to mind Isaac for the reader.[64]

The reference to *Jacob* (Mt. 1:2; also 8:11 and 22:32) functions to remind the reader of the people of Israel – the twelve tribes of the people, especially since he is described as the father of '*Judah* and his brothers' (1:2). This phrase ('and his brothers') added to the succinctly patterned structure is a marker of emphasis in the genealogy, as is its recurrence at 1:11 ('Jechoniah and his brothers'). It may be that the two-fold formula functions to highlight the time that the people of Israel are displaced from their land: (1) Judah and his brothers migrate to Egypt because of famine where they are eventually enslaved; and (2) Jechoniah and his brothers are deported to Babylon, with the latter providing an explicit addition to the genealogical framework at 1:11 ('at the time of the deportation to Babylon').[65]

Additionally, Judah is highlighted through his part in the story of Genesis 38, which is also evoked by the inclusion of his twin sons, *Perez* and *Zerah*,[66] as well as their mother *Tamar* (Mt. 1:3).[67] Tamar is the first of four women referenced in the early part of Matthew's genealogy, a significant inclusion since ancient genealogies as a genre were patrilineal and so usually omitted

64   Huizenga, *New Isaac*, p.141.
65   J. K. Brown, 'Matthew', in G. M. Burge and A. E. Hill (eds), *The Baker Illustrated Bible Commentary* (Grand Rapids: Baker, 2012), p.955.
66   The birth of the twins Perez and Zerah is described in Gen. 38:27-30. Perez's son *Hezron*, the final Genesis personage in Matthew's genealogy, is mentioned in Gen. 46:12, in the tracing of Judah's lineage.
67   Nolland, *Matthew*, p.73.

women. Matthew's purpose in evoking the story of Genesis 38 has been variously construed, but its interpretation should follow from the inclusion of all four women (Rahab and Ruth in 1:5; 'the wife of Uriah' in 1:6).[68] Most likely, Matthew means to emphasize the Gentile origins of these four women. Tamar is not from the people of Israel; she is chosen by Judah for his son Er while staying in an area of Canaan apart from his brothers (Gen. 38:1-6).[69] Rahab is a Canaanite from Shittim (Joshua 2:1-2), and Ruth is a Moabite (Ruth 1:4, 22). The clearest indication of Matthew's intention is the inclusion of Bathsheba, not by that name but by reference to her husband, 'the wife of Uriah'. This circumlocution places attention on Uriah, who is frequently described as 'Uriah the Hittite' in the Old Testament, emphasizing his non-Jewish origins.

Genesis Persons and Places across Matthew

Rachel, matriarch of Israel, is referred to once in Matthew at 2:18 in the infancy narrative, and specifically within the quotation of Jer. 31:15 that connects Rachel with the town of Ramah (Jer. 38:15; LXX). According to Genesis 35:16-20 and 48:7, Rachel was buried 'on the way to Ephrath (that is Bethlehem)'. Another tradition, represented in 1 Sam. 10:2 and Jer. 31:15, indicates that her tomb was located in Ramah (see 1 Sam. 7:17; 8:4).[70] It appears that Matthew draws upon both traditions to link Rachel with *Bethlehem* (see Mt. 2:1, 5, 6, 8, 16). 'Matthew is happy to make the most of the variety of traditions at his disposal.'[71] The association of Rachel with Bethlehem provides the story connection between the massacre of the innocents in Mt. 2:16 and the Jeremiah fulfilment quotation in 2:17-18. It is also the case that Matthew may be drawing his audience's attention to an exilic-restoration theme that derives from Jeremiah 31 (see especially 31:16-17). Relevant in this regard is Ramah's use as 'a transit station for the exiles from Jerusalem and Judah to be deported in 587 B.C.E.'.[72]

Two pericopae in Matthew 10–11 reference the cities of *Sodom* or *Sodom and Gomorrah*.[73] These place names occur within judgment pronouncements

---

68   Mary is the fifth woman in Matthew's genealogy (1:16). I understand her presence and role to be distinct from those of the women who are mentioned early in the genealogy. If not, then the common element among the five women would be the unusual or suspicious circumstances surrounding the births of their children. Evans, for example, emphasizes 'the question of legitimacy that hangs over [the] respective offspring' of the five women ('Incipit', p.70).

69   Davies and Allison (*Matthew*, I, p.170) suggest that Tamar was a Canaanite, although they note that some Jewish texts deny this ancestry (e.g. *Jub.* 41:1-2; *T. Jud.* 10:1-2).

70   1 Sam. 10:2 refers to Rachel's tomb as 'in the territory of Benjamin at Zelzah'. For Nolland, '[t]his is presumably not too far from Zuph (1 Sam. 9:5), which is probably to be identified with the Ramah [of 7:17 and 8:4]' (*Matthew*, p.125).

71   Nolland, *Matthew*, p.125.

72   Menken, *Matthew's Bible*, p.146.

73   Both pericopae derive from Q and are found in the same context in Luke (10:12, 13-15).

by Jesus and evoke the story of the cities' destruction in Gen. 18:16–19:29. According to Genesis, Sodom and Gomorrah are destroyed because of the greatness and scope of their wickedness (18:20, 32; 19:7, 13).[74] In Matthew's Mission Discourse (10:1–11:1), Sodom and Gomorrah are paragons of evil to be compared (favourably!) with any who would choose not to welcome and listen to Jesus' disciples (10:12–15).

In similar fashion, Sodom and Gomorrah (along with Tyre and Sidon) are cities that epitomize wickedness in Jesus' judgment upon the cities of Chorazin, Bethsaida, and Capernaum that have seen his miracles yet had not repented (11:20-23). Again, Sodom and Gomorrah are placed in favourable light when compared to the judgment that will come upon the cities that have rejected the ministry of Jesus (11:22, 24). Once more, Matthew evokes storied elements of Genesis by referencing these proper names.

Canaan as a place name is evoked in the description of a Canaanite woman (γυνὴ Χαναναία) from the region of Tyre and Sidon who comes to Jesus for the healing of her daughter (15:21-22). This is the only reference to Canaan in the entire New Testament; it does not derive from the evangelist's Markan source, which uses Συροφοινίκισσα (Mk 7:24-30).[75] Especially if Χαναναία reflects Matthean redaction, the evangelist is likely evoking Old Testament associations of the enmity between Israel and the people of Canaan and the promise to the patriarchs that they would inherit the land of the Canaanites (e.g. Gen. 9:25–27; 15:18–21; 27:8).[76] It is also possible that this association would recall for Matthew's audience the promise to Abraham that the nations would be blessed through him (Gen. 12:3), especially since Abraham has figured prominently in Matthew's narrative and since the import of this pericope is precisely the inclusion of this Gentile and her daughter into Israel's blessing (15:24–28).[77]

Noah is mentioned in Matthew's fifth and final discourse (Matthew 24–25) in relation to Jesus' *parousia* (παρουσία, 24:37, 39).[78] It is clear that, in referring to Noah, the evangelist is providing an analogy between the situation that will typify Jesus' *parousia* and the circumstances at the time

---

74   Note the frequent reference to Sodom (and Gomorrah) in subsequent parts of the Old Testament as examples of wickedness and/or judgment and destruction; e.g. Deut. 29:23; 32:32; Isa. 1:9-10; 13:19; Jer. 49:18; 50:40; Lam. 4:6; Ezekiel 16; Amos 4:11; and Zeph. 2:9.

75   Because of a number of significant differences between the parallel accounts in Mark and Matthew, some commentators have suggested that Matthew may (also) be using another source (M). Alternately, Davies and Allison argue that the differences are fairly well accounted for by Matthean redaction (*Matthew*, II, p.542).

76   For a range of possible purposes of this redaction, see Davies and Allison, *Matthew*, II, p.547.

77   France, *Matthew*, p.595.

78   For a helpful discussion of the referents of ἔρχομαι and παρουσία in Matthew 24 and the argument that the teaching about Jesus' *parousia* begins at 24:36, see France, *Matthew*, pp.889–94.

of Noah.[79] In fact, Matthew introduces the analogy with the comparative clause 'as the days of Noah were' (using ὥσπερ, 24:37). The analogy is made explicit in 24:38-39, highlighting the unexpectedness of the flood in Noah's generation.

> For as in those days before the flood they were eating and drinking, marrying and giving in marriage, until the day Noah entered the ark,[80] and they knew nothing until the flood came and swept them all away, so too will be the coming of the Son of Man.[81]

The activities assigned to Noah's contemporaries (four periphrastic participles: τρώγοντες καὶ πίνοντες, γαμοῦντες καὶ γαμίζοντες, 'eating and drinking, marrying and giving in marriage') are not drawn from the Genesis flood story and seem, at first, to be innocuous actions. Yet 'eating and drinking' can have a negative cast in the biblical text (e.g. Exod. 32:6) and does so in the immediate context of Matthew 24 (24:49, using ἐσθίω rather than τρώγω). It is also the case that the language of 'marrying and giving in marriage' would likely have evoked the introduction to the flood account (Gen. 6:1-4), in which the evil of humanity is illustrated by the intermarriage of 'the sons of God...[and] the daughters of humans' (6:4).[82]

The focus of these activities in Matthew, however, is to emphasize that the judgment of the flood catches people unaware.[83] The implication is clear: as the judgment of the flood caught those in Noah's generation by surprise, so the *parousia* will come unexpectedly. The specific teaching on Noah in relation to the *parousia* concludes with Jesus' exhortations to be awake and ready (24:42, 44).

---

79   Streett provides evidence that an analogical ('typological') reading of the flood story in relation to eschatological judgment is not a New Testament invention but has precursors in second temple literature (e.g. *1 En.* 10:1–11:2) as well as in Old Testament prophetic material (e.g. Isa. 26:20; 54:8-10). D. R. Streett, '"As It Was in the Days of Noah": The Prophets' Typological Interpretation of Noah's Flood', *CTR* 5 (2007), pp.33–51.

80   This temporal clause follows quite closely the LXX at Gen. 7:7:...εἰσῆλθεν... Νῶε εἰς τὴν κιβωτόν.

81   In this pericope (24:37-44), Matthew uses Q material (see Lk. 17:26-35; also 12:39-40). For likely Matthean additions to Q – such as the inclusion of παρουσία at 24:37, 39 and καὶ οὐκ ἔγνωσαν at the beginning of 24:39, see Hagner, *Matthew*, pp.718–19. For the complexities of determining Q and its redaction by Matthew and Luke in this passage, see Davies and Allison (*Matthew*, III, pp.375–6).

82   Davies and Allison, *Matthew*, III, p.380, n.46.

83   The likely Matthean addition to Q, 'and they knew nothing' (24:39) further emphasizes this point.

Conclusion: Hermeneutical Considerations

Genesis is invoked in Matthew's Gospel in a variety of ways for various purposes. It is frequently the case that the first evangelist draws upon Genesis personages, places, or texts to evoke story elements of Genesis. For example, Gen. 38:8 is alluded to in Mt. 22:24 to signal the story of Onan and Tamar as a backdrop to Deuteronomy legislation of the levirate marriage.

Matthew also uses Genesis material for its covenantal associations – associations that have both story and thematic purchase in Genesis. Covenant is evoked with a number of references to Abraham or the three patriarchs. Most of the Genesis persons in Matthew's genealogy also highlight covenantal themes from the story of Israel. Even the Gentile Tamar signals God's covenantal promises to Abraham to be a blessing to all peoples (Gen. 12:1).

Another storied evocation consists in the three allusions to Genesis 4. The story of Cain and Abel provides for Matthew a meta-narratival theme of sin and restoration. At 18:23 Jesus exhorts a life of forgiveness in contrast to the revenge typified by Lamech, Cain's progeny. The Genesis 4 narrative also provides Matthew with paraenetic value – his readers should avoid being like Cain in his anger that led to murderous actions (Mt. 5:21-25) and should emulate Abel (23:35).

Matthew uses story in the service of paraenesis by referencing Noah and the flood (to warn of judgment and to exhort toward readiness) and Sodom and Gomorrah (to announce and warn of judgment). In Mt. 19:4-5, Matthew uses Gen. 1:27 and 2:24 to provide the creational basis for human moral expectations regarding marriage. This provides another example of Genesis stories and themes leading to paraenesis.

Matthew also draws upon certain Genesis persons and texts to highlight his Christology. The martyrdom of the 'righteous Abel' (Mt. 23:35) offers an analogy for the death of the innocent Jesus. It may also be the case that Isaac is referenced or evoked at a number of points in Matthew to provide a pattern for Jesus' own faithful and willing participation in the plan of God.

In conclusion, by careful attention to Matthew's use of Genesis, numerous features of his gospel are illuminated. In particular, this chapter has shown that Matthew's theological and paraenetic purposes are enhanced by story features from Genesis evoked by reference to its persons, places, and texts.

Chapter 4

GENESIS IN LUKE-ACTS

Peter Mallen

Introduction

When one thinks of the OT in Luke-Acts, the book of Genesis does not immediately spring to mind as an obvious conversation partner or source for quotations. In fact, quotations from Genesis are found in just two places: at the end of Peter's speech in Acts 3:25; and in the beginning parts of Stephen's speech in Acts 7:3-7. These are references to the promises made to Abraham. Luke does not, however, develop these references in a sustained or nuanced way comparable to Paul's treatment of similar references in Galatians 3 and Romans 4. At first glance, then, it may appear that Genesis is not that important for Luke.

On further reflection, though, there are numerous allusions to Genesis in Luke's writing – especially to the figure of Abraham, whose name appears some twenty-two times. Many of these references are brief, often just the name Abraham with a word or two of description. Yet Abraham is such a towering figure in the Scriptures and traditions of Israel that mention of his name evokes numerous echoes. There are also several mentions of God as the sovereign Creator of the world and as the ancestral god of the patriarchs, a genealogy going all the way back to Adam, reference to Noah and the flood, and a summary of Israel's early history. In addition, there are other implicit references that rely on similarities in narrative pattern, some of which are probably intentional on Luke's part and some of which may be unintended.[1] The cumulative

---

1   There are probable echoes of the Abraham story in Luke 1, which we will explore shortly, but it is less certain when it comes to an account such as Pentecost in Acts 2. While some commentators see here a reversal of the confusion of language that occurred at Babel in Genesis 11, there are reasons for caution. There is almost no verbal overlap between the two stories and the main point of the accounts is widely divergent. One can draw up possible points of contact, but in each case they are opposites (e.g. the builders at Babel plan to build a tower *up to* heaven while the Holy Spirit descends *from* heaven). Hence while such an exercise may aid our appreciation of the Pentecost account, it is asking a lot of Luke's audience to hear the possible echoes, invert them, and then draw an opposite conclusion. Hence one concludes that it is unlikely that Luke intended to allude to the Babel account here.

effect of all these references is to suggest that Genesis was a significant dialogue partner for Luke.[2]

One sign of the importance of Genesis is that it is used to help set the scene for the narrative from the opening chapter of the Gospel. Two references to the Abrahamic covenant (Lk. 1:55, 72-73) establish expectations that reverberate through the rest of the narrative each time the name of Abraham is mentioned. Recurring questions for the audience include 'Who are the descendants of Abraham that will be blessed?', 'Who is the God who makes and fulfils such promises?', and 'How will God bring about this blessing?'. We suggest that such questions form threads through the narrative of Luke-Acts and receive instructive answers.

Before engaging with the text in detail, it may be helpful to set out some brief assumptions for this chapter. First, only modest attention will be given to the textual affinities of the Genesis text used by Luke. The main reason for this is that there are only three brief quotations cited by Luke and it will be demonstrated that these generally follow the form of the LXX text. The allusions rely mainly on recognition of a well-known person or event from Genesis and are therefore less reliant on the form of the text.

Second, the book of Genesis is part of the Scriptures designated by Luke as the Law of Moses (Lk. 24:44). Modern debates about the sources, authorship and development of these books, while important, will be treated as contemporary concerns and therefore not relevant to Luke and his readers. Likewise it appears that characters in Genesis, such as Abraham, Lot and Noah, were considered to be historical figures and the matter-of-fact way that the story of the Flood is treated in Jesus' teaching (Lk. 17:26-27) suggests that Luke's audience would hear it in a similar way.

Third, Luke-Acts will be taken as a unified narrative in two parts, having a form somewhat akin to Hellenistic historiography but with a heightened focus on the purposes and actions of God (Lk. 1:1-4; Acts 1:1-2).[3] The audience for Luke-Acts will be taken as predominantly Gentile, but having some previous association with the synagogue and Scriptures of Israel (e.g. God-fearers in Acts 13:26). Hence it is assumed that they will have heard of the figure of Abraham and have a sense of his place in Jewish history.

---

2   Important contributions to the discussion include N. A. Dahl, 'The Story of Abraham in Luke-Acts', in L. E. Keck and J. L. Martyn (eds), *Studies in Luke-Acts* (Nashville: Abingdon Press, 1966), pp.139–58; J. S. Siker, *Disinheriting the Jews: Abraham in Early Christian Controversy* (Louisville: Westminster/John Knox, 1991), particularly ch. 4; J. B. Green, 'The Problem of a Beginning: Israel's Scriptures in Luke 1–2', *BBR* 4 (1994), pp.61–86; R. L. Brawley, 'The Blessing of All the Families of the Earth: Jesus and Covenant Traditions in Luke-Acts', in E. H. Lovering Jr. (ed.), *SBLSP, 1994* (Atlanta: Scholars Press, 1994), pp.252–68; and R. L. Brawley, 'Abrahamic Covenant Traditions and the Characterization of God in Luke-Acts', in J. Verheyden (ed.), *The Unity of Luke-Acts* (BETL, 142; Leuven: Leuven University Press, 1999), pp.109–32.

3   The prologue to the Gospel highlights that the work is a narrative (διήγησις) concerning events that have been fulfilled (πεπληροφορημένων), which we interpret as a divine passive. The opening words of Acts suggest a continuation of the same narrative.

The layout of the chapter will follow the narrative order of Luke-Acts. This means that significant allusions in the Gospel will be addressed before turning to the relatively few quotations in Acts. The reason for this approach is to illustrate better how Luke uses themes, people and events from the book of Genesis to develop his narrative.[4] As we explore both allusions and quotations, we will reflect on what their purpose may be in the narrative.

Origins

The Scriptures have their beginning point in the book of Genesis, a book about origins. In the opening chapters of the Gospel, Luke chooses to present the origins of his chief character, Jesus, in terms that take the hearer back to Genesis. Luke does this in a way unique to his Gospel, with numerous echoes of the Abraham story.[5] There are no quotations from Genesis but as we hear of an elderly childless couple, the impossible promise of God, a repeated promise of blessing and the covenant with Abraham we are caught up in the echo chamber of the story of Abraham. These echoes merge seamlessly with the promises to David and later the hopes of an Isaianic New Exodus. Already it is clear that this narrative is some sort of continuation of the history of Israel.

These opening chapters, then, are about the *origins* of Jesus. Given the extensive space they occupy in the narrative, this is clearly an important matter for Luke.[6] One can likewise infer that it was an important topic for Luke's audience, in whose culture a 'new' religion was likely to be viewed with some suspicion and animosity.[7] Hence Luke is careful to show that far from being a recent arrival on the religious marketplace, Christianity has ancient roots in Judaism. These roots include the figure of Abraham, who is traditionally viewed as the founder or father of the Jewish people.[8] The connection with Abraham is made in two explicit references in the opening chapter. Mary's song (the *Magnificat*) ends with the statement:

> [God] has helped his servant Israel,
>   remembering mercy

4   The opposite approach is taken by Dahl, 'Abraham', who begins with a detailed examination of Stephen's speech in Acts 7 and then works backwards, finishing with brief comments on the Gospel. This writer feels that such an approach does not give adequate consideration to the intention of Luke's narrative.

5   The prologue of the Gospel of John also takes the reader back to Genesis with its striking opening verses, but focuses on Jesus' active presence at creation rather than on the formation of Israel through Abraham and his seed.

6   The amount of narrative space given to Jesus' origins in Luke 1–2 plus the genealogy in Luke 3 is comparable to that given to the passion account. Both topics are clearly important for Luke.

7   See, for instance, the discussion in F. S. Spencer, *The Gospel of Luke and Acts of the Apostles* (Nashville: Abingdon, 2008), pp.60–62.

8   See discussion in Siker, *Disinheriting*, pp.19–21.

>   – as he said to our fathers –
>   to Abraham and to his seed forever.

>   (Lk. 1:54-55)

Zechariah's song (the *Benedictus*) contains a similar statement:

>   ... showing mercy to our fathers,
>   and remembering his holy covenant,
>   the oath he swore to Abraham our father,
>   that, having rescued us from the hand of our enemies,
>   we might worship him without fear ...

>   (Lk. 1:72-74)

Neither of these statements quotes a known scriptural text but each contains phrases reminiscent of other texts.[9] Whether Luke (or his sources) had these particular texts in view is a moot point. But given that Luke later quotes two key verses from the Abraham cycle of stories in Genesis 12–25 (in Acts 3:25; 7:3), it seems likely that he is familiar with these chapters from Genesis.

The two references to Abraham in Luke 1 recall the covenant made with Abraham (Gen. 17:1-14), which God later swore by oath (Gen. 22:16-17). The blessings associated with this covenant focus on many descendants and the gift of the land. These promises form the origin of Israel's relationship with God and are repeated in summary form to both Isaac and Jacob. The two references to Abraham in Luke 1 not only remind the hearer of these promises, but also God's long history with the people of Israel. The vocabulary used – remembering, mercy, covenant, oath, servant, Israel, seed, fathers – suggests that God is acting once again to bless the descendants of Abraham in view of the special covenant relationship between God and Abraham.

While the songs of Mary and Zechariah mention Abraham by name, the perceptive hearer has possibly already heard numerous echoes of the Abraham story through the earlier parts of the narrative.[10] Zechariah and Elizabeth are introduced as righteous and blameless, advanced in years but having no children since Elizabeth is barren (Lk. 1:6-7). Abraham is likewise considered righteous (Gen. 15:6) and is called to be blameless (17:2). Both Abraham and Sarah are advanced in years (18:11) but have no children for Sarah is barren (11:30; 15:2; 16:1).[11] When Abraham is told by the Lord

---

9   See Mic. 7:20 ('... mercy to Abraham as you swore to our fathers'); Isa. 41:8-9 ('You are Israel, my servant ... the seed of Abraham ...'); Ps. 104[105]:8 ('remember his covenant forever ... which he made with Abraham'); and Exod. 2:24 ('God remembered his covenant with Abraham').

10   For further detailed comparisons, including a helpful table, see Green, 'Beginning', pp.68–77.

11   Note the verbal overlap in the following verses: Gen. 18:11a LXX reads Αβρααμ δὲ καὶ Σαρρα πρεσβύτεροι προβεβηκότες ἡμερῶν while Lk. 1:18b reads ἐγὼ γάρ εἰμι πρεσβύτης καὶ ἡ γυνή μου προβεβηκυῖα ἐν ταῖς ἡμέραις αὐτῆς; Gen. 11:30

that his wife will bear a son (17:15), he questions the promise because he is one hundred years old and Sarah is ninety (17:17). Yet Sarah conceives and bears a son (21:2). Similarly, Zechariah doubts and questions the angel who appears to him in the temple, telling him that his wife will bear a son (Lk. 1:11-13), since he and his wife are old (1:18). Yet Elizabeth does conceive (1:24) and bear a son (1:57).

Shifting the focus to Mary, she will bear a son who will be considered great (Lk. 1:31-32), which may recall the original promise made to Abraham (Gen. 12:2). Mary also questions the announcement (Lk. 1:34), to which the angel Gabriel replies that nothing will be impossible with God (1:37). This echoes the similar reply given to Abraham that nothing is too hard with God (Gen. 18:14) when he doubts that his elderly wife is to have a son.[12] When Mary visits Elizabeth, the latter's response emphasizes blessing – of Mary and the child she bears – with three occurrences of the word blessing (Lk. 1:42-45). This may echo the original promise to Abraham with its repeated emphasis on blessing (Gen. 12:2-3).

These various echoes may not have all been intended by Luke, yet their frequency, linguistic overlap with relevant Genesis texts and narrative fit suggest that Luke has consciously reflected on the Abraham and Sarah story and shaped this early part of his narrative with it in mind.

Luke's exploration of Jesus' origins in the early chapters of the Gospel has one other significant strand, which is the relationship between God and Jesus. Gabriel's announcement to Mary has already indicated that Jesus will be called the Son of God and will be mysteriously conceived by the power of the Holy Spirit (Lk. 1:35). This connection is confirmed at Jesus' baptism when an authoritative voice from heaven affirms Jesus to be God's Son (3:22) and the Holy Spirit descends upon him in bodily form. The wording of the announcement 'You are my Son, the Beloved…' is probably taken from Mk 1:11, which appears in part to echo the command to Abraham to 'Take your beloved son, whom you love, Isaac…' in Gen. 22:2 LXX.[13] It is difficult to gauge the extent to which Luke or his audience may have heard this echo. While Paul and John make the connection clearer between the near sacrifice of Isaac and the death of Jesus (Rom. 8:32; Jn 3:16), the earlier echoes of the Abraham story in Luke 1 may bring it to mind here.[14]

---

introduces Sarah as follows: καὶ ἦν Σαρα στεῖρα καὶ οὐκ ἐτεκνοποίει while Elizabeth is introduced in a similar way in Lk. 1:7, καὶ οὐκ ἦν αὐτοῖς τέκνον, καθότι ἦν ἡ ᾽Ελισάβετ στεῖρα.

12   This could almost qualify as a quotation, except for the several grammatical changes. Gen. 18:14a LXX reads μὴ ἀδυνατεῖ παρὰ τῷ θεῷ ῥῆμα; while Luke's text reads οὐκ ἀδυνατήσει παρὰ τοῦ θεοῦ πᾶν ῥῆμα.

13   Gen. 22:2 reads Λαβε τὸν υἱόν σου τὸν ἀγαπητόν, ὃν ἠγάπησας and Lk. 3:22b reads Σὺ εἶ ὁ υἱός μου ὁ ἀγαπητός. The heavenly announcement also echoes Ps. 2:7 and Isa. 42:1.

14   As noted by J. B. Green, *The Gospel of Luke* (NICNT; Grand Rapids: Eerdmans, 1997), p.187.

Luke defers further explanation about the significance of Jesus' baptism (Lk. 4:1, 14, 18) and launches instead into the genealogy of Jesus, which is traced in reverse linear fashion back through Joseph to Adam, son of God (Lk. 3:23-38). The compressed genealogy shows the human origins of Jesus and his legal ancestry. Unlike Matthew's genealogy that has been deliberately fashioned to highlight David and Abraham (Mt. 1:1, 17), Luke's genealogy is simply an extended list from Joseph back to Adam. While one can use it to trace Jesus' lineage back to David (Lk. 3:31) and the patriarchs of Israel, Abraham, Isaac and Jacob (3:34), Luke continues the line further back from Abraham to Noah and then all the way back to Adam, son of God (3:38).[15] In this way, Jesus may be seen to represent all of humanity rather than just the descendants of Abraham. There is thus a subtle suggestion that the story of Jesus has universal implications for all humanity, a theme that recurs in Acts (cf. Acts 17:26, 28-29).

From a human perspective, then, Jesus has strongly Jewish roots and may lay claim to be the legitimate Davidic Messiah of Israel, a line of argument that will be taken up in various ways in the speeches in Acts. Yet that is not the whole story. Luke's careful wording in Lk. 3:23 shows that Jesus was *thought to be* Joseph's son (cf. 4:22), although the audience already know that this is not the case (1:27, 31-35). Jesus is *God's* son, conceived by the power of the Holy Spirit. This is publicly announced at his baptism, is confirmed by the final words of the genealogy and is appropriated by the devil and evil spirits (4:3, 9, 41). The genealogy is thus included as another piece of evidence exploring the origins of Jesus. On one level, it represents a human perspective on Jesus' origins that his narrative sheds further light on (cf. 9:18-20). At another level, the genealogy points all the way back to God as the Creator of humanity, who is at work even now through the person of Jesus.[16]

These opening chapters thus show the origins of major characters in the narrative as lying firmly within the history and hopes of Israel. The God of Israel is actively at work through the births of John and Jesus and is acting to bless Abraham and his seed. Going further back, Jesus is descended from Adam, son of God, which suggests that the unfolding narrative will have implications for the whole of humanity. These early chapters thus suggest continuity and coherence with the history of Israel, indeed its fulfilment (cf. Lk. 1:1). It is not yet clear, however, whether Luke's account is simply another chapter of this long history or is perhaps a fresh beginning, just as God made a fresh beginning with Abraham.

---

15   The latter part of the genealogy, backwards from Abraham, summarizes Gen. 11:10-26 and 5:1-32. Its source is clearly the LXX, which includes an extra name (Cainan) between Arphaxad and Shelah that is not in the MT.

16   See similar conclusion in J. A. Fitzmyer, *The Gospel According to Luke 1–9: Introduction, Translation, and Notes* (AB, 28; Garden City: Doubleday, 1981), p.498.

Who is a descendant of Abraham?

The opening chapter of the Gospel confidently states that God is acting afresh to bring mercy to Abraham and his seed (Lk. 1:54-55, 72-75). The question of who will be included in this blessing is raised by John the Baptist and then reappears several more times through the Gospel. In Acts, the issue becomes pressing as many Jews reject the good news of salvation while many Gentiles embrace it. In this section we will consider only evidence from the Gospel, while in a later section we will consider material from Acts showing how all the families of earth will be blessed through Abraham's seed.

The theme of election is quite contentious within the book of Genesis. Abraham's promised descendants will not come through his firstborn son, Ishmael, but through his second son, Isaac (Gen. 21:8-13). Similarly, the line of blessing continues through Isaac's second son, Jacob, rather than through his firstborn, Esau (28:13-15; 35:11-12). Later events in Israel's history raise the question of who is the true Israel, the rightful descendants of Abraham (e.g. the division of the kingdom after Solomon, the return of the exiles from Babylon, responses to Greek and Roman rule). Similar – and often bitter – debates were active at the time of Jesus with various Jewish groups suggesting different criteria to answer the question.[17] Debate continued in the late first century as Christian and Jewish groups both claimed to be the legitimate descendants of Abraham.[18] This was a significant question for Gentile Christians of course, since they were not physical descendants of Abraham.

In Luke's narrative, it is John the Baptist who first brings this issue to the fore. John urges the crowds coming to him not to say 'We have Abraham as our father' (Lk. 3:8b; cf. Mt. 3:9a). The preaching of John suggests that a common understanding was that physical descent from Abraham was sufficient to guarantee blessing from God.[19] As we have already seen, such a view is built on the foundational promises made to Abraham in Genesis 12–25, and reiterated in later Jewish writings (e.g. Isa. 41:8-10; 51:1-3; *Ps. Sol.* 18:3). While such texts appear to offer unconditional blessing to Israel based on descent from Abraham, they imply that a faithful response is needed. Abraham himself is called to walk blamelessly before the Lord (Gen. 17:1) and receives a final promise of blessing only after he passes a severe test of his obedience (22:1-2, 16). John's call to repentance and righteous living (Lk. 3:8, 10-14) may therefore be seen as a reworking of the frequent prophetic

---

17   See the helpful summary of election and factionalism within Israel in J. D. G. Dunn, *New Testament Theology: An Introduction* (Library of Biblical Theology; Nashville: Abingdon Press, 2009), pp.99–105.

18   Signposts to these debates are found in places such as Gal. 4:21-31 and Jn 8:31-40.

19   According to Brawley, 'Blessing', pp.256–8, this was part of the dominant Jewish national culture and is reflected in the songs of Mary and Zechariah, namely that God will bless Israel – in its entirety.

message that nominal cultic practice is not enough to secure God's blessing unless accompanied by righteous living.

The second part of John's allusion to Abraham is more controversial – that God can raise up children for Abraham from the desert stones (Lk. 3:8c; Mt. 3:9b). Commentators offer divergent interpretations of this image. Just as God created the first human being from the dust of the earth (Gen. 2:7), so his creative power can bring life and even cries of praise from lifeless stones (Lk. 19:40). Alternatively, just as God quarried Israel out of a single rock, Abraham, so God can create new descendants from desert stones (Isa. 51:1b // 51:2a). Luke's mainly Gentile audience may well also hear that they are among these stones – so that lack of physical descent from Abraham is no barrier to being blessed. Hence John undermines the notion – perhaps being spoken by members of the synagogue – that physical descent from Abraham is both necessary and sufficient to receive God's blessing. John's response is that it is neither sufficient nor necessary.

From the outset of Jesus' ministry, he challenges prevailing notions of who can receive God's blessing (e.g. Lk. 4:25-27). While other Jewish groups excluded various people who failed to meet their standards of purity, Jesus welcomes those on the margins of Jewish society who are considered unclean (5:12-13) or 'sinners' (5:22-24, 30-32). On two occasions, which are only recorded in Luke's Gospel, Jesus deliberately identifies such a person as a child of Abraham and hence a legitimate recipient of God's blessing: the woman bent over in 13:10-17 and Zacchaeus the tax collector in 19:1-10.

In each of these cases there is a plausible reason why the person would be excluded from their community – the woman due to her physical deformity and Zacchaeus due to his vocation on behalf of the Romans.[20] Yet Jesus sees each of them as they truly are – a child of Abraham.[21] By restoring each to community, Jesus extends to them the mercy promised to Abraham's descendants (1:54-55, 72-75) and demonstrates that they are included in the family of God's people.[22] Each responds in a way that shows this familial resemblance: the woman begins praising God (Lk. 13:13; cf. Gen. 12:8) and Zacchaeus becomes generous and just with his possessions (Lk. 19:8; cf. 3:10-14; Gen. 14:18-24).

A third – negative – example of this theme is found in the parable of the rich man and Lazarus (Lk. 16:19-31). To the outsider, the rich man

20   M. C. Parsons, *Body and Character in Luke and Acts: The Subversion of Physiognomy in Early Christianity* (Grand Rapids: Baker Academic, 2006), explores further reasons for exclusion based on the pervasive practice of physiognomy, in which a person's physical appearance was related to their inward character. The woman may thus be viewed as weak, feeble and of evil disposition (p.86), with Zacchaeus seen as small-spirited, and either greedy or lacking self-esteem (p.99).

21   In Lk. 13:16 the woman is described as a daughter of Abraham using a present participle while in 19:9 Zacchaeus is described as a son of Abraham using the present indicative. Hence in each case their status as a child of Abraham is not changed by Jesus' action, but rather their community now recognizes their status.

22   See Green, *Gospel*, pp.525–6; 672–3.

appears blessed by God while Lazarus appears cursed and afflicted by God (16:20-21; cf. Job 2:7). When the two men die, however, there is a reversal: Lazarus ends up at Abraham's side, the place traditionally reserved for the righteous; and the rich man ends up in Hades, separated from Abraham. The rich man calls out to Abraham as 'Father' and asks for mercy (Lk. 16:24), but Abraham replies that the rich man should remember how he lived (16:25). He completely ignored the needs of Lazarus rather than show hospitality in the manner of Abraham (Gen. 18:1-8). This lack of hospitality towards Lazarus confirms him as unworthy to receive the promises of Abraham and the eschatological reversal affirms this.

This parable illustrates a more general principle that there will be a reversal when God's kingdom comes in its fullness (Lk. 1:51-53; 6:20-26; 13:30; 14:11). At the eschatological banquet of the kingdom, many who feel assured of their salvation will be turned away as unrighteous while people from the four corners of the earth will come and feast with Abraham, Isaac and Jacob (13:24-29). The rich man from the parable is an example of the first group while Lazarus, the bent over woman and Zacchaeus form part of the second group. Gentiles in Luke's audience may see themselves as among those from east and west, north and south who will participate in God's kingdom. This teaching reaffirms John's earlier words that not everyone who names Abraham as their father will inherit the promised blessing and that God will raise up unexpected children for Abraham (3:8).

Two preliminary conclusions may be drawn concerning the descendants of Abraham. First, the people who will inherit the blessing promised to Abraham are those who live like Abraham, those who demonstrate generosity, justice, hospitality and faithful trust (cf. 3:10-14). These are the true and rightful descendants of Abraham, with Abraham seen as a model or archetype for this way of living. Second, there will be a reversal at the consummation of God's kingdom as intimated by Mary (cf. 1:50-55). Many of the people who are regarded as excluded from God's blessing – for reasons of purity, gender or vocation – will be included and vice versa. Luke thus reshapes and subverts aspects of the Jewish culture by challenging notions of election and the basis for salvation. This reshaping will continue and expand in Acts.

Judgment

Judgment is the counterpoint to salvation in the narrative. John and Jesus have come to announce the good news of salvation to Israel, but if the people refuse to listen or to change their ways then they will face God's judgment. While Luke can draw on contemporary events to tease out this theme (e.g. 13:1-5), his more common approach is to draw on well-known scriptural examples. Two of these are taken from the book of Genesis: the flood (Genesis 6–9) and the destruction of Sodom and Gomorrah (Genesis 18–19).

The first reference to Sodom occurs in relation to the mission of the seventy-two disciples (Lk. 10:1-16; cf. Mt. 10:5-16).[23] In his instructions to the disciples, Jesus emphasizes that any town that refuses to welcome them will, on the day of God's eschatological judgment, face worse punishment than Sodom (Lk. 10:12; cf. Mt. 10:15; 11:23-24).[24] This is because rejection of the disciples is tantamount to the rejection of Jesus, which, in turn, is a rejection of God (Lk. 10:16). Echoes of the Sodom story from Genesis include the sending ahead of messengers (Gen. 19:1), the disregard for hospitality (19:4-9) and God's impending judgment (19:12-15, 24-25). In Luke's text, the sting is that the places facing God's punishment are the Galilean towns where Jesus' message has been preached – but apparently rejected. Those who expected to benefit from God's salvation instead face severe judgment, unless they repent. This judgment still lies in the future, but its seriousness is highlighted by use of this classic example of judgment from Genesis.

In a second episode, Jesus speaks of the eschatological coming of the Son of Man and illustrates its unexpected arrival by comparison to both the flood and the destruction of Sodom (Lk. 17:20-37; cf. Mt. 24:23-28, 37-39). People will be going about their routine activities – eating, drinking, marrying, building and so forth – when destruction will suddenly come upon them, like the flood in Noah's day (Lk. 17:26-27) or the fire from heaven in Lot's day (17:28-29). Luke provides sufficient verbal overlap to bring these events from Genesis to mind (Noah, entered the ark, flood; Lot, Sodom, rained fire and sulphur from heaven). The point of these illustrations seems to be that the coming of the Son of Man will be unexpected, inescapable and catastrophic to those who are unprepared. Disciples are further warned that they must not turn back, lest they too perish, like Lot's wife (17:31-32; cf. Gen. 19:17, 26).[25]

Rather than focusing on the wickedness of the people or God's rescue of a righteous remnant, as in Jewish tradition, Luke instead emphasizes the plight of the majority. They are portrayed as unaware of God's purposes and therefore unprepared for the impending judgment they face.[26] The everyday activities being practised by the people are described in neutral terms (contra to the descriptions in Gen. 6:5, 11-12; 13:13; 19:13). Earlier in the Gospel, however, Jesus warns against a life focused on food and drink, or building

---

23   Early texts are evenly divided between the number seventy and seventy-two, which reflect the table of nations in Genesis 10 in the MT and LXX respectively. In either case, it points ahead to the mission to all nations in Lk. 24:47 and Acts 1:8.

24   Lk. 10:12 simply reads 'on that day' while 10:14 reads 'at the judgment'. Both terms refer to the eschatological day of Yahweh, as described in prophetic texts such as Mal. 3:1-6.

25   This warning is similar to Jesus' later warning to flee to the mountains when Jerusalem is attacked (Lk. 21:20-21) and echoes the similar instruction given to Lot's family in Gen. 19:17.

26   J. Nolland, *Luke 9:21–18:34* (WBC, 35B; Dallas: Word Books, 1993), p.860, notes that the key issue is 'the unwillingness [of Jesus' contemporaries] to reckon with the prospect of such a judgment'.

projects (e.g. Lk. 12:18-19, 29-31). Instead, disciples are to actively seek after God's kingdom (e.g. showing generosity towards the poor, hospitality to the outsider).

Luke's use of judgment imagery from Genesis, which largely mirrors that in Matthew, is consistent with its usage elsewhere in the NT. The judgment expected to be part of the Messiah's reign awaits a future time, but its object includes many from among Abraham's descendants who would be expecting blessing rather than judgment. This continues the theme of reversal described above and shows, negatively, that failure to accept Jesus and his message will lead to unexpected but inevitable judgment.

Blessing all the families of earth

Acts 3 contains the first quotation from Genesis in Luke's writing, which refers to God's promise to Abraham to bless all the families of earth through his seed (3:25).[27] It occurs in Peter's speech following the healing of a lame man at the gate of the Jerusalem temple (Acts 3:1-11). The joyous response of the healed man quickly attracts a crowd, who provide the audience for Peter's speech (3:12-26).[28] This original audience presumably comprised Jewish worshippers coming to the temple and those working in the temple precincts. Luke's mainly Gentile hearers form a second distinct audience.

Jesus is the focus of Peter's speech and the one to whom the healing is attributed (3:16). The God who has now glorified his servant Jesus and raised him from the dead is none other than the God of Abraham, Isaac and Jacob (3:13a). This same God, whom the gathered crowd worship, spoke through Moses and the prophets (3:22-24), and made a covenant with their fathers (3:25a) saying to Abraham, 'through your seed all the families of the earth shall be blessed' (3:25b). Peter concludes the speech by linking this promise with recent events – God has sent the risen Jesus first to Israel, to bless them and to turn them from their wicked ways (3:26).

The textual form of the Genesis quotation resembles several similar but variously worded promises from the LXX:

Acts 3:25   καὶ ἐν τῷ σπέρματί σου ἐνευλογηθήσονται πᾶσαι αἱ πατριαὶ
              τῆς γῆς
Gen. 12:3   καὶ ἐνευλογηθήσονται ἐν σοὶ πᾶσαι αἱ φυλαὶ τῆς γῆς

---

27   For a thorough exploration of this Genesis quotation in Acts 3:25 see J. A. Meek, *The Gentile Mission in Old Testament Citations in Acts: Text, Hermeneutic and Purpose* (LNTS, 385; London: T&T Clark, 2008), ch. 6.

28   While this speech is attributed to Peter, it is likely to have been composed by Luke from material in his sources, along with the other significant speeches in Acts. They are thus primarily written for Luke's audience and convey Luke's theological and mission-ary understandings. See M. L. Soards, *The Speeches in Acts: Their Content, Context and Concerns* (Louisville: Westminster/John Knox, 1994), especially ch. 4.

Gen. 18:18   καὶ ἐνευλογηθήσονται ἐν αὐτῷ πάντα τὰ ἔθνη τῆς γῆς

Gen. 22:18   καὶ ἐνευλογηθήσονται ἐν τῷ σπέρματί σου πάντα τὰ ἔθνη τῆς γῆς

Gen. 26:4   καὶ ἐνευλογηθήσονται ἐν τῷ σπέρματί σου πάντα τὰ ἔθνη τῆς γῆς

Gen. 28:14   καὶ ἐνευλογηθήσονται ἐν σοὶ πᾶσαι αἱ φυλαὶ τῆς γῆς καὶ ἐν τῷ σπέρματί σου

The quotation is closest though not identical to the LXX text of Gen. 22:18 and 26:4. Of these two texts, it is more likely to be a citation of 22:18 since this text is addressed to Abraham, as noted in Luke's introductory formula, while 26:4 is addressed to Isaac. Luke has changed the emphasis of the promise by placing 'through your seed' (ἐν τῷ σπέρματί σου) at the beginning of the quotation and has substituted the word 'families' (πατριαί) for 'nations' (ἔθνη). Although one cannot be definitive, an indication that Luke has followed the LXX rather than the MT is that the verbal form used by Luke is passive ('be blessed') rather than the reflexive hithpael ('bless themselves').[29]

The promise of blessing the nations through Abraham is the last element or strand of the programmatic promises first made to Abraham in Gen. 12:2-3, and repeated several more times with slight variation to each of Abraham (18:18; 22:17-18), Isaac (26:3-4) and Jacob (28:13-14). This blessing follows promises of many descendants and land. Christian commentators typically see this universal element as the climax or goal of the promises, namely that Abraham will mediate blessing to the whole world.[30] Within Israel's theology, however, this strand of blessing was far less prominent than the other strands of the promise. In part this may have been because the promise was read as a reflexive (bless themselves), making Abraham and his seed the model rather than the mediator of blessing.[31] In this reading of the promise, those seeking God's blessing will model themselves after Abraham's faith and obedience (e.g. Gen. 15:6; 22:18).[32] In addition, from the book of Exodus onwards, the nations were more often viewed by Israel – and experienced – as a threat rather than as a worthy object of God's blessing. The prophetic writings and literature of Second Temple Judaism abound with judgment oracles against

---

29   Whether the Hebrew verb 'bless' in these various Genesis texts is to be taken as a passive or a reflexive is a well-known interpretative crux. The LXX interprets each occurrence as a passive.

30   For a recent example of this trend, see B. T. Arnold, *Genesis* (NCBC; Cambridge: Cambridge University Press, 2009), p.133.

31   This line of interpretation is developed by R. W. L. Moberly, *The Theology of the Book of Genesis* (Cambridge: Cambridge University Press, 2009), pp.148–61. See also N. M. Sarna, *Genesis* (JPS Torah Commentary; Philadelphia: The Jewish Publication Society, 1989), p.89.

32   See earlier discussion that those who receive God's blessing are those who live like Abraham.

the nations, with only a few suggestions that they may be blessed.[33] If the promises of descendants and land are seen as core to Israel's theology, then perhaps this last part of the promise was sometimes viewed as a 'non-core' promise.[34]

Several aspects of Luke's use of this Genesis text deserve attention. First, who are the intended recipients of this blessing? Peter's speech is addressed to a predominantly if not entirely Jewish audience, within the Jerusalem temple precinct. This suggests that the blessing is intended especially for Israel, as Luke has intimated from the infancy narratives onward, in accordance with God's covenant with Abraham (Lk. 1:54-55, 72-75). The healing of the lame man continues Luke's earlier focus on marginalized individuals who were described as descendants of Abraham and hence worthy of receiving God's mercy (e.g. 13:16; 19:9). The change in wording from 'nations' in Gen. 22:18 LXX to the more racially neutral 'families' may have been made to ensure that the Jewish audience were included in the blessing.

The ending of Peter's speech indicates that the blessing is intended first for Israel (Acts 3:26), with the strongly Jewish co-text suggesting that Israel remains the primary heir of the promises made to Abraham.[35] The priority for Israel remains unchanged through the rest of the Acts narrative, with Paul later reiterating the need to bring the good news first to Israel in the programmatic description of his ministry (13:46). This pattern is followed consistently and coheres with Paul's stated theology elsewhere (Rom. 1:16). Hence although this Genesis text lends itself to supporting Gentile inclusion, as developed by Paul in Galatians 3, Luke does not utilize it in this way.

A promise to bless 'all the families of the earth', however, will naturally be heard by a Gentile audience as including them, with a mission *first* to Israel implying a *subsequent* mission to the nations. This inclusive understanding has been anticipated twice in the Gospel narrative with respect to Abraham (Lk. 3:8; 13:28-29), confirmed in Jesus' commissioning of the disciples (Lk. 24:47; Acts 1:8) and suggested by Peter's interpretation of the Joel quotation at Pentecost (Acts 2:21, 39). The incident with Peter and Cornelius in Acts 10 sets a significant precedent for God accepting Gentiles while the recurring mission pattern established by Paul at Antioch in Acts 13 is initial proclamation to Jews followed by proclamation to Gentiles (13:46-48).

A second aspect of the quotation is what form the blessing will take. In Genesis, blessing includes elements of fertility, prosperity, protection, military

---

33   See discussion in P. Mallen, *The Reading and Transformation of Isaiah in Luke-Acts* (LNTS, 367; London: T&T Clark, 2008), pp.111–13.

34   Australian Prime Minister John Howard famously declared some of his election promises 'non-core' after winning the 1996 election.

35   The Jewish milieu of the episode is emphasized by its location (Jerusalem temple), the identification of God (as God of the patriarchs), and by reference to Moses and Torah. The syntax of Peter's speech also indicates that the Jewish audience are the primary recipients through the emphatic placement of 'you' in 3:25-26 ('*you* are the descendants of the prophets and of the covenant ...'; 'to *you* first God sent ...').

success and peace.[36] Examples of the nations being blessed through Abraham and his seed include Abraham's intercession on behalf of Sodom and Gomorrah (Gen. 18:16-33), the healing of Abimelech's household (20:17-18) and Joseph's wise governance of Egypt during the famine (Genesis 41). The blessings of the covenant with Abraham envisaged in the songs of Mary and Zechariah in Luke 1 cover a similar sphere (prosperity for the poor and hungry, rescue from enemies, peace). Later in Luke's narrative, however, the blessings that are specifically linked to Abraham include healing, forgiveness and restoration to community (e.g. Lk. 13:12-13; 19:8-9; cf. Acts 3:7-8). Thus, there is a subtle shift from mostly physical blessing in Genesis more towards social and spiritual blessing, especially the forgiveness of sins and right relationship with God and neighbour. Luke also emphasizes that receipt of God's blessing cannot be assumed but rather depends on repentance and putting God's priorities into practice (Acts 3:19, 26; cf. Lk. 3:7-9; 19:8-9; 24:47; Acts 2:38).

A third consideration is the instrument or agency of blessing. In Genesis 12–50, blessing for the nations comes through the direct intercession of Abraham (Gen. 18:23-33; 20:17-18) or through the actions of one of his descendants (e.g. Joseph). The 'seed' in the promises made to Abraham, Isaac and Jacob was normally interpreted as a collective noun, indicating the nation, Israel, the descendants of Abraham (e.g. Lk. 1:55; Sir. 44:21).[37] Hence in the last days when it is envisaged that the nations will be blessed through the teaching of God's Torah and justice (e.g. Isa. 2:2-4; 51:4-5), it is implied that this blessing will come through God's people, Israel. In Peter's interpretation of the promise, however, blessing comes through the seed of Abraham (singular), namely God's servant Jesus, in whose name the man was healed (Acts 3:6, 16). The syntax of the Genesis quotation puts emphasis on this seed by placing it first. Hence Luke continues to reshape the promises made to Abraham, highlighting that they are indeed being fulfilled in the present – through the agency of Jesus (cf. Gal. 3:16).

Fourth, this promise continues to build on Luke's characterization of God.[38] Whatever exclusive claims Luke's audience may have heard from the synagogue, this quotation from Genesis shows that God's intention is to bless all people. Luke's narrative has consistently portrayed barriers being broken down, such that God's blessing is potentially available to all, irrespective of gender, vocation, status or race. God is the gracious Benefactor who chooses to freely bestow blessing on people, without expectation or demand of

36   See discussion in J. McKeown, *Genesis* (The Two Horizons Old Testament Commentary; Grand Rapids: Eerdmans, 2008), pp.226–33.

37   Sir. 44.21 LXX makes reference to blessing the nations through the seed (ἐν σπέρματι) of Abraham. His seed will be as numerous as the stars and God will give them (αὐτούς) an inheritance. Hence the singular seed of Abraham is the collective nation of Israel.

38   See discussion in Brawley, 'Covenant', especially pp.121–6.

reciprocity.[39] Although Luke includes several references to God's judgment, the dominant note is that God is bringing near times of refreshing through his chosen agent, Jesus (3:20; cf. Lk. 4:19). Further, the whole narrative shows the faithfulness of God to the promises made to Abraham – to individuals, to the nation of Israel and in ever widening ripples to all people. This is in keeping with the original promise to Abraham – to bless him, to bless his seed (Israel) and through his seed to bless all people (cf. Acts 1:8).

This short quotation from Genesis forms part of the core promises made to the patriarchs and is thus foundational to Israel's faith. In Luke's account, this promise is both affirmed and revised. The promise includes blessing for Israel, which Luke has highlighted from the very beginning of the narrative, and which in this instance involves the healing of a lame man. The surprising new twist for a Jewish audience is that the blessing comes through the agency of Jesus, recently rejected and crucified but now raised to life by God and glorified. For Luke's Gentile audience, they too are included within this promise to Abraham, for it is intended for all families of the earth. This is indeed the goal or plan of Israel's God who is seen here as the great Benefactor of all peoples.

Israel's History

Two of the longest speeches in Acts, given by Stephen in Acts 7 and by Paul in Acts 13, give a selective recital of Israel's history. Each begins with God's choosing of Abraham and ends with God's recent action through Jesus. While the style and content of these speeches are unique to the NT canon, there are several scriptural precedents for such historical summaries (e.g. Neh. 9:5-37; Psalms 78, 105, 106). As in these other retellings, the two Acts speeches offer a particular interpretation of Israel's history.

When Stephen is falsely accused of speaking against the temple and the Mosaic law (Acts 6:8-14), he does not respond directly to these charges but instead recounts some key moments in the history of Israel.[40] Our focus will be on the first sections of Stephen's speech, which show the most sustained engagement with the narrative and characters of Genesis in Luke-Acts. We will first show the many connections with Genesis (through quotation, verbal allusion and allusion) before exploring several implications. We will then briefly consider Paul's synagogue speech in Acts 13.

---

39   For discussion of God as Benefactor in Luke's narrative, see Green, *Gospel*, pp.202–3; 274–5; 495–6.

40   For various perspectives on Stephen's speech, see J. Kilgallen, *The Stephen Speech: A Literary and Redactional Study of Acts 7,2-53* (AnBib, 67; Rome: Biblical Institute Press, 1976); and T. Penner, *In Praise of Christian Origins: Stephen and the Hellenists in Lukan Apologetic Historiography* (ESEC, 10; New York: T&T Clark International, 2004).

Acts		Genesis	
7:2	The God of glory appeared (ὤφθη) to our father Abraham … in Mesopotamia	12:7 11:31	The Lord appeared to Abraham … (verbal allusion) … country of the Chaldeans (allusion)
7:3	Ἔξελθε ἐκ τῆς γῆς σου καὶ ἐκ τῆς συγγενείας σου, καὶ δεῦρο εἰς τὴν γῆν ἣν ἄν σοι δείξω Leave your country and your relatives and go to the land I will show you	12:1 (LXX)	Ἔξελθε ἐκ τῆς γῆς σου καὶ ἐκ τῆς συγγενείας σου … εἰς τὴν γῆν, ἣν ἄν σοι δείξω
7:4	Abraham settled (κατῴκησεν) in Haran (Χαρράν) … … moved to this country	11:31 12:5	… settled in Haran (verbal allusion) … went to land of Canaan (allusion)
7:5	… promised to give (δοῦναι) the land to Abraham and to his seed (σπέρματι) as a possession (κατάσχεσιν) Abraham had no children	17:8, 48:4 15:2	The land of Canaan I give to you and your seed as an everlasting possession (verbal allusion) Abraham is childless (allusion)
7:6-7:7a	ἔσται τὸ σπέρμα αὐτοῦ πάροικον ἐν γῇ ἀλλοτρίᾳ καὶ δουλώσουσιν αὐτὸ καὶ κακώσουσιν ἔτη τετρακόσια καὶ τὸ ἔθνος ᾧ ἐὰν δουλεύσουσιν κρινῶ ἐγώ His seed will be strangers in a foreign land, and they will be enslaved and mistreated four hundred years. The nation which they serve as slaves I will judge	15:13-14a (LXX)	… πάροικον ἔσται τὸ σπέρμα σου ἐν γῇ οὐκ ἰδίᾳ, καὶ δουλώσουσιν αὐτούς καὶ κακώσουσιν αὐτούς … τετρακόσια ἔτη. τὸ δὲ ἔθνος, ᾧ ἐὰν δουλεύσωσιν, κρινῶ ἐγώ
7:7b	μετὰ ταῦτα ἐξελεύσονται After that they will come out καὶ λατρεύσουσίν μοι ἐν τῷ τόπῳ τούτῳ. and worship me in this place	15:14b (LXX) (Exod. 3:12b LXX)	μετὰ δὲ ταῦτα ἐξελεύσονται ὧδε μετὰ ἀποσκευῆς πολλῆς … καὶ λατρεύσετε τῷ θεῷ ἐν τῷ ὄρει τούτῳ … and worship God on this mountain

7:8	God gave the covenant of circumcision ...	17:10-14	God explains the covenant of circumcision (allusion)
	Abraham becomes the father of Isaac ...	21:2-3	Sarah bears a child to Abraham who is named Isaac (allusion)
	Abraham circumcised Isaac (περιέτεμεν) on the eighth day (τῇ ἡμέρᾳ τῇ ὀγδόῃ) ...	21:4	Abraham circumcised Isaac on the eighth day (verbal allusion)
	Isaac becomes father of Jacob ...	25:26	Jacob born (allusion)
	... Jacob of the twelve patriarchs	35:23-26	The twelve sons of Jacob (allusion)
7:9	Patriarchs are jealous (ζηλώσαντες) of Joseph ...	37:11	Joseph's brothers jealous (verbal allusion)
	... they sell (ἀπέδοντο) him into Egypt (εἰς Αἴγυπτον)	37:28	Joseph sold to merchants who take him to Egypt (verbal allusion)
	... God was with him (ἦν μετ᾿ αὐτοῦ)	39:2-3, 21, 23	The Lord was with him (verbal allusion)
7:10	Joseph shows wisdom before Pharaoh ...	41:33-39	Joseph described as wise and discerning by Pharaoh (allusion)
	Joseph appointed ruler over Egypt	41:40-44	Joseph placed in charge of all Egypt (allusion)
7:11	Famine comes upon Egypt	41:54	Famine in Egypt (allusion)
	Ancestors cannot find food	42:5	Famine in Canaan (allusion)
7:12	Jacob sends ancestors to Egypt because there is grain there	42:1-2	Jacob sends ten of his sons to Egypt to buy grain (allusion)
7:13	Joseph makes himself known to his brothers	45:1-4	Joseph reveals his identity to his brothers (allusion)
	Joseph's family become known to Pharaoh	45:16	Pharaoh hears that Joseph's brothers have come (allusion)
7:14	Joseph invites Jacob and all his relatives to come to Egypt ...	45:9-13	Joseph sends word back to Jacob to come to Egypt (allusion)
	...seventy five (ἑβδομήκοντα πέντε) people in all	46:27 (LXX)	Seventy five of Jacob's family move to Egypt (verbal allusion)[41]

41 Gen. 46:27 LXX puts the total number at seventy five people, while the MT puts the total as seventy.

7:15	Jacob goes to Egypt and dies there	46:26	Jacob goes to Egypt (allusion)
		49:33	Jacob dies (allusion)
7:16	The bodies brought back to Shechem and placed in a tomb bought by Abraham	50:12-13	Jacob's body brought back to Mamre and placed in tomb bought by Abraham (allusion)[42]
7:17	Time draws near for God to fulfil his promise to Abraham … the people increased (ηὔξησεν) and multiplied (ἐπληθύνθη)	47:27	The people of Israel increased and multiplied greatly (verbal allusion)

A quick perusal of the table shows that most of the references to Genesis take the form of allusions. While some of these have verbal overlap with the relevant Genesis text, many allude to an incident or character without making any direct verbal connection with the Genesis text. These indicate that the speech is best regarded as a summary of selected events and people with some key verses quoted in full. These quotations have been taken from the LXX with mostly minor modifications. The most significant change occurs in 7:7b where the final four words of Gen. 15:14 (…come out 'with many possessions') have been replaced with a phrase that appears based on Exod. 3:12 (…'and you will worship God on this mountain'). This change makes an important connection between the promise to Abraham and the promise to Moses and provides a key to understanding the entire speech.

First, God is shown to be active in history, working out his purposes.[43] God is thus shown to be the one who graciously initiates and shapes Israel's history. He even works through Joseph's unfortunate circumstances to enable Abraham's descendants to survive a great famine. Stephen's portrayal of God's kindness and active intervention for Israel is consistent with how Luke portrays God's activity in Luke 1–2 and more recently in Acts 2:22-36 and 3:13-26 where God is at work to bring his favour and blessing to Israel.

Second, God is shown to be faithful to his promises, even though the people are later shown to be unfaithful towards God's chosen agents (i.e. Moses, Jesus, Stephen). God's faithfulness is shown by the fulfilment

---

42   Genesis states that Jacob was buried at Mamre in a tomb that Abraham purchased from Ephron the Hittite (50:12-13; cf. 23:7-20). The book of Joshua states that Joseph was buried at Shechem in a tomb that Jacob purchased from the sons of Hamor (Josh. 24:32; cf. Gen. 33:18-19). Stephen (or Luke) appears to have confused these two burial accounts.

43   Kilgallen, *Stephen*, p.43, notes that God is the subject of all but one verb in vv.2-8 so that 'God is the one who brings about all that happens to Abraham'.

of the prophetic word quoted from Gen. 15:13-14 about Abraham's descendants being enslaved in a foreign land and then coming out to worship in 'this place' (Acts 7:6-7). While not a major part of the Abraham story, it serves to tie the early part of the speech to what follows.[44] The subsequent references to Joseph basically explain how and why God's people moved from Canaan to Egypt (7:9-15),[45] while the reference to the people multiplying there (7:17) sets the scene for the Exodus story (7:18-39). The reference to worship in 7:7 anticipates later arguments about the worship of Israel and the temple (7:40-50).[46]

The comment that the time was drawing near for God to fulfil the promise made to Abraham (7:17) has two possible antecedents: the prophetic word that the people would come out from Egypt (7:7b); and the promise of the land (7:5). The changed ending to the quotation from Gen. 15:13-14 appears to be an attempt to tie these two threads together and so link the Abraham and Exodus stories in terms of promise and fulfilment. In order for the promise of land to be fulfilled, the people must first be freed from Egypt. The command to worship God on 'this mountain' (Exod. 3:12) refers to Mt Horeb but the subtle change to 'this place' in Stephen's speech most probably refers to the land promised to Abraham where the audience is now living (Acts 7:5).[47] God's faithfulness is shown both by the Exodus and the fact that Abraham's descendants are now living in the promised land. In a similar way, God has been faithful in recent history to another promise – to raise up a prophet like Moses, namely Jesus (7:37; cf. 3:22).

Third, Luke's audience is implicitly invited to view Israel's history as their own. Stephen aligns himself with 'our fathers' through the majority of the speech, which makes sense in the original setting, but which also invites Luke's audience to view Abraham as their father and to hear the history as their own history. This pattern is broken only in the last few verses of the speech when Stephen abruptly changes to 'your fathers' (7:51-52). Unlike the exemplary obedience of Abraham (7:4, 8), the current Jewish leaders in Jerusalem are presented as resisting God and being disobedient to God's law over their rejection of the Righteous One, Jesus (7:53). In this way they are behaving like their faithless fathers who rejected Moses, even though he was sent by God (7:35, 39).

---

44   Penner, *Origins*, pp.94–6, argues that vv.6-7 provide both the inner logic and major themes of the speech. See also Kilgallen, *Stephen*, pp.37–42.

45   The brief narrative mentions that Joseph is given grace and wisdom before Pharaoh (7:10), two terms also used to describe Stephen (6:3, 8, 10). Hence some commentators see here a deliberate comparison between Joseph and Stephen.

46   The ultimate purpose of God's promise to Abraham – worship in this place – has been corrupted through Israel's idolatry (7:40-43) and wrong thinking about the temple (7:44-50). See discussion in Penner, *Origins*, pp.308–18.

47   As argued, for instance, by Dahl, 'Abraham', pp.145–7; and Siker, *Disinheriting*, pp.122–3. Alternatively, 'this place' refers to the Jerusalem temple, which will become the dominant theme in the latter part of the speech.

Paul's later speech in Acts 13:16-41 continues to rehearse Israel's history, this time to a mixed synagogue audience comprising Israelites and God-fearing Gentiles (13:16). The calling of the patriarchs and the Exodus, the focus of Stephen's speech, are summarized in just a few verses (13:17-19). Paul then describes the time of the Judges, the demand for a king and the choice of Saul and then David (13:20-22). Unlike Stephen's speech, Paul's focus falls on Jesus, the promised Saviour from the line of David (13:23-41). This promise is intended for the descendants of Abraham (13:26, 32), which has the effect of connecting the promises made to David with promises made to Abraham. A similar interpretative move was made in Luke 1 where Gabriel announces to Mary that she will have a son who will rule on David's throne (Lk. 1:31-33), and Mary responds by praising God for remembering his promise to Abraham (1:54-55).[48]

In these two speeches, then, the promises made to Abraham have merged with promises made to Moses and David. These promises are fulfilled in Jesus who is both the promised prophet like Moses and the promised messianic Saviour from the line of David. Luke thus shows how key promises made to Abraham, Moses and David all converge in the person of Jesus. Luke's narrative is thus more than a continuation of Israel's past history, but not a brand new beginning. Rather, Luke sees the hopes and promises of Israel's long history being fulfilled in Jesus.[49] The selective history that Luke recalls demonstrates the ancient roots of Christian faith, but also shows that Israel's history has a specific trajectory that points forward from Abraham and the patriarchs to fulfilment in Jesus Christ. God is shown to be faithful to these promises and to his people, Israel, which provides assurance that the God of Abraham can be trusted.

The promises, however, have been reshaped in Luke's hands. The key promise of the land to Abraham (Acts 7:5; 13:19) is not mentioned again in Paul's proclamation about Jesus, of which Acts 13 is presented as typical. Neither is it mentioned in Zechariah's summary of the Abrahamic covenant where it has been replaced by worship and right living (Lk. 1:72-75; cf. Acts 7:7).[50] Likewise, the centerpiece of the Mosaic covenant, the law, has been marginalized in light of the coming of the prophet like Moses (Acts 3:22; 7:37), Jesus, who is able to release people from their sins in a way not possible under the law (13:38-39). Finally, the hope of a Davidic king to free Israel from their political enemies (Lk. 1:69-71) has been transformed into an eternal Saviour who reigns at God's right hand in heaven (Acts 2:33-35; 13:22).

---

48   For discussion about Luke's merging of covenant traditions see Brawley, 'Blessing', pp.254–6, 265–6.

49   B. Witherington III, 'Finding Its Niche: The Historical and Rhetorical Species of Acts', in *SBLSP, 1996* (Atlanta: Scholars Press, 1996), pp.67–97, here p.82, notes that Luke-Acts is the fulfilment rather than the continuation of or sequel to the OT.

50   As discussed by Siker, *Disinheriting*, pp.123–4, who notes that 'The promise to Abraham finds its fulfilment not in the possession of the land per se but in the worship and service rendered to God by God's people'.

The Creator God

Three passages in Acts identify and characterize God as the sovereign Creator (Acts 4:24; 14:15-17; 17:24-29), with allusion back to the creation accounts in Genesis 1–2. The repetition of this theme and the way the three passages build from each other suggest its importance to Luke. We will briefly explore these passages to see how Luke uses these references to build his audience's understanding of God.

The first reference occurs in a prayer of the Christian community, which addresses God as 'the one who made the heaven and the earth and the sea and everything in them' (4:24). The same expression occurs when Paul speaks to a pagan crowd in Lystra (14:15). Paul encourages the audience to turn from worthless things (i.e. idols, worship of false gods) to the living God (14:16-17; cf. 1 Thes. 1:9; Rom. 1:20).[51] In a later speech given to Greek philosophers in Athens, Paul describes God as 'the one who made the world and everything in it, who is Lord of heaven and earth' (Acts 17:24). This speech continues by asserting that God gives life and breath to all people (17:25), and made all the nations from one man to inhabit the whole earth (17:26). Paul concludes by speaking against idolatry (17:29) and calling the audience to repent or face God's judgment through Christ (17:30-31).

These references allude to the creation accounts in Genesis and form the basis for unique claims about the power, authority, will and wisdom of Israel's God. The latter two speeches sound like a Jewish apology for monotheism but also provide a starting point for proclamation of the gospel. The one Creator God who provides for all people has now acted through Jesus Christ. Earlier speeches in Acts address the descendants of Abraham with their explicit reference to Israel's Scriptures, but the appeal to creation widens the scope of the gospel message to all people. The Creator of the whole world, who will judge every person through Christ, may legitimately make claims on Gentiles as well as Jews.

Conclusion

The book of Genesis provides a significant echo chamber for the narrative of Luke-Acts. There are only a few brief quotations but many allusions to the key characters and events of Genesis. Foremost among these is the figure of Abraham and the promises God made to him, along with reference to Noah and the flood, to Lot and the destruction of Sodom, and to Joseph. The other key actor from Genesis is of course God, about whom Luke draws several important inferences based on this book. While some of the references to Genesis can be traced to Mark or Q (e.g. imagery of judgment, preaching of

51   See discussion of Luke's anti-idol polemic in D. W. Pao, *Acts and the Isaianic New Exodus* (WUNT, 2/130; Tübingen: Mohr Siebeck, 2000), pp.193-204.

John the Baptist), the majority are distinctly Lukan, including those found in the infancy narratives and the speeches in Acts. This suggests that Luke has consciously reflected on these stories, especially the story of Abraham.

The three quotations taken from Genesis occur in Acts 3:25 (Gen. 22:18), Acts 7:3 (Gen. 12:1) and Acts 7:6-7 (Gen. 15:13-14). While each is based on the LXX text, there are minor changes in word order and lexical selection from any known LXX text. In two instances, these changes appear to have been made to deliberately make a point (Acts 3:25, 7:7). Since the quotations occur in speeches most likely composed by Luke, they show his willingness to modify the text to stress or clarify the point being made. The most significant change involves replacement of a phrase from Gen. 15:14 with a phrase from Exod. 3:12 in Acts 7:7, which serves to link the sections of Stephen's speech more closely together. Other indications that Luke has used the LXX text of Genesis rather than the MT are the inclusion of an extra name in the genealogy of Jesus (Lk. 3:35; cf. Gen. 11:12-13) and the number of Jacob's family who moved to Egypt (Acts 7:14; cf. Gen. 46:27).

Luke's interest in Genesis appears to fall into three main areas. The first stems from Luke's approach as a writer of historiography with its attention to the past and to origins as a way of understanding recent events (Lk. 1:1). What has been fulfilled are God's ancient promises and plan to bless all people through Jesus. These promises go back to the figure of Abraham, who is regarded as the father of the Jewish people. Hence the importance of the covenant made with Abraham (Lk. 1:55, 72-73) and the other promises of blessing made to Abraham (Acts 3:25; 7:3-5; 13:32). These promises, along with promises made to Moses and David, all find their fulfilment in Jesus. It is important for Luke's audience to grasp, then, that Christianity is not a 'new' religion but rather the fulfilment of these ancient promises made to the founding fathers of Israel.[52] Thus there is continuity and coherence between recent events centred on Jesus and the promises made to Abraham and his descendants. These help to tie the Jesus story and the emerging Christian community back to God's past dealings with Israel.

Second, the promises made to Abraham are being fulfilled in some unexpected ways. For instance, not every Jew who claims physical descent from Abraham will be blessed (Lk. 3:8), but rather those who repent and live like Abraham (3:8, 10-14; 19:8-9). Otherwise they will face judgment. A further sign of reversal is that outsiders who may have been considered excluded from God's blessing through Abraham become recipients of blessing (1:51-55; 13:11-16, 28-30; 19:1-10). The promise of blessing is potentially available to all people (Acts 3:25), but comes through the singular seed of Abraham, namely Jesus. Hence Luke has read Genesis in light of the Jesus event and the emergence of the mixed Jewish/Gentile church and so

---

52   As Witherington, 'Niche', p.91, notes, 'Christianity is not to be seen as a purely new religion, but rather the fulfilment in a more universal mode of a very old one, bringing to fruition ancient prophecies to God's people.'

has reshaped some of the promises made to Abraham. Focus falls on the recipients of blessing (all who repent and believe in Jesus, including Gentiles and other outsiders) and the breadth of blessing (social and spiritual as well as physical).

Third, Luke draws on Genesis to help characterize the nature of God. The God whom Christians worship is the faithful covenant-making God of Israel who remembers and acts upon his promises to Abraham (and to Moses and David). This God of the patriarchs of Israel (Acts 3:13) is also the Creator of heaven and earth (4:24; 14:15; 17:24) who brings blessing to all people (3:25; 14:17). Hence the good news of the gospel is for all people, Gentiles as well as Jews. While God's nature is to bless, God will also bring judgment on those who reject Jesus (Lk. 3:7-9; 10:10-16; 17:26-32). Here Luke draws on two classic images of judgment from Genesis, namely the flood and the destruction of Sodom and Gomorrah. The God who acted through Jesus Christ thus has a particular history with the nation of Israel but also universal claims on all people.

These various allusions to Genesis join with other scriptural voices in Luke-Acts to show that recent events find their meaning and place in continuity with God's activity in history and the promises made to the patriarchs and to Israel. These promises have taken a surprising direction through Jesus but readers may be assured that they are included in these promises and have now joined in the story of God's people.

Chapter 5

GENESIS IN JOHN'S GOSPEL AND 1 JOHN

Maarten J. J. Menken

Introduction

For Jews at the beginning of our era, the book of Genesis had significance in at least three respects. Genesis was the narrative of the beginnings of Jewish history, from creation to Israel's sojourn in Egypt. It was also the first book of the Torah, the Law that regulated Jewish life. Although it hardly contained law in the strict sense, it provided the basis for certain laws (such as those concerning Sabbath and circumcision), and presented examples of law-abiding behaviour in the patriarchs. And thirdly, it was a source of important theological ideas, such as creation, election and covenant. The significance of the book had materialized in diverse interpretative works (such as *Jubilees* or the works of Philo).

Christianity started as a Jewish movement. It read Scripture, including Genesis, with Jewish eyes. This holds even for Johannine Christianity, although the outcome of its reading of Scripture may sometimes look anti-Jewish. That, however, is the consequence of a split between Johannine Christian Jews and other Jews.

In the Johannine literature,[1] there are no marked quotations from Genesis. There is one unmarked quotation (in Jn 1:51), and there are several allusions.[2] There are also some evident references which cannot be characterized as quotations or allusions, and which I would provisionally label 'straightforward references'. They consist in the mention of names and events known from Genesis. They are not quotations because there is hardly any verbatim borrowing. They are not allusions either: an allusion requires some effort on the part of the reader to be recognized and can be missed without the alluding text becoming incomprehensible, whereas a straightforward reference is easily recognized and missing it makes the referring text incomprehensible. The use of straightforward references in combination with a lack of explicit quotations shows that

---

1   That is, the Gospel and Epistles of John. They come from the same early Christian 'school', and probably even from the same author.
2   On the concept of 'allusion', see M. J. J. Menken, 'Allusions to the Minor Prophets in the Fourth Gospel', *Neot* 44 (2010), pp.67–84, esp. 68–71.

in the Johannine literature, Genesis is functioning more as a *narrative* than as a *text*.[3]

I shall start with those instances in John where the use of Scripture in John is easily recognized, and then move on to less easily recognized ones. I make an exception for the various references to Abraham in Jn 8:31-59; because they occur in one continuous dialogue, it is best to discuss them in one section. I will finally give attention to the Genesis reference in 1 Jn 3:12. Lack of space forbids discussion of all possible references to Genesis in the Johannine literature,[4] but my selection covers, at least to my mind, the most important ones.

Genesis in John's Gospel

Some Straightforward References

In Jn 4:5-6, at the beginning of the story of the meeting between Jesus and the Samaritan woman, the evangelist locates the Samaritan city Sychar 'near the plot of ground that Jacob had given to his son Joseph',[5] and he tells his readers that 'Jacob's well was there'. Later in the narrative, the woman speaks of 'our ancestor Jacob, who gave us the well, and with his sons and his flocks drank from it' (4:12). According to Gen. 48:22, the dying Jacob says to his son Joseph: 'I now give to you one portion more than to your brothers, the portion that I took from the hand of the Amorites with my sword and with my bow.' The Hebrew word translated in the NRSV as 'portion' is שְׁכֶם, which can also be interpreted as the toponym Shechem (so the LXX: Σικιμα). Read in this way, Gen. 48:22 can be connected to Gen. 33:19 and Josh. 24:32, verses that taken together show that this Shechem that Jacob gave to Joseph is the plot of land that Jacob bought from the sons of Hamor, the father of Shechem, and in which Joseph's bones were buried after Israel's entrance into the land of Canaan.[6] The well of Jacob is not

---

3   For discussions of references to Genesis in John and 1 John, see G. Reim, *Studien zum alttestamentlichen Hintergrund des Johannesevangeliums* (SNTSMS, 22; Cambridge: Cambridge University Press, 1974), pp.98–105; A. J. Köstenberger, 'John', in G. A. Beale and D. A. Carson (eds), *Commentary on the New Testament Use of the Old Testament* (Grand Rapids, MI: Baker; Nottingham: Apollos, 2007), pp.415–512; D. A. Carson, '1–3 John', in Beale and Carson (eds), *Commentary on the NT Use of the OT*, pp.1063–7.

4   Examples of possible allusions not discussed here are the allusions to Gen. 27:35 in Jn 1:47, Gen. 2:2 in Jn 5:17, Gen. 2:7 in Jn 9:6, and Gen. 49:10 in Jn 9:7. The quotation from Zech. 9:9 in Jn 12:15 was probably also influenced by Gen. 49:10. For other possible allusions in John to Genesis 1–2, see J. K. Brown, 'Creation's Renewal in the Gospel of John', *CBQ* 72 (2010), pp.275–90.

5   Unless otherwise indicated, English translations of biblical passages come from the NRSV.

6   For details, see P. van Veldhuizen, *Geef mij te drinken: Johannes 4,4-42 als waterputverhaal* (Zoetermeer: Boekencentrum, 2004), pp.86–96.

mentioned in Genesis (although the story of Genesis 29 on Jacob watering the flock of Laban may well have given rise to the idea of a well of Jacob), but it must have been (and still is) a locally well known source of water.[7] These straightforward references do not immediately imply interpretation of the text of Genesis, but they serve the comparison of Jesus' gift of living water with the gifts of Jacob.

Another instance of a straightforward reference to Genesis is found in Jn 7:22. In 7:19-24, the Johannine Jesus defends his healing of a sick man on the Sabbath (5:1-9) by means of an argument *a minori ad maius*: if his Jewish opponents circumcise their male children even if the eighth day after their birth is a Sabbath,[8] they have no reason to be angry with Jesus because he made a whole human person well on the Sabbath. In v.22, Jesus says to his opponents that Moses gave them circumcision, and he adds by way of correction: 'It is, of course, not from Moses but from the patriarchs.' The command to circumcise a male child on the eighth day after his birth is found among the laws given by God to Moses (Lev.12:3), but its first mention in the Torah is found in Genesis 17. There, God gives the circumcision command to Abraham (vv.10-14), and Abraham executes it (vv.23-27; see also Gen. 21:4; 34:13-24). Jesus' correction of his own previous statement on Moses may serve to enhance the authority of the circumcision command: it is even older than Moses, it dates back to the patriarchs.[9]

The Quotation from Gen. 28:12 in Jn 1:51

In Jn 1:45-51, the evangelist narrates the call of Nathanael. Philip puts Nathanael in contact with Jesus, who demonstrates his omniscience. Nathanael then confesses Jesus as 'the Son of God' and 'the King of Israel', and Jesus promises him that he will see 'greater things than these', that is, greater than Jesus' demonstration of omniscience. The scene ends in v.51 with Jesus saying to Nathanael:

ἀμὴν ἀμὴν λέγω ὑμῖν, ὄψεσθε τὸν οὐρανὸν ἀνεῳγότα καί τοὺς ἀγγέλους τοῦ θεοῦ ἀναβαίνοντας καὶ καταβαίνοντας ἐπὶ τὸν υἱὸν τοῦ ἀνθρώπου.

Very truly, I tell you, you will see *heaven* opened *and the angels of God ascending and descending* upon the Son of Man.

The italicization in this fragment is that of NA[27]; together with the marginal reference it suggests that part of the saying constitutes an unmarked quotation from Gen. 28:12. This verse is part of Jacob's dream on his journey to Haran (Gen. 28:10-17), a dream in which God appears to him, makes

---

7   See Van Veldhuizen, *Geef mij te drinken*, pp.96–9.
8   See *m. Shabb.* 18:3–19:2; *m. Ned.* 3:11.
9   Cf. C. K. Barrett, *The Gospel according to St John* (London: SPCK, [2]1978), p.320.

him a promise and assures him of his presence. The dream begins in v.12 with Jacob seeing a ladder with its bottom on the earth and its top reaching 'to heaven, and the angels of God were ascending and descending on it'. The words between quotation marks read in the LXX, which gives here an adequate translation of the Hebrew: εἰς τὸν οὐρανόν, καὶ οἱ ἄγγελοι τοῦ θεοῦ ἀνέβαινον καὶ κατέβαινον ἐπ' αὐτῆς. It is important to note that the Hebrew text is ambiguous in one detail. The final word of the verse is בּוֹ; this can be translated as 'on it', that is, on the ladder, but also as 'on him', that is, on Jacob. The LXX translator has preferred the former, more obvious possibility (αὐτῆς refers to the κλίμαξ, 'ladder', mentioned earlier in the verse), but we know from rabbinic literature (*Gen. Rab.* 68:12; 69:3) that there was discussion on which of the two possibilities to prefer.[10]

Can we indeed speak of an unmarked quotation in this case? Jn 1:51 and Gen. 28:12 LXX have eleven Greek words in common (including ἐπί, not italicized in NA[27]). These words occur in exactly the same order, and they encompass at least a complete clause ('the angels of God were ascending and descending'). Moreover, the verbs 'to ascend' and 'to descend' occur in both John and Genesis in the same slightly illogical sequence: from the perspective of one who is on earth, one would expect that the angels (who are supposed to dwell with God in heaven) first descend and then ascend. It is therefore legitimate to perceive in Jn 1:51 an unmarked quotation from Gen. 28:12.

Was the quotation derived from the LXX? The verbal agreement may suggest that it was, but we should take into account that all substantives and verbs in the quotation are standard translations of their Hebrew equivalents (οὐρανός of שָׁמַיִם, ἄγγελος of מַלְאָךְ, θεός of אֱלֹהִים, ἀναβαίνειν of עלה, and καταβαίνειν of ירד), and that the word order is the same as in the Hebrew text. This means that any translator could easily arrive at this result.

In three particulars, the quotation deviates from its source: (1) 'heaven' has become the subject of the participle 'opened'; (2) the clause on the angels ascending and descending has become an *accusativus cum participio* depending on 'you will see'; (3) the angels are now said to ascend and descend not on the ladder, but 'upon the Son of Man'. The first and second particular are no more than consequences of the new context into which the quotation is inserted: the announcement of an apocalyptic vision[11] in which part of Jacob's dream is re-enacted. The third particular is important and will be discussed below, but before we can do so, we have to consider the provenance of the saying in Jn 1:51.

There are reasons to assume that the saying is of pre-Johannine origin, and was inserted here by the evangelist: (1) although Jesus is speaking in v.50 and continues to do so in v.51, the latter verse starts with 'And he said to him'; (2)

10   The discussion partners are R. Chiyya the Elder and R. Yannai, two Tannaim of the beginning of the 3rd century.

11   A look into opened heaven is a characteristic element of apocalyptic visions, see Ezek. 1:1; Mt. 3:16; Mk 1:10; Acts 7:56; 10:11; Rev. 4:1; 19:11; *2 Bar.* 22:1; *T. Ab.*, rec. A 7:3; *Jos. Asen.* 14:2; Herm. *Vis.* 1.1.4; *Ap. John* 1:30–2:2.

although Jesus is speaking to Nathanael in v.50 and addresses him according
to the beginning of v.51 ('And he said to him'), the saying itself is addressed
to a group of disciples (the double 'you' is plural in Greek: ὑμῖν, ὄψεσθε); (3)
the content of the saying is not very Johannine: elsewhere in his gospel, John
betrays a positive interest in realistic apocalyptic imagery or in angels only
in a few passages where he evidently depends on tradition (1:32; 20:12);
(4) a literal fulfilment of the promise of v.51 is lacking in John. Originally,
the saying may have referred to Jesus' resurrection or his parousia.[12] John
connects it to Jesus' ministry in its entirety: he uses it to flesh out the seeing
of 'greater things' than Jesus' omniscience (v.50), that is, the witnessing of the
ministry of Jesus as it will be narrated in the gospel, including Jesus' death
and resurrection.

What is the Johannine meaning of Jn 1:51 with the quotation from Gen.
28:12?[13] The clue is to be found in the final words of the saying: 'upon the
Son of Man' (ἐπὶ τὸν υἱὸν τοῦ ἀνθρώπου). With 'the Son of Man' Jesus
refers to himself; so the angels ascend and descend on Jesus. This twist in the
quotation must be based on the ambiguity of בו in the Hebrew text of Gen.
28:12. We saw that it can mean both 'on it', referring to the ladder, and 'on
him', on Jacob, and that there was a strand in rabbinic exegesis preferring the
latter interpretation. In the quotation this interpretation of בו as 'on him', on
a human person on earth, is obviously presupposed, and Jesus is substituted
for Jacob. If the Son of Man were substituted for the ladder, we would rather
expect ἐπὶ τοῦ υἱοῦ τοῦ ἀνθρώπου, with a genitive after the preposition ἐπί
(answering the question 'where') instead of an accusative (answering the
question 'whither'), just as in the LXX (ἐπ' αὐτῆς). In the quotation the Son
of Man is not the medium via which the angels ascend and descend, but the
place to which they descend (and, by implication, from which they ascend).[14]

That the angels first ascend and only then descend means that they are
already accompanying the Son of Man on earth; otherwise they could not
first ascend. In this respect, there is an interesting parallel between our

---

12   See, e.g. R. E. Brown, *The Gospel according to John (i-xii)* (AB 29; Garden City,
NY: Doubleday, 1966), p.89. According to M. Casey, *The Solution to the 'Son of Man'
Problem* (London: T&T Clark, 2009), pp.277–81, the saying is a Johannine rewrite of Mt.
26:64.

13   For the interpretation that follows, cf. C. Rowland, 'John 1.51, Jewish
Apocalyptic and Targumic Tradition', *NTS* 30 (1984), pp.498–507. For different interpre-
tations, see J. H. Neyrey, 'The Jacob Allusions in John 1:51', *CBQ* 44 (1982), pp.586–605;
D. Burkett, *The Son of the Man in the Gospel of John* (JSNTSup, 56; Sheffield: Sheffield
Academic Press, 1991), pp.112–19; M. Theobald, 'Abraham – (Isaak –) Jakob. Israels
Väter im Johannesevangelium', in M. Labahn, K. Scholtissek and A. Strotmann (eds),
Israel und seine Heilstraditionen im Johannesevangelium (FS J. Beutler; Paderborn:
Schöningh, 2004), pp.158–83, esp. 159–63.

14   See F. Blass and A. Debrunner, *Grammatik des neutestamentlichen Griechisch*,
ed. F. Rehkopf (Göttingen: Vandenhoeck & Ruprecht, [16]1984), §§233 and 234. The
assumption that the disciples have been substituted for Jacob implies that the Son of Man
has been substituted for the ladder – which is improbable on account of ἐπί + acc.

quotation and the version of Gen. 28:12 in the Palestinian Targums (see *Tg. Neof.*, *Tg. Ps.-J.* and *Frg. Tg.* Gen. 28:12). In this version, angels are accompanying Jacob since he left his father's house, and these are the angels Jacob sees ascending to heaven in his dream. They invite the angels who are in heaven to descend to earth and to consider Jacob, whose image they have already seen engraved in the celestial throne of God, and the angels in heaven answer the invitation and descend. Something similar is the case in Jn 1:51. Jesus is already accompanied by angels, that is, in Johannine terms, he is already the place of God's presence. From this point in John's narrative onward, the disciples will see heaven opened and the angels ascending and descending on Jesus, that is, they will see God's presence in Jesus manifest itself in word and deed. In Johannine perspective it is appropriate that Jesus is called here 'the Son of Man', for the Johannine Son of Man is characterized by his heavenly origin and destination (see Jn 3:13; 6:62), by virtue of which he can exercise the divine prerogatives of giving life and judging (see Jn 3:14-15; 5:27; 6:27, 53). As the Son of Man, Jesus is greater than Jacob (cf. Jn 4:12), he is the true 'house of God' and 'gate of heaven' of Gen. 28:17.

In the above, early Jewish exegesis has proved helpful in explaining Jn 1:51 by drawing attention to two aspects of Gen. 28:12: the ambiguity of בו, and the odd sequence of ascending and descending. The early Jewish texts in question are no doubt post-Johannine, but the exegetical problems to which they respond must have been observed much earlier. In any case, the explanation of Gen. 28:12 in Jn 1:51 becomes transparent if we assume that it exploits an ambiguity and an oddity of the biblical text.

The Allusion to Gen. 1:1 in Jn 1:1

The first clause of John ('In the beginning was the Word', 1:1a) contains an allusion to the first clause of Genesis ('In the beginning when God created the heavens and the earth ...', 1:1), a clause that was well known in John's environment.[15] There are several signals in Jn 1:1a pointing to Gen. 1:1. First of all, there is the combination of words ἐν ἀρχῇ, 'in the beginning', which occurs in both Gen. 1:1 LXX and Jn 1:1a, and is repeated for the sake of emphasis in Jn 1:2. But it is not just the combination of words that matters, because the expression 'in the beginning' in itself does not need to be very significant;[16] it is also that ἀρχή is used here in the sense of the absolute beginning of all, and that the expression ἐν ἀρχῇ occurs not only at the beginning of a sentence but even at the beginning of a book.[17] The Word

---

15   Quotations in Greek are found in Philo, *Opif.* 26, 27; *Her.* 122; *Aet.* 19; Josephus, *Ant.* 1:27; see further B. H. McLean, *Citations and Allusions to Jewish Scripture in Early Christian and Jewish Writings through 180 C.E.* (Lewiston, NY: Mellen, 1992), p.17.

16   See LXX Judg. 20:18 B; 2 Kgdms 17:9; 2 Chr. 13:12; 2 Esd. 9:2; Jer. 28(51):58; Acts 11:15; Josephus, *Ant.* 15:179; 16:384.

17   Emphasized by D. Muñoz León, 'El Pentateuco en San Juan', in I. Carbajosa and L. Sánchez Navarro (eds), *Entrar en lo Antiguo: Acerca de la relación entre Antiguo y*

(λόγος) of Jn 1:1a turns out to belong to God (1:1b-2), and to be the Word through which all things came into being (1:3, with γίνεσθαι); this theme of creation by God's word constitutes another link between John and Genesis, for the pattern of Genesis 1 as a whole is that God speaks and his creatures come into being (γίνεσθαι in the Greek versions).[18] So the signals pointing to Gen. 1:1 are: a combination of words, the specific meaning of one word, the position of the combination, and theme. The allusion has apparently more than enough volume.

The allusion makes sense in two respects: one concerns John's Gospel as a book, the other concerns John's Christology. That John's Gospel begins in the same way as the first book of the Torah and of the entire Bible[19] suggests quite strongly that the evangelist intended to write a book that would constitute to his audience a new Torah or even a new Bible. The first verses of John's Prologue are then very probably meant to parallel the creation story at the beginning of Genesis.

Concerning the significance of the allusion for John's Christology,[20] it is essential first to establish that the present tense φαίνει in 1:5 ('the light shines') and the reference to John the Baptist in 1:6-8 show that, at least from 1:5 onward, John is speaking of the incarnate Word, the human being Jesus of Nazareth. And if we take into account that in the rest of the Gospel Jesus speaks in the first person singular about his pre-existence with God (see, e.g. 8:26, 38), we may assume that from the first clause of the Gospel onward, the Word and Jesus are identical. So John identifies Jesus with God's creative word in Genesis 1. But there is more. The Johannine Word exists before creation with God, and 'all things came into being through him' (1:2-3). John apparently interprets Genesis 1 by means of Jewish wisdom literature, in which Wisdom is not only personified, but also exists before creation and is the mediator of creation (see Proverbs 8; Sir. 24:11-22; Wis. 9:9), and he identifies Jesus with Wisdom.[21] The evangelist then goes one step further, and ascribes divine status to the Word identified with Jesus (1:1c, 18; see also 20:28; 1 Jn 5:20). All this means that there is some shift in the meaning

---

Nuevo Testamento (Presencia y diálogo 16; Madrid: Facultad de Teología 'San Dámaso', 2007), pp.107–66, esp. 153.

18   Ps. 33:6 ('By the word [LXX: λόγος] of the Lord the heavens were made') may have functioned as an intermediary between Genesis and John.

19   We do not precisely know which books were considered to belong to the Scriptures in John's time and environment, but we can be fairly certain that the Torah, the Prophets and the Psalms were part of them, with the Torah ranking first in sequence and importance.

20   A recent study, with many references to older literature, is J. Painter, 'Rereading Genesis in the Prologue of John?', in D. E. Aune, T. Seland and J. H. Ulrichsen (eds), *Neotestamentica et Philonica* (FS P. Borgen; NovTSup 106; Leiden: Brill, 2003), pp.179–201.

21   'Word' and 'wisdom' are identified in Wis. 9:1-2. In John's preference for the term λόγος Middle Platonism such as found in Philo must also have been influential.

of 'beginning' (ἀρχή) between Genesis and John: in Genesis the beginning is the moment of creation, in John it lies before creation.

The allusion having been established, other points of contact between the beginning of John and the beginning of Genesis appear. In the Word 'was life, and the life was the light of all people' (Jn 1:4). 'Life' (ζωή), together with the verb 'to live' (ζῆν), and 'light' (φῶς) occur in the Greek versions of the creation account of Genesis 1: 'light' is the very first thing God creates (vv.3-5), and later on God creates 'living creatures' (vv.20, 24), and speaks of 'everything that has the breath of life' (v.30). In the second creation account in Genesis 2, God breathes 'the breath of life' into man, so that he becomes 'a living being' (Gen. 2:7), God makes 'the tree of life' grow in the midst of the garden (v.9), and man gives a name to 'each living creature' (v.19). John makes use of concepts that also occur in Genesis 1–2, but transposes them from the physical to the spiritual and eschatological level: 'life' and 'light' are now God's own life and light, his eschatological gifts which are present in the person of Jesus (see Jn 8:12; 11:25-26; 14:6).[22] 'Darkness' also occurs in both John's Prologue and Genesis (σκοτία in Jn 1:5, σκότος in the Greek versions of Gen. 1:2, 4, 5, 18), but its narrative role has completely changed: from primeval chaos and part of God's good creation in Genesis to creation opposed to God in John.

Some Minor Allusions

John's story of Jesus changing water into wine at a wedding in Cana (2:1-11) starts with Jesus' mother telling her son that the wine has run out. He gives her an enigmatic response; she says to the servants: 'Whatever he tells you, do' (ὅ τι ἂν λέγῃ ὑμῖν ποιήσατε, v.5),[23] and the miracle takes place. The words of Jesus' mother to the servants constitute an allusion to the words of Pharaoh to the Egyptians at the beginning of the seven years of famine, when Joseph is in charge of the distribution of grain: 'Whatever he will tell you, do' (LXX, correctly translating the Hebrew: ὃ ἐὰν εἴπῃ ὑμῖν ποιήσατε, Gen. 41:55). The verbal agreement between the two commands is evident. It is definitely stronger than the agreement between Jn 2:5 and any of the other passages that have been suggested as the source: the assenting words of the people to Moses' proclamation of God's commandments in Exod. 19:8 and 24:3, 7 ('All [the words] that the Lord has spoken we will do').[24] Apart from the different wording of the latter passages, they also differ from Jn 2:5 and Gen. 41:55 in that they concern what God says whereas Jn 2:5 and Gen. 41:55 concern the words of a human being. An allusion to Gen. 41:55 makes sense: faithfully carrying out the commands of Joseph and

---

22   Cf. Muñoz León, 'Pentateuco en San Juan', pp.116-17.

23   English translations of biblical texts in this paragraph are my own. In the NRSV, agreements are less visible.

24   See, e.g. F. J. Moloney, *The Gospel of John* (SP, 4; Collegeville, MN: Liturgical Press, 1998), p.72.

Jesus leads to the removal of a lack of food or drink, while Joseph and Jesus differ in that the former brings salvation by wise government and the latter by performing a miracle.

Jesus' monologue on the identity of the real father of 'the Jews' in Jn 8:42-47 contains in v.44 an allusion to Genesis 3–4. Jesus says to his opponents: 'You are from your father the devil, and you choose to do your father's desires. He was a murderer from the beginning and does not stand in the truth, because there is no truth in him. When he lies, he speaks according to his own nature, for he is a liar and the father of lies.' That 'the devil' is said to have been 'a murderer from the beginning', alludes in the first place to the story of the fall in Genesis 3. The serpent, whose deceit introduced death into the world, was in Jewish tradition identified with the devil (see Wis. 2:24: 'Through the envy of the devil death came into the world'). The murderous activity of the devil also alludes to the fratricide of Genesis 4: as we shall see below in connection with 1 John 3:12, Cain was supposed to have killed his brother Abel under the influence of the devil. Further, Jesus' remarks in Jn 8:44 on the devil being a liar and not standing in the truth refer to the misleading role the devil plays in Genesis 3 vis-à-vis Eve. The allusion serves to make clear that – in the view of the evangelist, of course – 'the Jews', who try to kill Jesus (8:37, 40), are part of a history of murder and deception that has started with the fall.

After his resurrection, the Johannine Jesus imparts the Holy Spirit to his disciples. He 'breathed (ἐνεφύσησεν) on them and said to them: Receive the Holy Spirit' (20:22). In the LXX version of the second creation story, the same verb ἐμφυσᾶν in the same form is used: after God formed man from dust, he 'breathed (ἐνεφύσησεν) into his nostrils the breath of life' (Gen. 2:7). The verb ἐμφυσᾶν seems to have become a more or less usual rendering of the Hebrew נפח qal in Gen. 2:7, for it is also found in Aquila's translation of Gen. 2:7 and in the evident reference to the creation story in Wis. 15:11, where God is called 'he who breathed (ἐμφυσήσαντα) a life-giving spirit'.[25] Apart from this verb, there is agreement between Jn 20:22 and the creation story in the object of breathing: πνεῦμα ἅγιον, 'the Holy Spirit', in John, πνοὴ ζωῆς, 'the breath of life', in Genesis (πνεῦμα and πνοή both derive from πνεῖν, 'to breathe'), πνεῦμα ζωτικόν, 'a life-giving spirit' in Wis. 15:11. The allusion shows that John intends to present the giving of the Spirit as a new creation (cf. 2 Cor. 5:17; Gal. 6:15).

Abraham in Jn 8:31-59

Jn 8:31-59 constitutes the final phase and the climax of the series of debates between Jesus and his Jewish opponents in the temple in Jerusalem (John 7–8). The ongoing main theme of the various conversations is the identity of Jesus as God's eschatological envoy, but other themes are woven into this main theme, such as the identity of Jesus' discussion partners in 8:31-47.

---

25   Cf. also Ezek. 37:9 LXX, in a context of re-creation.

From a dramatic point of view, 8:31-59 constitutes one continuous dialogue between Jesus and a group characterized as 'the Jews who had believed in him' (v.31). Whatever their belief may mean or have meant, later on they are simply called 'the Jews' (v.48). Several interrelated topics are dealt with in the dialogue: freedom and ancestry, paternity in relation to the acts of the children, Jesus' claim of a unique relation with God, his Father. One factor making the dialogue into a literary unit is the fact that Abraham occurs several times in it (vv.33, 37, 39-40, 52-53, 56-58). What is said of him by Jesus and his opponents calls to mind the Abraham narratives from Genesis together with their early Jewish interpretations. We will now investigate the character, sources and meaning of John's references to Abraham.[26]

In response to Jesus' promise of freedom to whoever remains in his word, his audience retorts: 'We are seed (NRSV: descendants) of Abraham (σπέρμα 'Αβραάμ) and have never been slaves to anyone' (v.33). The expression 'seed of Abraham' is found a few times in the Old Testament (Isa. 41:8; Ps. 105:6; 2 Chron. 20:7); in addition, the combinations 'your seed' and 'his seed' occur (e.g. Gen. 12:7; Neh. 9:8). If these expressions do not denote Abraham's immediate physical offspring, they denote Israel as a people elected by God, and they are used in the same sense in early Jewish and early Christian literature (e.g. *Ps. Sol.* 9:9; 3 Macc. 6:3; Lk. 1:55; Heb. 2:16). So 'seed of Abraham' is not an allusion to a Genesis passage but a reference to a well-known biblical theme. Jesus' opponents then continue by saying that as 'seed of Abraham', they 'have never been slaves to anyone', so there is no need to make them free. In a typically Johannine misunderstanding they speak of freedom in the literal sense, whereas Jesus spoke of spiritual freedom. Their statement is in flagrant contradiction to their own history as recorded in Scripture: the Israelites have been slaves in Egypt, and there is a link to Abraham in that God himself has announced the slavery of 'your seed (NRSV: offspring)' to Abraham (then still called Abram) in the famous vision of Genesis 15 (vv.13-14).[27] Alluding to this passage, the opponents deny what God predicted to Abraham.

In his answer, Jesus first makes clear that he is speaking of slavery under sin (v.34). Then he says: 'The slave does not have a permanent place in the house (NRSV: household), the son has a place there for ever' (v.35). Finally, he concludes that only the Son brings real freedom (v.36). It is not easy to establish the precise logic of these verses; in any case, v.35 may well allude to a passage from the Abraham cycle in Genesis. One could think of Gen. 21:8-14, when Ishmael, the son of the slave woman, is cast out (see already Gen. 17:15-22), but Gen. 15:2-4, where God announces to Abraham that his own son will be his heir and not his servant Eliezer,

---

26   A relevant study with a good collection of materials is T. de Lange, *Abraham in John 8,31-59: His Significance in the Conflict between Johannine Christianity and Its Jewish Environment* (Amsterdam: Amphora, 2008).

27   Compare δουλώσουσιν, 'they will enslave them', and δουλεύσωσιν, 'they will be slaves', in Gen. 15:13-14 LXX with δεδουλεύκαμεν, 'we have been slaves', in Jn 8:33.

might be the better option, for it contains the word 'house' (vv.2, 3), which is pivotal to Jn 8:35.

In v.37 the Johannine Jesus affirms that his audience are 'seed of Abraham', and he moves the discussion to the question of paternity. He declares what he has seen with the Father (God); his opponents should do what they heard from the Father (v.38). They immediately counter: 'Abraham is our father' (v.39), characterizing Abraham in a way that is usual in the Old Testament (e.g. Josh. 24:3; Isa. 51:2) and in early Jewish and early Christian literature (e.g. Lk. 1:73; Josephus, *Ant.* 1:158; *m. Ta'an.* 2:4-5). Jesus says to them that being 'children of Abraham'[28] ought to imply 'doing the works of Abraham (NRSV: what Abraham did)' (v.39), but his opponents try to kill him, 'a man who has told you the truth that I heard from God'; this is in his view definitely not what Abraham did (v.40). What does the straightforward reference to 'the works of Abraham' precisely mean? Abraham's works are obviously the opposite of killing God's messenger, but that still leaves many possibilities. The book of Genesis speaks of Abraham's faith (ch. 15, esp. v.6), of his hospitality (18:1-16), of his obedience, manifest in his willingness to sacrifice his son (ch. 22, esp. v.12), of his observance of God's commandments (26:5); these materials have been interpreted and elaborated in later tradition (e.g. 1 Macc. 2:52; Sir. 44:20; Philo, *Abr.* 107). Because John's Jesus refers to the works of Abraham in general terms and in Johannine language,[29] it is difficult to decide which of the passages on Abraham is in view. To my mind, Genesis 15 is again a serious candidate. Jn 8:40 implies that unlike 'the Jews', Abraham would have accepted God's messenger, and this theme returns at the end of John 8, when Jesus says that Abraham was glad to see Jesus' day (v.56). Abraham's joy when seeing Jesus' day can be linked, as we shall see, to Genesis 15, and his acceptance of God's messenger could then also refer to John's interpretation of the vision of Genesis 15.

Following these words to his opponents (Jn 8:39-40), Jesus continues: 'You are indeed doing what your father does' (v.41a); he does not yet say who this father is. The audience appeal to God as their father (v.41b), and Jesus explains to them that by not accepting him as God's envoy, they show that the devil is their father (vv.42-47). In the course of the discussion that follows (vv.48-59), Jesus claims that he will safeguard believers from death (v.51), and in their reaction, 'the Jews' make a straightforward reference to Abraham's death (vv.52-53). They say that 'Abraham died ('Aβραὰμ ἀπέθανεν)', and ask Jesus: 'Are you greater than our father Abraham, who died ('Aβραάμ, ὅστις ἀπέθανεν)?'. The source of this information is Gen. 25:8: 'Abraham died (MT: אַבְרָהָם וַיָּמָת; LXX: ἀπέθανεν Aβρααμ).' One

---

28   John apparently distinguishes between 'seed of Abraham' (his natural offspring) and 'children of Abraham' (his spiritual offspring), see De Lange, *Abraham*, pp.69, 160.

29   Ποιεῖν τὰ ἔργα, 'to do the works' (also in v.41, and nine more times in John), is characteristic of Johannine style, see G. Van Belle, *Les parenthèses dans l'évangile de Jean* (SNTA, 11; Leuven: Leuven University Press – Peeters, 1985), p.152.

might be tempted to consider the references as quotations, because of their literal agreement with Gen. 25:8 LXX. This is, however, not advisable, firstly because Abraham's death could hardly be recorded in other terms, secondly because in John the death of Abraham is paired with the death of the prophets. John makes Jesus' opponents here simply refer to the fact of the death of Abraham and the prophets, in an effort to combat Jesus' statement that whoever keeps his word will not die.

Jesus responds by appealing to his unique relation with God, his Father, and his response ends with another straightforward reference: 'Your father (NRSV: ancestor) Abraham rejoiced that he would see my day; he saw it and was glad' (v.56). In Genesis, there is one possible mention of Abraham's joy: he laughs when God promises him a son by Sarai although he and his wife are already aged (17:17). This laughter, however, is an expression of scepticism, not of joy,[30] and a link to Abraham's vision of 'my day' is not easily made. A view of future things is ascribed to Abraham in various early Jewish interpretations of Genesis 15: according to *4 Ezra* 3:14, God showed only to Abraham 'the end of times, secretly at night', and in *2 Bar.* 4:4, God says to Baruch about the new Jerusalem: 'I showed it to my servant Abraham in the night between the portions of the victims'[31] (see further *Apoc. Ab.* 15–30; *L.A.B.* 18:5; 23:6-7). Although these interpretations do not speak of joy, the retelling of Genesis 15 in *Jubilees* 14 closes with the words: 'And Abram rejoiced' (v.21).[32] John has apparently made use of extant Jewish re-readings of Genesis 15, and 'christianized' these by making Jesus' day the object of Abraham's vision of future things and of his joy. Just as Isaiah has seen the glory of the pre-existent Jesus in his temple vision (Jn 12:41), so Abraham has seen in his vision in Genesis 15 the heavenly Jesus to be revealed on earth.

'The Jews' respond in v.57: 'You are not yet fifty years old, and have you seen Abraham?'. Jesus then ends the debate with the words: 'Very truly, I tell you, before Abraham was, I am' (v.58). Both utterances build on the reference to Abraham in v.56. The reaction of the audience is another instance of misunderstanding: Jesus spoke of Abraham having seen his day, 'the Jews' speak of Jesus having seen Abraham. 'Fifty years' stand for a normal human lifetime (Num. 4:3, 47; 8:25), so they ask how Jesus, who is not yet at the end of his life, can have seen Abraham, who lived many centuries earlier. In his final word, the Johannine Jesus contrasts Abraham's origin in history with Jesus' eternal being. The audience consider Jesus' final statement as blasphemy, and try to stone him (v.59, cf. Lev. 24:16).

Looking back on the references to Abraham in Jn 8:31-59, we can observe that almost all of them, insofar as they can be tied to specific Old

---

30   For early Jewish efforts to arrive at a more positive view of Abraham's laughter, see De Lange, *Abraham*, pp.131–2.

31   Trans. A. F. J. Klijn, in *OTP*, Vol.1.

32   Trans. O. S. Wintermute, in *OTP*, Vol.2.

Testament passages, concern Genesis 15 (at least as a serious possibility).[33] Even the death of Abraham can be tied to this chapter: God announces it in Gen. 15:15. Genesis 15 contains many elements that were apparently interesting to early Jewish and early Christian readers:[34] Abraham's vision, his faith, the promise of a son and numerous offspring, Abraham's sacrifice, God announcing slavery and exodus, God's covenant with Abraham. In the conflict between the Johannine community and its Jewish environment, John uses Genesis 15 to make Abraham side with Jesus and against 'the Jews'.

Genesis in 1 John

While John's Gospel contains many Old Testament materials in the form of quotations, allusions and other references, biblical materials are almost absent in the Johannine Epistles. This conspicuous difference between Gospel and Epistles should very probably be explained by a change of situation: the Gospel is addressed to Christians who are in conflict with Jews (see Jn 9:22; 12:42; 16:2), the Epistles are addressed to Christians who are in conflict with fellow Christians (see 1 Jn 2:18-27; 4:1-6; 2 Jn 7). In the former situation scriptural arguments are required, in the latter, the arguments mostly concern confession and ethics.

It is all the more striking that in 1 Jn 3:12 the figure of Cain and his murder of his brother Abel, known from Gen. 4:1-16, appear. In 3:11 the author reminds his audience of 'the message you have heard from the beginning, that we should love one another', and in v.12 he presents, by way of contrast, an example of not loving one another: 'We must not be like Cain who was from the evil one and murdered his brother. And why did he murder him? Because his own deeds were evil and his brother's righteous.' This reference to Genesis is not a quotation[35] nor an allusion; the category of straightforward reference probably comes closest, but we must again take into consideration that the reference is not only to the Genesis story but also to its interpretive development. In the story of Cain and Abel in Genesis, it is not evident why God rejects Cain's sacrifice and why Cain kills his brother; early interpretations try to fill in these 'gaps'.[36] In what follows I will first present some aspects of this development, briefly and with a limited amount of textual materials for comparison, and then

---

33   'More than other passages in Genesis, Genesis 15 appears to be the key passage for an adequate understanding of John's view on Abraham' (De Lange, *Abraham*, p.160).

34   See, apart from the materials already mentioned, the quotations in Acts 7:6, 7; Rom. 4:3, 9, 18; Gal. 3:6; Jas 2:23.

35   Verbatim agreement is limited to the name 'Cain' and 'his brother', said of Abel.

36   This process already starts in the LXX, according to J. N. Lohr, 'Righteous Abel, Wicked Cain: Genesis 4:1-16 in the Masoretic Text, the Septuagint, and the New Testament', *CBQ* 71 (2009), pp.485–96.

try to explain why this story in its developed form appealed so much to the author of 1 John that it became the only Old Testament passage explicitly referred to in this writing.[37]

First of all, we can observe that in 1 Jn 3:12 new elements have been introduced into the Genesis story: Cain was 'from the evil one (ἐκ τοῦ πονηροῦ)', that is, he belonged to and found his spiritual origin in the devil, he performed 'evil deeds (ἔργα πονηρά)' whereas those of Abel were 'righteous (δίκαια)', and for Cain's killing of Abel a verb with a connotation of heavy violence is used (σφάζειν, 'to murder'). These new elements are documented in other contemporary sources: according to *Apoc. Ab.* 24:5, Cain 'had been led by the adversary [the devil] to break the law',[38] Josephus describes Cain as 'very evil' (πονηρότατος, *Ant.* 1:53), Abel is called 'righteous (δίκαιος)' in Mt. 23:35 and Heb. 11:4, and Josephus uses the verb σφάζειν, 'to murder', in *Ant.* 1:67 for Cain's killing of Abel.

Relevant to 1 John are also descriptions of Cain's character given in the interpretive development of the Genesis story. Cain's motive for murdering his brother is sometimes said to have been hatred. According to a fragment that may have been part of the Prologue or the Epilogue of the *Exagoge* of Ezekiel the Tragedian,[39] the devil prompted Cain to kill Abel and equipped his 'brother-hating arms'. In *T. Benj.* 7:5, Cain is characterized by 'envy leading to hatred of brothers'. Another trait ascribed to Cain is godlessness; it is implicitly present in many texts, and made explicit especially by Philo. In his view, Cain was 'godless and impious…, because, opening wide the inner chambers of his complex being, he stood agape for all outward things' (*Det.* 103).[40] Cain was also supposed to have been greedy. According to Josephus,[41] Cain 'had an eye only to gain' (*Ant.* 1:53), and after his expulsion, he went on with his evil behaviour of 'increas[ing] his substance with wealth amassed by rapine and violence' (1:61).

Taking all this together, we can say that four characteristics are ascribed to Cain in early interpretations of Genesis 4: (1) he was evil, inspired by the

---

37   For a more elaborate argument, see M. J. J. Menken, 'The Image of Cain in 1 John 3,12', in J. Verheyden, G. Van Belle and J. G. van der Watt (eds), *Miracles and Imagery in Luke and John* (FS U. Busse; BETL, 218; Leuven: Peeters, 2008), pp.195–211. See also J. Byron, 'Slaughter, Fratricide and Sacrilege: Cain and Abel Traditions in 1 John 3', *Bib* 88 (2007), 526–35; T. Thatcher, 'Cain and Abel in Early Christian Memory: A Case Study in "The Use of the Old Testament in the New"', *CBQ* 72 (2010), pp.732–51.

38   Trans. R. Rubinkiewicz, in *OTP*, Vol.1.

39   The fragment has been preserved in Epiphanius, *Pan.* 64.29.6–30.1. On its authenticity, see C. R. Holladay, *Fragments from Hellenistic Jewish Authors. 2: Poets* (SBL Texts and Translations, 30; Pseudepigrapha Series, 12; Atlanta, GA: Scholars Press, 1989), pp.526-8; A.-M. Denis, *et al.*, *Introduction à la littérature religieuse judéo-hellénistique* (Turnhout: Brepols, 2000), pp.1205–6.

40   Trans. F. H. Colson, in the Loeb Classical Library-edition of Philo, vol.2.

41   The translation is that of H. St. J. Thackeray, in the Loeb Classical Library-edition of Josephus, vol.4; see also L. H. Feldman, *Flavius Josephus, Judean Antiquities 1-4: Translation and Commentary* (Leiden, Brill, 2000), pp.18–23.

devil; (2) he murdered Abel out of hatred; (3) he was godless; and (4) he was greedy, driven by his own material advantage.

Before I can show the relevance of these four characteristics of Cain to 1 John, something has to be said on the opponents combated in this epistle. The reason for writing the epistle must have been the secession from the Johannine community of members whose ideas and conduct were wrong in the view of the author. Two passages in 1 John (2:18-27; 4:1-6) explicitly concern these secessionists and their ideas on Christology: they apparently denied that Jesus is the Christ who has become a fully human being. In addition, there is a series of polemical statements in which the author opposes assertions about an alleged positive relation with God to actual negative conduct over against fellow Christians (1:6-10; 2:4-9; 4:20); these may be supposed to concern the secessionists as well, but implicitly. In any case: the Christological view of the secessionists as attacked in the overtly polemical passages coheres well with their ethical stance as attacked in the covertly polemical passages. Both Christological view and ethical stance testify to some sort of 'realized eschatology': Jesus is a heavenly Christ, whose humanity is irrelevant, and his followers already participate fully in heavenly reality.

Now it is interesting to see that the characteristics ascribed to Cain in early interpretations of Genesis 4 are also ascribed to the secessionists in 1 John:

1.   Just as Cain was 'from the evil one' (3:12), so 'the whole world lies under the power of the evil one' (5:19). The secessionists belong to 'the world' (4:5, cf. 4:1, 3), and are consequently under the power of the devil.

2.   Just as Cain was motivated by hatred, so the secessionists 'hate their brothers or sisters' (4:20; see also 2:9, 11). Hatred characterizes 'the world', to which the secessionists belong (3:13). The secessionists fall under the verdict that 'all who hate a brother or sister are murderers' (3:15), just as Cain was a murderer (3:12). Whether this verdict implies real murder is not quite clear; it implies at least the equation of murder with not sharing with the needy brothers and sisters (3:17).

3.   Just as Cain was godless, so the secessionists, who boast of their special relation with God, are in reality living in darkness (1:6; 2:9, 11), they belong to the realm of lie, not of truth (1:6; 2:4, 21, 22, 27; 4:20). 'The world', to which they belong, is far from God (2:15-17).

4.   Just as Cain was selfish, so the secessionists are greedy: they refuse to share with brothers and sisters who are in material need (3:17). As belonging to 'the world', they are guilty of 'the desire of the flesh, the desire of the eyes, the pride in riches' (2:16).

It becomes clear why the Cain story in its interpretive development became the only Old Testament passage explicitly used by the author of 1 John: the negative image of Cain exactly fitted his negative image of the secessionists. Cain was to him a useful means to vilify his opponents and to warn his community about them.

Conclusion

In the Johannine literature, there is a clear interest in the book of Genesis, in the form of one unmarked quotation and of several allusions and straightforward references. Various Genesis passages are used, but there are two foci of Johannine interest: the stories of creation and fall (Genesis 1–4), and the Abraham narratives. The stories of creation and fall are used in Jn 1:1; 8:44; 20:22, and in 1 Jn 3:12; the Abraham narratives in Jn 8:31-59. The Johannine author (or authors) is apparently aware of early Jewish interpretations of the Genesis materials he has incorporated, and reads the Old Testament texts through these interpretations (just as other early Christian authors did). To put it otherwise: his book of Genesis is not Genesis in itself, but an already interpreted Genesis.

The interest of the author in the stories of creation and fall can be explained by his wish to present Jesus as God's creative word of old that has now realized a new creation, and to vilify the opponents of Jesus and of his followers as children of the devil (identified with the serpent) and as adherents of Cain. His interest in the Abraham narratives can be explained by his wish to make Israel's ancestor into a supporter of Jesus and to withdraw his spiritual paternity from 'the Jews'. His incidental use of other passages from Genesis also serves his Christology. This is especially evident in the case of the quotation in Jn 1:51: Jesus will manifest himself as the place of God's presence.

One of the Johannine hermeneutical rules to interpret the Old Testament is that Moses has written about Jesus (Jn 1:45; 5:46). As Moses is considered to have been the human author of the five books of the Torah, the rule implies that in the Johannine view the book of Genesis is about Jesus. The above analysis of the use of Genesis in John's Gospel and in 1 John has shown what this means in practice.

Chapter 6

GENESIS IN PAUL

David Lincicum

Introduction

Genesis is a book of fundamental importance for the apostle Paul, in a manner that is not fully reflected in mere numerical tallies of his explicit citations. To be sure, Paul does often cite Genesis (15 times), but he also learns from it certain basic narratives, stories that order and make sense of his world: the creation of the cosmos, the formation of humanity, the sin of Adam, the covenant with Abraham and the promises to the patriarchs. In fact, if we ask about narrative elements in Paul, we will find that the vast majority of these come from Genesis, apart from a few significant exceptions (e.g. snippets from the exodus tradition in Romans 9 and 1 Corinthians 10, or the Elijah story in Romans 11).

Paul's interest in the book of Genesis is not an idiosyncrasy of the apostle to the nations. Genesis, as the great beginning to the Pentateuch, was a profoundly 'catholic' text, foundational to Second Temple Jewish authors of a variety of backgrounds and outlooks. Along with Psalms, Deuteronomy and Isaiah, Genesis ranks high among the number of manuscripts attested in the Dead Sea Scrolls (19 or 20 manuscripts).[1] We also find Genesis paraphrased (e.g. 4Q158, 4Q364, etc.), rewritten (e.g. in *Jubilees*, the Genesis Apocryphon [1Q20], Josephus, *Ant.* 1.27–2.200) and philosophically expounded (all of Philo's three great works, the *Quaestiones et Solutiones*, the Allegorical Commentary and the Exposition of the Law, devote sustained attention to Genesis).[2]

---

1   See E. Tov *et al.*, *The Texts from the Judaean Desert: Indices and an Introduction to the Discoveries in the Judaean Desert Series* (DJD, 39; Oxford: Clarendon, 2002), pp.167–8. The fluctuation reflects uncertainty as to whether 4Q8 represents one manuscript or two.

2   For the Dead Sea Scrolls evidence, see, e.g. K. Berthelot, T. Legrand and A. Paul (eds), *La Bibliothèque de Qumrân, 1: Torah – Genèse* (Paris: Editions du Cerf, 2008). One also finds, of course, various compositions spurred by individual figures or groups in Genesis, such as Adam (*Apoc. Mos.*; *L.A.E.*), the watchers (the Enochic literature), Noah (1Q19, 4Q534), Abraham (*Apoc. Ab.*; *T. Abr.*), Melchizedek (11QMelch), and the patriarchs (*T. 12Patr.*). See further Chapter 1 in this volume.

The widespread influence of Genesis arguably reflects the habituating impulses of liturgical reading in the synagogue, the context that supplies the most natural environment for Paul's own encounter with the book.[3] Given the popularity of the scroll of Genesis and the foundational nature of the themes it treats (the two phenomena are of course related), it will come as no surprise to find that Paul's citations and allusions range across the book and touch on some key elements in his theology. Together with Deuteronomy, Psalms and Isaiah, the scroll of Genesis proved one of the most fruitful sources for Paul's theological reflection and pastoral guidance to his fledgling communities.

Quotations from and Allusions to Genesis

In line with Paul's general citation practices, his quotations of Genesis in the undisputed letters are confined to the *Hauptbriefe* (in the deutero-Pauline epistles, note Gen. 2:24 in Eph. 5:31; cf. 1 Tim. 2:13-15). Also reflecting his usual preferences, his citations seem to rely on a Greek version of Genesis, though he has occasionally modified his citations to suit their new epistolary context or followed Greek texts that deviate from our standard editions of the Septuagint.[4]

The fact that Paul, even when writing to communities comprised of substantial numbers of Gentiles, so often alludes to figures from Genesis

---

3   For the public reading of the Torah in the first century, see Philo, *Hypoth.* 7.12-13 (in Eusebius, *Pr. Ev.* 8.7.12–13); Lk. 4:16-20; Acts 13:15; 15:21; Josephus, *Ant.* 16.43–45; *C. Ap.* 2.175–78; 1QS 6:6–8; 4Q251 1:5; 4Q266 5 ii:1–3 = 4Q267 5 iii:3–5; *T. Levi* 13:2; and the so-called Theodotus inscription from Jerusalem. What is more, early Greek manuscripts of the Torah show evidence of being designed for public reading, and the importance of such an act of public reading is strengthened when approached via the more sociological concerns with low literacy rates and an interpenetration of oral and written media on the one hand, and from the more particularly archaeological and literary attestation to the synagogue and its activities on the other; cf. D. Lincicum, *Paul and the Early Jewish Encounter with Deuteronomy* (WUNT, 2.284; Tübingen: Mohr Siebeck, 2010), chapter 2; M. Harl, *La Genèse* (La Bible d'Alexandrie, 1; Paris: Éditions du Cerf, 1986), pp.33–45.

4   There is a broad, though not unanimous, consensus about this point in Pauline scholarship. Apart from the fact that such a high degree of coincidence in verbatim renderings of the Hebrew would be remarkable if Paul were independently translating his *Vorlage* (note here the astute comments of Philo, *Mos.* 2.38!), there are a number of features in Paul's Genesis citations that could not be derived from the Hebrew as we know it. To take but two examples: the reference to 'two' (δύο) in Gen. 2:24 is not in the Hebrew (but is in the Peshitta and Vulgate, and perhaps the Samaritan Pentateuch; cf. J. W. Wevers, *Notes on the Greek Text of Genesis* [SBLSCS, 35; Atlanta: Scholars, 1993], p.35); and the passive form of λογίζομαι in Gen. 15:6 is likewise absent from the Hebrew. Many other such instances could be marshaled; for the textual character of Paul's Pentateuchal citations, see further D.-A. Koch, *Die Schrift als Zeuge des Evangeliums: Untersuchungen zur Verwendung und zum Verständnis der Schrift bei Paulus* (BHT, 69; Tübingen: Mohr Siebeck, 1986), pp.51–4 and *passim*.

without offering full explanations, may suggest that he passed on its substance to his converts as part of their catechesis. As Christopher Stanley has aptly noted with regard to Galatians,

> From the many unexplained references to Abraham and his family, we can deduce that Paul expected the Galatians to know at least the broad outlines of two story-cycles from the Abraham narrative: (a) the stories of the inauguration (Gen 12:1-3) and confirmation (Gen 13:14-17, 15:1-6) of God's covenant with Abraham, including God's promises to Abraham (Gal 3:8, 16, 18, 29), Abraham's faith in these promises (3:6, 9), and God's proclamation of Abraham's righteousness (3:6); and (b) the stories of Sarah and Hagar and their respective sons, including Isaac's birth as the fulfillment of a divine promise (Gal 4:23, 28), Hagar's son 'persecuting' Isaac (4:29), and Hagar and her son being cast out into the desert (4:30).[5]

Paul likewise mentions Adam and the Patriarchs without pausing to explain them, also suggesting that Paul presupposed a knowledge of their stories among his converts. This, then, also provides some indication of the importance of Genesis for the apostle.

Given that Paul often engages with stories from Genesis rather than simply isolated verses, in what follows the investigation will proceed by examining the evidence under five broad headings: creation, Adam and Christ, Abraham in Galatians, Abraham in Romans, and finally other references to Genesis in Romans.[6]

Creation

We find three major clusters of references to the creation account in Genesis, and a handful of other significant allusions. Paul's references to Adam as a type of Christ will be treated separately in the next section.

---

5   C. D. Stanley, *Arguing with Scripture: The Rhetoric of Quotations in the Letters of Paul* (New York and London: T&T Clark International, 2004), p.117. Stanley also plausibly suggests that Paul assumes his readers in 1 Corinthians and Romans are familiar with the story of Adam (pp.76, 139).

6   I have thus excluded from consideration some of the allusions suggested by NA[27]. For example, they suggest that Gen. 6:12 may be alluded to in Rom. 3:20 and Gal. 2:16, though the main allusion in each case appears to be to Ps. 142:2 LXX and only the phrase 'all flesh' (πᾶσα σάρξ) could be derived from Genesis. This phrase, however, is unlikely to recall Genesis specifically, as it is common in the Greek Scriptures. Other proposed allusions are similarly mere verbal similarities with little interpretative significance: e.g. Gen. 8:21 in Phil. 4:18 (sharing ὀσμὴν εὐωδίας); Gen. 15:16 in 1 Thess. 2:16 (sins being 'filled up' using ἀναπληρόω); and Gen. 32:31 in 1 Cor. 13:12 ('seeing' God [though different verbs of sight are used] 'face to face', πρόσωπον πρὸς πρόσωπον).

Quotation of Gen. 2:24 in 1 Cor. 6:16

In 1 Cor. 6:16, Paul adduces Genesis's classic statement about marriage (2:24: 'the two shall become one flesh') not to discuss that institution, which he will go on to do in 1 Corinthians 7, but to prohibit illicit sexual unions (πορνεία). The citation follows the LXX exactly, with an interspersed introductory word (φησίν).[7] Paul is arguing against a permissive Corinthian view of the body, which he counters in a series of staccato arguments against the possible sanction of fornication. The scriptural citation supplies grounds for Paul's assertion that the sexual act causes a union of persons – in this case, not the union of husband and wife, but the incongruous union of a Christian and a prostitute. Paul therefore takes Gen. 2:24 not (merely) as a statement about procreation, but as a claim concerning a type of union between two people, a union that can be either beneficial or harmful.[8]

Allusions to Genesis 1–2 in 1 Cor. 11:2-12

In the course of his difficult argument about women being veiled in the assemblies in 1 Cor. 11:2-12, Paul makes a number of allusions to Genesis. Most clearly, in 11:8-9, Paul argues from the manner of the creation account in Genesis 2. In 11:8, Paul writes that 'man was not made from woman, but woman from man (ἐξ ἀνδρός)', recalling Gen. 2:22-23 in which God takes one of Adam's ribs to form Eve 'from the man' (ἐκ τοῦ ἀνδρός). In 11:9 Paul writes that woman was created 'for the sake of man' (διὰ τὸν ἄνδρα), recalling Gen. 2:18 and the statement that God made the woman 'for him as a helper corresponding to him' (αὐτῷ βοηθὸν κατ' αὐτόν). This reading of Genesis 2 seems to control Paul's reading of Genesis 1: in 1 Cor. 11:7, Paul conceives of the man as the 'image and glory of God' (εἰκὼν καὶ δόξα θεοῦ), while the woman is the 'glory of the man' (δόξα ἀνδρός). In Gen. 1:27, it is 'humanity' (τὸν ἄνθρωπον) that is made 'male and female' (ἄρσεν καὶ θῆλυ) in the image of God (κατ' εἰκόνα θεοῦ). Paul appears to have read this through Genesis 2, which narrates the creation of the singular human (2:7: τὸν ἄνθρωπον), identified as Adam in 2:16, from whom woman is made at a subsequent point (2:18-24). This order of creation is taken by Paul to imply a corresponding social order that should be reflected in liturgical praxis (however difficult that may appear to his modern readers).[9]

---

7   This occurs only here in Paul as an introduction to a scriptural citation; cf. C. D. Stanley, *Paul and the Language of Scripture: Citation Technique in the Pauline Epistles and Contemporary Literature* (SNTSMS, 74; Cambridge: Cambridge University Press, 1992), p.195.

8   Note the different uses of the verse in Eph. 5:31; Mk 10:7; and Mt. 19:5.

9   NA[27] suggests an allusion to Gen. 3:16 in 1 Cor. 11:3, but to see the hierarchy as a result of the fall would seem to undercut Paul's subsequent argument from creation order in 11:7-9. Some have also seen a reference to the watcher tradition stemming from Gen. 6:1-4 in Paul's cryptic statement that women should cover their heads 'because of the angels'; this is possible, but by no means certain.

Allusions to Genesis 1 in 1 Corinthians 15:38-39

In the course of his argument about the reality of the resurrection in 1 Corinthians 15, Paul seeks to clarify the nature of the resurrected bodies by analogy to the different 'bodies' in creation. In 1 Cor. 15:38 ('God gives it a body as he wished, and to each of the seeds its own body'), Paul may be recalling the growth of plants which each had their 'seed' in them, according to their kind, in Gen. 1:11-12. In 1 Cor. 15:39 Paul explicitly mentions the different kinds of flesh in reverse order of that found in the creation story of Gen. 1:26 (cf. 1:20-27):

Gen. 1:26 LXX	1 Cor. 15:39
Ποιήσωμεν ἄνθρωπον ... καὶ ἀρχέτωσαν τῶν ἰχθύων τῆς θαλάσσης καὶ τῶν πετεινῶν τοῦ οὐρανοῦ καὶ τῶν κτηνῶν	Οὐ πᾶσα σὰρξ ἡ αὐτὴ σὰρξ ἀλλὰ ἄλλη μὲν ἀνθρώπων, ἄλλη δὲ σὰρξ κτηνῶν, ἄλλη δὲ σὰρξ πτηνῶν, ἄλλη δὲ ἰχθύων

Paul here seems to achieve interpretative mileage out of the repeated prepositional phrase κατὰ γένος ('according to its kind'), which occurs in Gen. 1:11, 12, 21, 24 and 25. Paul takes this to suggest that each category of creature has a different kind of flesh. Although σάρξ is not used in Genesis 1, it is used in Gen. 8:17 in connection with birds and beasts and reptiles, echoing Gen. 1:26-27. But whether Paul derived the term from Genesis is of negligible significance. Paul uses the conceptuality of the creation account to suggest that it is not unreasonable to think of another kind of body entirely, a spiritual body.

Other Allusions to Genesis 1–3

We also find a handful of other allusions to the creation account in Paul's letters. In 2 Cor. 4:6, Paul writes, 'For it is the God who said, "Let light shine out of darkness," who has shone in our hearts to give the light of the knowledge of the glory of God in the face of Jesus Christ.' Although there is 'no specific grounding in either the Hebrew or Greek Scriptures',[10] conceptually the connection is clear: God speaks and light is created (Gen. 1:3-4). This allusion thus recalls God's creative power and therefore stresses that '[t]he God of redemption is none other than the God of creation'.[11]

In 2 Cor. 11:3, Paul writes, 'But I am afraid that as the serpent deceived Eve by its cunning (πανουργίᾳ), your thoughts will be led astray from a sincere and pure devotion to Christ.' Paul has just suggested that the church is betrothed to one husband (Christ), and so this may recall Paul's arguments (to be examined below) which consider the Messiah to be a new

---

10   Stanley, *Paul and the Language of Scripture*, p.215.

11   M. J. Harris, *The Second Epistle to the Corinthians: A Commentary on the Greek Text* (NIGTC; Grand Rapids: Eerdmans, 2005), p.335.

Adam. The allusion is to the deception of the woman by the serpent in Genesis 3. Interestingly, while the Septuagint describes the serpent as 'most wise' (φρονιμώτατος), Aquila and Theodotion both describe the serpent as 'cunning' (πανοῦργος or in some manuscripts, πανουργότερος), using the same root word as Paul. It is possible that Paul had knowledge of a text that anticipated Aquila and Theodotion rather than the Septuagint at this point.[12]

Finally, Paul's oblique reference to the creation groaning under futility in Rom. 8:20 seems to recall the curse of Gen. 3:17-19, although the language of 'futility' occurs in Ecclesiastes rather than Genesis. One also finds references to a 'new creation' (Gal. 6:15; 2 Cor. 5:17) which ultimately hark back to Genesis, though perhaps through an Isaianic lens (cf. Isa. 66:22-23).

Adam and Christ

In two places Paul explicitly pairs Adam and Christ: 1 Cor. 15:21-22, 45-49 and Rom. 5:12-21.

Adam and Christ in 1 Corinthians 15

In the previous section it was noted that 1 Corinthians 15, Paul's great defence of the resurrection of the dead, contains several allusions to the creation account in Genesis 1–2. He continues his focus on creation by arguing that the correspondences between the first human, Adam, and Christ reveal certain parallels that must be taken seriously by his Corinthian hearers. First in 15:21-22 Paul uses the common humanity of Adam and Christ to suggest a certain necessity of inversion: just as death came through a human being (δι' ἀνθρώπου θάνατος), so the resurrection of the dead must come through a human being (15:21). Paul then repeats the same logic with explicit reference to Adam: 'for just as all die in Adam, so also all will be made alive in the Messiah' (15:22). Paul alludes to Gen. 3:17-19, in which Adam receives the punishment for eating the fruit. The prohibition in Gen. 2:17 warned that 'on the day that you eat of it, you shall die by death' (θανάτῳ ἀποθανεῖσθε),[13] and Paul sees Adam's disobedience as incurring the sanctions of this warning, and so ushering death into the world.[14] Death

---

12   Cf. also 1 Tim. 2:14; compare Sir. 25:24, which blames Eve for the 'beginning of sin' (ἀρχὴ ἁμαρτίας) and the resultant death. Some have also suggested that a reference to God's judgment on Eve in Gen. 3:16 may lie behind Paul's cryptic statement in 1 Cor. 14:34 (cf. 1 Tim. 2.12) that 'the law also says' that women should be subordinate. This is impossible to prove, and at any rate, the originality of 1 Cor. 14:33b-35 is disputable.

13   Following R. J. V. Hiebert's translation in the *New English Translation of the Septuagint*, which captures well the jarring Greek rendition of the Hebrew infinitive absolute.

14   Although other streams of Jewish tradition looked to the events of Gen. 6:1-4 as signalling the real decline of the human race (esp. Enochic literature), Paul is not alone in reading Adam's actions as signalling the entrance of death into the world; see esp. Wis.

entering the world through the actions of one human requires, according to Paul, an equal and opposite reaction, in which the dead are made alive again by the actions of one human, whom Paul here identifies as the Messiah.

This correspondence is developed further in 1 Cor. 15:45-49. In arguing that a physical body requires also a spiritual body, Paul cites Gen. 2:7. The citation differs slightly from the Septuagint:

Gen. 2:7 LXX	1 Cor. 15:45
καὶ ἐγένετο ὁ ἄνθρωπος εἰς ψυχὴν ζῶσαν	ἐγένετο ὁ πρῶτος ἄνθρωπος ᾿Αδὰμ εἰς ψυχὴν ζῶσαν

In light of his argument, Paul has clarified that this is the 'first' man, and also named him explicitly as Adam.[15] As Adam became 'a living being/soul', so the Messiah, here identified as 'the last Adam' (ὁ ἔσχατος ᾿Αδάμ), became a life-giving spirit (πνεῦμα ζῳοποιοῦν). The latter term appears to be modeled on the description of Adam in Gen. 2:7, and that Paul has already used the verb ζῳοποιέω in his earlier reference to the Adam/Christ parallel in 15:22 may suggest that he already had this in view. Paul goes on to contrast Adam, as the 'man of dust' (χοϊκός), with Christ, the 'man from heaven' (15:47). This alludes to the narration present in the first half of Gen. 2:7, in which God forms 'the man, dust from the earth' (τὸν ἄνθρωπον χοῦν ἀπὸ τῆς γῆς). Adam and Christ each represent one stage or type of humanity, and Paul argues that the progression from the first to the second comes via the resurrection. In 15:49 Paul expresses confidence that 'just as we have borne the image of the man of dust, we shall also bear the image of the heavenly man'. This may further recall Gen. 5:3, in which Adam's son Seth is born 'according to his image' (κατὰ τὴν εἰκόνα αὐτοῦ; cf. Gen. 1:27).[16]

2:23-24: by the envy of the devil which resulted in his tempting Adam, 'death entered the world' (θάνατος εἰσῆλθεν εἰς τὸν κόσμον). Note also Philo, *Leg.* 1:105-107 for death as both physical and spiritual; cf. also *4 Ezra* 3:7; 7:118-19. On the early reception of Genesis 2–3 in Second Temple Judaism, see K. Schmid, 'Loss of Immortality? Hermeneutical Aspects of Genesis 2-3 and Its Early Receptions', in K. Schmid and C. Riedweg (eds), *Beyond Eden: The Biblical Story of Paradise (Genesis 2-3) and Its Reception History* (FAT, 2.34; Tübingen: Mohr Siebeck, 2008), pp.58–78.

15   Symmachus and Theodotion both also add ᾿Αδάμ to ἄνθρωπος (for the reading, see Wevers' Göttingen edition, *ad loc.*). Stanley (*Paul and the Language of Scripture*, pp.207-9) suggests that Paul may be reliant on a variant Septuagintal text here, which is possible, though it is just as likely that Paul supplies the name Adam as a clarification for the sake of his audience. On the question of whether 1 Cor. 15:45b should be considered part of the citation, see Stanley, *Paul and the Language*, p.209, n.99.

16   Many have noted the parallel to the idea of a heavenly and an earthly man in Philo, *Opif.* 134-35. While there are some striking similarities, unlike Philo Paul nowhere clearly reads the two creation accounts as describing two different acts of creation. Against the position of Schmid ('Loss of Immortality', p.72), who follows M. Rösel in seeing a Platonic influence on the LXX translation of Genesis 1–3 (which, it is suggested, encouraged Philo's reading), see J. Cook, 'The Septuagint of Genesis: Text and/or Interpretation?'

Adam and Christ in Rom. 5:12-21

Similarly to his argument in 1 Cor. 15:21-22, in Rom. 5:12-21 Paul explores the similarities and points of contrast between Adam and the Messiah. His argument in Romans proceeds at greater length, affirming the assertion of 1 Cor. 15:21-22 that the sin of Adam brought death, but also moves beyond that argument. In Rom. 5:14, Paul suggests that Adam 'is a type of the one who was to come'. This conviction suggests that Paul sees Adam as prefiguring the Messiah in accordance with the divine plan that orders all of history. The argument of Rom. 5:12-21 is complicated and need not be fully expounded here.[17] But it is worth noting that Paul here conceives of Adam's act of disobedience to be not merely 'sin' but 'transgression' (παράπτωμα), the contravention of an explicit command or law. This is the difference between Adam and those who followed after him until Moses: Adam had a 'law' (presumably, Gen. 2:17), while those before the Torah was given at Sinai did not (Rom. 5:13-14). While in 1 Corinthians Paul suggests that death comes to all because of Adam's sin, in Romans he goes beyond this by arguing that not only death, but also sin spread to all because of Adam's action.[18] But similarly to 1 Corinthians, here Paul casts Adam as a contrast to the Messiah, and Paul alludes to the tragedy of Genesis 2–3 in order to celebrate the recovery now achieved in Christ.

Paul also subtly develops this representative status of Adam later in Romans. In Rom. 7:7-11, Adam's transgression likely lies behind the brief narrative Paul supplies. While this is a matter of some debate and judgments here are informed by broader perspectives about the nature of the speaker in Romans 7, certain links between Rom. 7:7-11 and Genesis 2–3, however, make an Adamic background likely: the sequence of a) being alive 'apart from law', b) commandment given, and c) the concept of the serpent (Gen. 3:13) or sin (Rom. 7:11) 'deceiving' with the result of death.[19]

The Story of Abraham in Galatians

Paul's engagement with Genesis in his letter to the Galatians is almost wholly centred on the story of Abraham. He conducts two sustained arguments about Abraham, first in 3:6-29 and then again in 4:21-31. He cites Gen. 15:6 in Gal. 3:6, Gen. 12:3/18:18 in Gal. 3:8, Gen. 13:15 par. in Gal. 3:16 and Gen. 21:10 in Gal. 4:30. In the course of his allegorical retelling of the

---

in A. Wénin (ed.), *Studies in the Book of Genesis: Literature, Redaction and History* (BETL, 155; Leuven: Peeters, 2001), pp.315–30.

17   See further O. Hofius, 'The Adam-Christ Antithesis and the Law: Reflections on Romans 5:12-21,' in J. D. G. Dunn (ed.), *Paul and the Mosaic Law* (Grand Rapids: Eerdmans, 2001), pp.165–206.

18   So Fitzmyer, *First Corinthians*, p.570.

19   See H. Lichtenberger, *Das Ich Adams und das Ich der Menschheit: Studien zum Menschenbild in Römer 7* (WUNT, 164; Tübingen: Mohr Siebeck, 2004).

story of Sarah and Hagar, he also alludes to Gen. 16:15 in Gal. 4:22, Gen. 17:16 in Gal. 4:23, Gen. 21:2 in Gal. 4:22 and Gen. 21:9 in Gal. 4:22, 29.

Abraham in Galatians 3

In Gal. 3:6-14, as part of his larger argument that Gentiles are children of Abraham through faith in Christ rather than by Torah observance (3:1-29), Paul seeks to ground in Scripture his assertion that the Galatian Gentile believers received the Spirit through the hearing of faith and not by law observance (3:2). In 3:6-9 Paul argues from the example of Abraham that 'those who are from faith will be blessed together with Abraham, the man of faith' (οἱ ἐκ πίστεως εὐλογοῦνται σὺν τῷ πιστῷ Ἀβραάμ). In 3:6 Paul begins an argument from Scripture about two things: how Abraham was blessed, and who gets to be called a child of Abraham and so a partaker in that blessing. This will stretch until at least 3:29, with the climactic assertion that 'you are Abraham's offspring', though Abraham remains 'on stage' until 5:1. Many have suggested that Paul here responds to an alternative reading of Genesis previously proposed by his opponents, in which Abraham's circumcision is held up as a model of obedience for the Galatians to emulate.[20] It is not unlikely that Paul is responding to the legitimation strategy of his opponents, at least as it has been reported to him, but since we cannot know much of the details of the account, overly elaborate reconstructions should be avoided. In some Jewish literature of the day, Abraham is seen as the archetypal convert: a pagan worshiper of the moon in Mesopotamia, he is called by God and responds to that call, founding the people that comes to be known as Israel.[21] What Paul engages in, especially in 3:6-9 and 3:15-18, is an argument about relative chronology in the telling of the story of Abraham from Genesis 12–22. It is possible that the agitators pointed to Genesis 14 with Abram's good deed of tithing to Melchizidek and rescuing Lot, and especially to Abraham's circumcision in 17:4-14. Paul, in response, draws attention to 15:6 and 12:3/18.18, the first emphasizing faith, the second, the promise.

Galatians 3:6 closely follows the LXX of Gen. 15:6, although Paul has brought the name Abraham forward[22] and substituted Ἀβραάμ for Ἀβράμ:

---

20   For one influential reconstruction of the agitators' (or teachers', as Martyn prefers) reading of Genesis, see J. L. Martyn, *Galatians: A New Translation with Introduction and Commentary* (AB; Yale: Yale University Press, 1997), pp.302–6; idem, *Theological Issues in the Letters of Paul* (Nashville: Abingdon Press, 1997), pp.7–24. But for cautions about our ability to reconstruct the situation in Galatia, see the classic article by J. M. G. Barclay, 'Mirror-Reading a Polemical Letter: Galatians as a Test Case', *JSNT* 31 (1987), pp.73–93.

21   Perhaps most fully in the *Apocalypse of Abraham* 1-8.

22   In fact, it is unclear whether 'Abraham' should be considered as belonging to the citation or to the introductory formula; for discussion, see R. N. Longenecker, *Galatians* (WBC, 41; Waco: Word Books, 1990), p.112.

'Abraham believed God and it was credited to him as righteousness'.[23] This is, in fact, the first occurrence of πιστεύω in the Pentateuch.[24] This is followed quickly by a citation of Gen. 12:3/18:18 in Gal. 3:8: Scripture 'declared in advance the gospel to Abraham, saying, "All the Gentiles shall be blessed in you" (ἐνευλογηθήσονται ἐν σοὶ πάντα τὰ ἔθνη)'. This citation most likely bears the marks of Paul's shaping. Rather than speak of 'all the tribes of the earth' (πᾶσαι αἱ φυλαὶ τῆς γῆς) as Gen. 12:3 originally does, Paul imports 'all the Gentiles/nations' (πάντα τὰ ἔθνη) from Gen. 18:18 (cf. also 22.18) for the strategic importance of τὰ ἔθνη in his argument.[25] In the citations of both Gen. 15:6 and Gen. 12:3/18:18, Paul stresses not the obedience of Abraham that finds its due reward, but rather that Abraham believes and receives a promise before he has obeyed anything that might be construed as law (a reading in contrast to many of Paul's Jewish contemporaries). The language of 'righteousness' in association with belief in Gen. 15:6 has been anticipated in Paul's argument in Gal. 2:15-21 and provides Paul with a lens by which to understand the promise to Abraham that he recalls from Gen. 12:3/18:18 in Gal. 3:8. The effect that Paul wants to draw from this is clearly stated in v.9: 'those who believe are blessed along with Abraham the believer'. That is, Abraham's story, rather than pointing to the necessity of circumcision, displays how faith is the *sine qua non* of God's dealing with those who want to be like Abraham.

Paul's argument about the relative chronology of the Abraham story is expanded to a broader salvation-historical plane in 3:15-18. In arguing that the later imposition of the law cannot nullify the previously-delivered promise, Paul writes, 'Now the promises were spoken to Abraham and to his offspring' (Gal. 3:16). He then goes on to indicate that he intends a citation by arguing that Scripture or God does not say 'and to offsprings' (καὶ τοῖς σπέρμασιν) but 'and to your offspring' (καὶ τῷ σπέρματί σου), whom Paul then identifies as the Messiah (ὅς ἐστιν Χριστός). The precise wording (καὶ τῷ σπέρματί σου), occurs several times in Genesis (13:15; 17:8; 24:7).[26]

---

23   In Genesis LXX, the shift in name comes in 17:5, after which Ἀβράμ does not occur again in the LXX or NT (the exception being a retelling of the change of name in 2 Esd. 19:7 = Neh. 9:7).

24   So Wevers, *Notes*, p.205.

25   Genesis 18:18 reads ἐνευλογηθήσονται ἐν αὐτῷ πάντα τὰ ἔθνη τῆς γῆς, and 22:18 reads ἐνευλογηθήσονται ἐν τῷ σπέρματί σου πάντα τὰ ἔθνη τῆς γῆς; for other possible allusions to these texts, see Rom. 4:13; Rev. 1:7. Stanley convincingly argues that Paul has introduced the substitution himself, whether intentionally or due to a slip in memory (*Paul and the Language of Scripture*, p.237). For Paul following a preexistent LXX text with ἐνευλογηθήσονται see Koch, *Schrift als Zeuge*, p.52. More generally on Gen. 12:3/18:18 in Gal. 3:8, see J. R. Wisdom, *Blessing for the Nations and the Curse of the Law: Paul's Citations of Genesis and Deuteronomy in Gal 3:8–10* (WUNT, 2:133; Tübingen: Mohr Siebeck, 2001), pp.129–53.

26   Cf. also Gen. 12:7 (τῷ σπέρματί σου, lacking καί). NA[27] suggests 13:15; 17:8; 24:7, while S. Moyise suggests Gen. 12:7 (*Paul and Scripture: Studying the New Testament Use of the Old Testament* [Grand Rapids: Baker Academic, 2010], p.131). Stanley (*Paul and the Language of Scripture*, p.248, n.230) does not note the parallel in 17:8, but suggests that contextually Gen. 13:15 makes most sense.

Who is the original recipient of the promise? Abraham, Paul answers, and 'his seed'. Here Paul atomizes the word 'offspring', and suggests that it refers to the Messiah, even though the singular noun had a collective sense, which Paul probably well knew. But this is an interpretative technique to imbue the Genesis narrative's forward horizon (the promise) with a focus. The point Paul draws is simply this: if the 'inheritance' really came through the law (as Paul construes his opponents' argument to suggest), then God spoke falsely to Abraham. Clearly this is a *reductio ad absurdum* argument.

Sarah and Hagar in Gal. 4:21-31

In the next chapter, Paul's argument takes a surprising turn towards an allegorical reading of the Sarah and Hagar narrative, once more returning to Genesis, this time to chapters 16–21. Some have even suggested that the section is misplaced or a mere afterthought on Paul's part. But when viewed in light of the argument Paul has been conducting since 3:1, this forms a sort of conclusion to Paul's argument, as he labours to cast his Galatian hearers in the roles which he believes will ultimately lead to them living faithfully in the new age under the Messiah. The fact that Paul here returns to the Abraham story has been taken by many as an indication that he is here continuing his project of rereading Genesis in dispute with the agitators and the reading they had bequeathed to the Galatian congregations.[27] Given the tortured nature of the argument, such a state of affairs is not unlikely, though it should be treated with suitable caution.

Intriguingly, in 4:21b, the 'law' is spoken of positively – in fact, for the first time in the letter. Paul writes, 'Tell me, you who desire to be subject to the law, will you not listen to the law?' He then provides a summary of what he hopes to persuade the Galatians that the law does in fact say, though this is not unproblematic as a straightforward reading of Genesis. Key to Paul's presentation is the verb he mentions in 4:25, συστοιχέω, which originally referred to soldiers standing in the same line, but came to denote the correspondence of categories in lists.[28] Thus, Paul reads the story with a binary hermeneutic, and aligns the two columns roughly as follows:

Abraham had two sons (4:22)

one by a slave	and one by a free woman (4:22)
born according to the flesh	born through promise (4:23)

---

27   So, e.g. C. K. Barrett, 'The Allegory of Abraham, Sarah, and Hagar in the Argument of Galatians', in J. Friedrich, W. Pohlmann and P. Stuhlmacher (eds), *Rechtfertigung. FS E. Käsemann* (Tübingen: Mohr Siebeck, 1976), pp.1–16. On Gal 4:21-31 and contemporary Jewish exegesis see, e.g. Koch, *Schrift als Zeuge*, pp.204–11; Longenecker, *Galatians*, pp.200–6 (though he includes many much later Jewish sources).
28   Cf. LSJ s.v.; so also, e.g. Martyn, *Galatians*, pp.431–66 and many others.

Allegorically, the women correspond to two covenants (4:24)

Mount Sinai for slavery (4:24)	free (4:26)
Hagar (4:24)	(Sarah, though not explicitly mentioned)
the present Jerusalem (4:25)	the Jerusalem above (4:26)
bearing children in slavery (4:25)	children of promise (4:28)
according to the flesh (4:29)	born according to the Spirit (4:29)

We should recall Paul's earlier contentions about his independence from the Jerusalem apostles. Here the polemic reaches perhaps its sharpest point: the present Jerusalem is in slavery, and so are all those who want to align themselves with it (i.e. her children, and so the agitators). As J. D. G. Dunn writes, 'This is the language of polemic, an exegetical *tour de force*, a virtuoso performance, rather than sober theological argument'.[29] Paul's reference to the contrast between the present Jerusalem and the Jerusalem that is above has its roots in apocalyptic. This seems to be based on the idea found in Exod. 25:9, 40 (and the tradition stemming from it), where Moses is shown a pattern and told to construct a tabernacle according to that pattern, thus implying that the original is in heaven and awaiting revelation.

The main thrust of the section is an interpretation of the story of Sarah and Hagar from Genesis 16–21 (the written text: γέγραπται), although with a contemporizing hermeneutic that sees the story as directed ultimately to the present (ἅτινά ἐστιν ἀλληγορούμενα). Gal. 4:22 does not introduce a direct citation, but refers in broad strokes to the stories of sons borne by Hagar (Gen. 16:15; 21:9) and Sarah (Gen. 21:2). Both Hagar (Gen. 16:10) and Sarah (Gen. 17:16) were promised numerous descendants, and so to read them as symbolic figures is in itself not a novel interpretative move, especially after Paul has established a similar significance for Abraham in Galatians 3. What is novel, however, is the inversion Paul attempts to achieve, regarding those who had historically viewed themselves as children of Sarah now to be children of Hagar. Paul does this in part by citing Isa. 54:1 ('Rejoice, O barren one, you who bear no children, burst into song and shout, you who endure no birth pangs; for the children of the desolate woman are more numerous than the children of the one who is married'). As Paul identifies Sarah implicitly with this woman, we may see some of the path along which Paul travelled to arrive at this allegory.[30] Moreover, Paul

---

29   J. D. G. Dunn, *The Theology of Paul's Letter to the Galatians* (Cambridge: Cambridge University Press, 1993), p.97.

30   This may also align with Paul's tendency elsewhere to read negative epithets as references to the Gentiles; cf. J. R. Wagner, *Heralds of the Good News: Isaiah and Paul in Concert in the Letter to the Romans* (NovTSup, 101; Leiden: Brill, 2002), pp.83, 188.

follows a prominent stream of Jewish tradition in seeing Ishmael's 'playing' with Isaac in Gen. 21:9 as involving malicious behaviour; Paul characterizes this as 'persecution' (Gal. 4:29), though the choice of word is likely determined by Paul's present circumstances more than the exegetical detail of the Genesis story itself.

But the practical point of his comparison is clear. In Gal. 4:30 Paul writes, 'But what does the scripture say? Drive out the slave woman and her child; for the child of the slave will not share the inheritance with the child of the free woman'. Paul here cites Gen. 21:10, having probably introduced a number of minor alterations to the citation that enhance his ability to contemporize it.[31] When Gen. 21:10 here speaks, Paul claims, it tells the Galatian congregations exactly what they need to do. Once more, we see Genesis as a word directed to the present. But with the emphatic position of Gen. 21:10, Paul promptly and forcefully brings to a climax the argument he has been developing since 3:1.

To describe the function of the Abraham story in Galatians is to touch the central concerns of the letter: the Galatians must hold fast to the faith of Abraham and his promise, not allowing themselves to be circumcised and persuaded to keep the calendrical observances they have set out upon. To keep the Torah in the present time as Gentiles is to deny the reality of God's invasive, new apocalyptic action in Christ, and to align oneself with the former things: the period of slavery, of adolescence, of discipline, of restraint, of the earthly Jerusalem, of the elements of the world. But, as Paul will say in chapter 6, there has come about 'a new creation' (a concept also indebted to a reading of Genesis and Isaiah together), and this, Paul is labouring to argue, changes everything. What is more, this new state of affairs is precisely that which was *promised*. Paul places a stress on *promise* as opposed to law: this is constitutive for the people of God, the promise that was given to Abraham, then to his seed, that is Christ, and those who believe in Christ through faith, and so realize the promise for themselves.

The Story of Abraham in Romans 4

The story of Abraham plays an equally significant role in the letter to the Romans. In what is one of the most sustained interpretative expositions in his epistles, Paul spends nearly twenty-five verses arguing from the story of Abraham. Following on from his rejection of boasting, Paul asks whether Abraham had reason to boast. In diatribe style, Paul asks, 'What does the Scripture say?' (4:3a). He cites Gen. 15:6, which follows the Septuagint with only minor changes, in response: 'Abraham believed God, and it

---

31   He omits from Genesis two deictic words (ταύτην and ταύτης) and substitutes 'the free one' (τῆς ἐλευθέρας) for 'Isaac'. By contrast, he probably followed a Greek text that included μή. See Koch, *Schrift als Zeuge*, p.52; Stanley, *Paul and the Language of Scripture*, pp.248–51; and Wevers, *Notes*, p.303.

was credited to him as righteousness' (paraphrased again in 4:9, 22-23). As in Galatians, though with a more measured tone, Paul subsequently argues from the relative chronology of the Abraham story that he was reckoned as righteous 'not after, but before he was circumcised' (4:10; cf. Gen. 17:10-11). This supports first of all the conclusion that Abraham was reckoned righteous when he was ungodly, and so has no boast, in contrast to some contemporary Jewish portraits of the patriarch.[32] But second, that this occurred before he was circumcised, means that Abraham is father of both the circumcised and uncircumcised (4:11-12) – expressed here in more conciliatory tones than in Galatians.

As in Galatians 3, Paul pairs a concern with Abraham's justification by faith in Gen. 15:6 with the promises given to the patriarch. In 4:13-15, Paul speaks of 'the promise that he would inherit the world'. Such a breadth of promise does not appear in the patriarchal narratives as such, but Paul seems to be generalizing from the promise for land and descendants that is repeated to Abraham several times (Gen. 12:1-3; 18:18; 22:17-18). By dissociating the promise from the law, as in Galatians 'Paul's primary interest here is to overcome the ethnic prerogative with regard to the promise'.[33]

In Rom. 4:16-25 Paul argues that the promise of Abraham, because it is based on faith, is guaranteed for all who share in Abraham's faith. Paul cites Genesis twice in these verses, and alludes to the story of Isaac's miraculous conception. In Rom. 4:17 Paul cites Gen. 17:5: 'I have made you the father of many nations', following the LXX exactly. This citation supports Paul's contention that both Jew and Gentile comprise the heirs of Abraham, since otherwise God's statement that Abraham was the father of many nations would be void. Paul goes on to characterize the faith of Abraham: 'hoping against hope' he believed the promise of God for an heir, the *sine qua non* of fathering many nations. In Rom. 4:18, Paul cites Gen. 15:5, again exactly following the LXX: 'so numerous shall your descendants be'. This brief phrase encapsulates the repeated promise in Genesis that God would multiply Abraham's descendents.[34] Although both he and Sarah were advanced in age (note Gen. 17:17 in Rom. 4:19), Abraham believed the promise fully, and this same faith is counted to him as righteousness. Here Paul has brought together once more the two important resources he takes from Abraham's story: justification by faith, and the promise of many nations as Abraham's heritage. The two themes are, of course, closely related for Paul.

---

32   See, e.g. the *Apocalypse of Abraham*; *Jub.* 12:1-24; *Tg. Ps.-J.* Gen. 15:1; *Tg. Neof.* Gen. 15:1; cf. further Francis Watson, *Paul and the Hermeneutics of Faith* (London: T&T Clark, 2004), pp.167–269.

33   R. Jewett, *Romans: A Commentary* (Hermeneia; Minneapolis: Fortress, 2007), p.326.

34   In Romans, some MSS (F G a) add 'as the stars of the heaven and the sand of the sea' in apparent harmonization to Gen. 22:17; cf. also 26:4 and, more loosely, 12:2.

Other References to Genesis in Romans

Paul's letter to the Romans also includes three citations of the Patriarchal narratives and one major allusion. All three of his citations occur in the argument of Romans 9:6-13, in which Paul seeks to support his contention that 'the word of God has not failed' (9:6) by charting a revisionist history of election within Israel in anticipation of the current inflow of the Gentiles into the church.

Quotation of Gen. 21:12 in Rom. 9:7

One important stage in this argument is Paul's strategy of redefining 'Israel'.[35] Paul makes a division within the history of Israel, contending that 'not all Israel is Israel'. He then adduces Gen. 21:12 in Rom. 9:7 to support this position. Paul's citation corresponds precisely to the Septuagint.[36] It is introduced somewhat abruptly, and an audience would probably only be aware that Paul is citing by the syntactical tension within its new epistolary context.[37] Recalling the story of Isaac and Ishmael which Paul allegorically expounded in Gal. 4:21-31, Paul calls attention to the fact that not all of Abraham's sons were considered to be the line of Israel, but only those descended from Isaac ('in Isaac will seed be called for you'). Paul anticipates the citation by speaking of the 'seed of Abraham' as the true Israel that does not correspond entirely with physical descent (9:7a).[38] In the following verse Paul offers an explanation (τοῦτ᾿ ἔστιν) in which he states what he takes Gen. 21:12 to prove: 'those who are children of the flesh, these are not children of God, but the children of the promise are reckoned as seed'. The contrast between children of the flesh and children of the promise once more recalls Paul's exposition of the Sarah and Hagar story in Gal. 4:21-31.

Quotation of Gen. 18:10, 14 in Rom. 9:9

Immediately after his brief exposition of Gen. 21:12, Paul introduces the supporting witness of the promise itself. Paul has made alterations to the citations that enhance its contemporary ring. As the following table shows, Paul has introduced a prepositional phrase from Gen. 18:10 into 18:14, substituted 'I will come' for 'I will return' (probably to avoid the distraction

---

35   Cf. Wagner, *Heralds of the Good News*, pp.49–51
36   This citation also occurs in Heb. 11:18 (possibly dependent on Paul) though there it is used for a slightly different end; cf. C. K. Rothschild, *Hebrews as Pseudepigraphon: The History and Significance of the Pauline Attribution of Hebrews* (WUNT, 235; Tübingen: Mohr Siebeck, 2009), pp.95–6.
37   So Koch, *Schrift als Zeuge*, p.23.
38   The term σπέρμα ᾿Αβραάμ occurs in 2 Chr. 20:7; Ps. 104:6; *Ps. Sol.* 9:9; 18:3; Isa. 41:8; cf. also 2 Cor. 11:22; Jewett, *Romans*, 575.

of his listeners wondering about the first visit), and abbreviated the whole. The changes should be laid at Paul's feet, though they do not substantially alter the meaning of the text.[39]

Gen. 18:10, 14 LXX	Rom. 9:9
18:10: ἐπαναστρέφων ἥξω πρὸς σὲ κατὰ τὸν καιρὸν τοῦτον εἰς ὥρας, καὶ ἕξει υἱὸν Σάρρα ἡ γυνή σου. 18:14: εἰς τὸν καιρὸν τοῦτον ἀναστρέφω πρὸς σὲ εἰς ὥρας, καὶ ἔσται τῇ Σάρρᾳ υἱός.	κατὰ τὸν καιρὸν τοῦτον ἐλεύσομαι καὶ ἔσται τῇ Σάρρᾳ υἱός.

Paul does not identify the speaker here and so probably sees the speaker (one of the three men who visited him by the oaks of Mamre) as the Lord (cf. Gen. 18:1, 13). Paul thus takes this to be the divine promise that guarantees that Isaac will be born and so indicates that Isaac is to be favoured to Ishmael. This citation functions to support the assertion of 9:8 that election is a selective phenomenon in Israel's history, and that the promise is what defines the lineage of true Israel (υἱός here being the concrete example of the τέκνα of 9:8).

Quotation of Gen. 25:23 in Rom. 9:12

The next stage in Paul's argument carries his point forward a generation, from Sarah to Rebecca. In contrast to Isaac and Ishmael, who shared the same father but had different mothers, Jacob and Esau were twins, conceived 'by one husband' (Rom. 9:10). Therefore, they serve to demonstrate that the choice between them did not depend on physical descent, which was identical in their case, but on divine initiative. In fact, to exclude any suggestion that divine favour was not an initiative but a response to the actions of Jacob and Esau (and here Paul seems to presuppose a knowledge of the divergent paths taken by the brothers in Genesis), he draws attention to the fact that God's decisive word is delivered *before* those actions had taken place – and in fact before they had even been born. This decisive word was spoken (ἐρρέθη) to Rebecca: 'the elder shall serve the younger', a clear reversal of normal Ancient Near Eastern family practice. In fact, a major theme in Genesis is reversal, and the younger son overtaking the elder recurs throughout the book.[40] Thus Paul's citation of Gen. 25:23, which follows

---

39　　Stanley (*Paul and the Language of Scripture*, pp.103–5) disputes the claim that this is the result of a conflation of vv.10 and 14. But he rightly calls attention to the 'dehistoricizing treatment accorded the Genesis passage' (p.104) and suggests that Paul introduced these changes to ensure that his point was duly emphasized.

40　　For the reception of this theme in early Christianity, see Harl, *Genèse*, pp.45–6.

the LXX exactly, picks up a recurrent motif in the book expressed in pithy fashion. Paul finds this reading of Genesis confirmed with Mal. 1:2-3 ('Jacob have I loved, but Esau have I hated'). This further confirms the significance of these figures as representing peoples. Although Paul does not extend his argument to Gentiles explicitly at this point (contrast *Barn.* 13:1-6 in which Gen. 25:23 is read in a fiercely supersessionist manner), Paul does find in Genesis a divine purpose that cannot be encompassed by physical lineage and so prepares for his argument that the Gentiles have been grafted into the true Israel.

Allusion to Gen. 22:12/22:16 in Rom. 8:32

In the course of offering assurance of the love of God for believers, Paul marshals the handing over of God's own son to death as proof of his willingness to 'give us all things'. Paul's wording in Rom. 8:32 (τοῦ ἰδίου υἱοῦ οὐκ ἐφείσατο ἀλλὰ ὑπὲρ ἡμῶν πάντων παρέδωκεν αὐτόν, God 'did not spare his own son but delivered him up for us all') recalls the description of God's commendation of Abraham when he displayed a willingness to kill Isaac, the child of promise, in response to the divine command (Gen. 22:12/22:16: οὐκ ἐφείσω τοῦ υἱοῦ σου τοῦ ἀγαπητοῦ, 'you did not spare your beloved son'). Given Paul's widespread use of the Abraham story elsewhere in his letters and the unique verbal correspondence (not sparing a son), it is likely that Paul here describes God's giving of his own son with echoes of Abraham's willingness to sacrifice Isaac. Within early Christianity, the *akedah*, or 'binding' of Isaac (Genesis 22), was often read as typologically anticipating God's giving of his son, and Paul seems to be an early (perhaps the earliest) example of that tendency.

Conclusion

In his reconstruction of Paul's theological reading of the Pentateuch, Francis Watson argues that Paul finds in Genesis above all the self-commitment of God to act for salvation, and so derives from Genesis 'the hermeneutical priority of the promise'.[41] This is an apt characterization of Paul's reading of the Abraham material in particular: in both Romans and Galatians, Paul wants to stress the inclusive and prevenient nature of the promises to Abraham and the subsequent community created in Christ. But Paul also derives ethical guidance from Genesis, which he applies to problems of sexual ethics or disunity in worship. Especially in Paul's correspondence with the Corinthians, Paul has repeated recourse to the opening chapters

41   Watson, *Paul and the Hermeneutics of Faith*, p.15, n.5 and *passim*; cf. pp.167–269. For a brief response to Watson's larger construal of Paul's reading of the Pentateuch, see D. Lincicum, 'Paul's Engagement with Deuteronomy: Snapshots and Signposts', *Currents in Biblical Research* 7 (2008), pp.37–67, esp. pp.53–6.

of Genesis, perhaps because he needs to stress the materiality of creation and new creation in his argument concerning the resurrection. And in both Romans and 1 Corinthians, the eschatological horizon of Paul's hermeneutic becomes clear, as he sees Adam pointing beyond himself to the coming Messiah. Above all, one sees that Paul has read and listened to Genesis intently, pondering not simply individual verses or pithy phrases, but its narrative elements in particular. These stories – of creation and ruination, of election and promise – order Paul's world of thought, and he attempts to pass on this storied world to his Gentile audiences.

Chapter 7

GENESIS IN THE DEUTERO-PAULINE EPISTLES

James W. Aageson

Introduction

Examining the use and function of Genesis in the Deutero-Pauline Epistles invariably raises broader questions of how the early church writers used Scripture and how these approaches relate to interpretive practice in early Judaism. As the scholarly conversation has developed, distinctions between quotations, allusions, and echoes have often been used to differentiate or categorize scriptural usage in the Pauline epistles, and together they have normally been grouped under the more general heading intertextuality.[1] Whatever the nuances attributed to the term intertextuality, it also relates to a variety of methodological approaches commonly described as source criticism, midrash, typology, and inner biblical exegesis, to name the more obvious examples.[2] Standing behind these terms and concepts are questions of authorial intention and audience reception, both of which beg the question of how the readers or hearers would have understood the Pauline arguments and exhortations.

The use of scriptural material in these letters is always in a literary context, and it is also presumably shaped by some Pauline socio-historical context as well, though that may not always be clearly discernable to us based on the evidence available from the text. However the scriptural material is incorporated into the Pauline text, it is being placed in a new context and that context is critical to understanding its Pauline pastoral or theological function. In the case of the Deutero-Pauline letters, that context is doubly complicated by the fact that the historical Paul may not

---

1   The work of Richard Hays has precipitated and shaped much of this conversation during the past generation. See especially *Echoes of Scripture in the Letters of Paul* (New Haven and London: Yale University Press, 1989) and *The Conversion of the Imagination: Paul as Interpreter of Israel's Scripture* (Grand Rapids, Michigan: Eerdmans, 2005).

2   Steve Moyise, 'Intertexuality and the Study of the Old Testament in the New Testament', in Steve Moyise (ed.), *The Old Testament in the New Testament: Essays in Honour of J. L. North* (JSNTSup, 189; Sheffield: Sheffield Academic Press, 2000), pp.14–18.

have written these letters, in which case they were written presumably by someone in the Pauline tradition seeking to emulate or perhaps valorize the apostle.[3] But what makes this especially complicated, if we conclude the apostle did not actually write these letters, is that we now must contend with the possibility that Scripture is echoing through the undisputed Pauline epistles on the way to being reflected in the Deutero-Pauline letters.[4] This is still more complicated should Richard Pervo be correct that all of the Pauline material was reworked, perhaps at a Pauline school in Ephesus, prior to reaching the form with which we are familiar today.[5] If this is correct, the use of Scripture in the undisputed Pauline texts, let alone the Deutero-Pauline texts, is complicated in a variety of ways, and standing behind the scriptural quotations, allusions, and echoes in these texts may be a process more complex than is immediately apparent to us today. For the sake of making the present task manageable, the epistolary texts will be taken as they currently stand, while recognizing that behind those texts may stand a complex textual history no longer readily available to us.

A final feature of the Deutero-Pauline letters to be noted at the outset is that Ephesians and Colossians are community letters and the Pastoral Epistles are ostensibly written to individuals, associates of Paul. The individual character of the Pastorals, however, does not preclude that communities read or heard these letters. Yet the literary axis of each epistle turns on the instructions given by Paul to a junior associate and that shapes how the language, pastoral theology, and exhortations, including the use of Scripture, are framed.

Pastoral Epistles

Gen. 1:27, 2:7, 2:22, 3:6, 3:13, 3:16 in 1 Tim. 2:13-15

The literary context for the cluster of references to Genesis includes the material from 2:8-12, which establishes church gatherings, presumably for worship, as the context for the discussion.[6] It begins in 2:8-9 with instructions for men to pray holding holy hands lifted and women to dress modestly

---

3   For my approach to the question of the authorship of the Pastoral Epistles, see *Paul, the Pastoral Epistles, and the Early Church* (Peabody, Massachusetts: Hendrickson, 2008), pp.3–5, 86–9, 207–8.

4   See e.g. 1 Cor 11:3, 7, 8; 14:34; 15:45, 47.

5   Richard I. Pervo, *The Making of Paul: Constructions of the Apostle in Early Christianity* (Minneapolis: Fortress Press, 2010), pp.2, 27.

6   See e.g. Jouette M. Bassler, *1 Timothy, 2 Timothy, and Titus* (Nashville: Abingdon, 1996), p.59; Ben Witherington III, *Letters and Homilies for Hellenized Christians: A Socio-rhetorical Commentary on Titus, 1–2 Timothy, and 1–3 John* (Downers Grove, Illinois: IVP Academic, 2006), p.224; Jerome D. Quinn and William C. Wacker, *The First and Second Letters to Timothy* (ECC; Grand Rapids and Cambridge: Eerdmans, 2000), p.223.

with appropriate clothes and without braided hair, gold, pearls, or expensive clothing. The men are to pray without anger or contention, and the women are to profess reverence to God through good works. Clearly the projected *Sitz im Leben* in 2:8 is prayer, and the use of ὡσαύτως to introduce 2:9 certainly suggests the same context is projected for the instructions directed towards women. Hence, it is reasonable to conclude that this setting extends all the way through 2:12 and that the use of Genesis material in 2:13-15 relates most specifically to women in that context. The projected context for these instructions might rightly be thought to limit the intended scope of these words and cautions against universalizing and applying them too quickly to other, broader contexts for women's lives in the early church. In any case, the use of Genesis in 2:13-14 and the instructions to which they relate in 2:11-12 are linked to the circumstances of church prayer gatherings and the author's desire for how these ought to be conducted.

This raises the question about how we ought to understand the nuances of the opening expression in 2:8, sometimes translated as 'I want you to know', 'I desire', or 'It is my wish' (βούλομαι). Is the author's desire or wish, and hence the subsequent instruction in 2:11-14, precipitated by an identifiable problem in the community, or is it a more general statement about what men and women are to do or not do in prayer gatherings, simply reflecting more generic moral expectations about good order and proper behaviour?[7] If it is the former, as the literary context would seem to suggest, the instruction functions as a guide to Timothy about how he should deal with a specific circumstance in the Ephesian church and where he might turn for support, viz. Genesis.[8] If the latter, the instruction would appear more generic, perhaps proactively and more generally addressing the behaviour of men and women in prayer gatherings regardless of any specific problems that have yet erupted. This could also lend itself more readily to the view that Paul's instructions to Timothy are driven more by a sense of normative order than controversy, an order less tailored or constrained by particular circumstances in the church and thus more open to having wider applicability for the behaviour of men and women.[9] In either case, however, the instructions about women seem to be modelled on Greco-Roman behavioural expectations, even though the Genesis material is actually cited. Wrestling with these subtle distinctions informs how we will understand the nuanced use of Genesis in 2:11-12 to relate to Paul's instructions to Timothy, while at the same time, they remind us that the instructions about women also play themselves out within an

7   Luke Timothy Johnson, *Letters to Paul's Delegates: 1 Timothy, 2 Timothy, and Titus* (Valley Forge, Pennsylvania: Trinity Press International, 1996), pp.134–6.

8   See the argument by Witherington, *Letters and Homilies.* pp.217–30. Cf. also Johnson, *Letters to Paul's Delegates.* pp.134–6, 140.

9   Philip H. Towner, '1–2 Timothy and Titus,' in G. K. Beale and D. A. Carson (eds), *Commentary on the New Testament Use of the Old Testament* (Grand Rapids, Michigan: Baker Academic, 2007), pp.894–8.

understanding of the church as the household of God, which in many ways reflects expectations for the Greco-Roman household.[10]

The injunctions to Timothy in 2:11-12, that women in church gatherings learn in silence (ἡσυχία) and all submission/obedience (ὑποταγῇ) and that women not be allowed (ἐπιτρέπω) to teach or have authority over a man (αὐθεντεῖν) but be in silence (ἡσυχίᾳ), set the stage for a two-part allusion to the Genesis story: 1) the account of Adam and Eve's creation; and 2) the temptation of Eve. This begs the question of whether 2:15, perhaps echoing the punishment of Eve in Gen. 3:16, is also part of the scriptural argument.[11] If it is, it would appear to be an echo rather than an unmistakable allusion, that is, if we accept that an allusion is an intertexual reference closer to the intention of the author and more readily accessible to the intended audience. In 2:13-15, it is by and large the Yahwist's narrative of creation that frames the specific references,[12] and it might be assumed that the narrative frame contextualizes for Timothy and any wider audience the familiar Genesis story. In some measure, those familiar with this story would have had it brought to mind by the specific catch phrases and would have understood Paul's instruction in a more normative way because of the larger narrative. Since the issues reflected in 2:9-12 address the behaviour of women and their proper roles, it is apparent that the specifically identified features of the relationship between Adam and Eve from the Genesis story are intended to underwrite support for the author's instruction to Timothy. To put it simply, what can be shown to have been the case in the creation story and in creation time is also the case now and is applicable to the present circumstance, perhaps controversy, in the Ephesian community.[13]

While it is normally not possible to identify specific textual traditions standing behind allusions and echoes, it is possible in this case to see verbal connections with the Greek text of Genesis. The most prominent are the names Ἀδάμ and Εὕα (see Gen. 3:20 MT, 4:1 LXX), which undoubtedly have a poignancy not found among the other biblical terms.[14] Even to this day, these names immediately catch our attention and conjure up the fuller Genesis story without missing a beat. We would assume the same was the case for the audience of 1 Timothy. Equally striking, the author uses the word ἐπλάσθη in 2:13, which is the same root as ἔπλασεν used in the Greek of Gen. 2:7, 8, and 15.[15] Only in Rom. 9:20 is this word used elsewhere in the Pauline corpus. As Philip Towner points out, this word is not used of Eve's creation in the Genesis account, but in 2 Macc. 7:23, Josephus *Ant.* 1:32, and 1 *Clem.* 33:4 it appears to refer to the creation of both man and woman.[16]

---

10   Aageson, *Paul, the Pastoral Epistles, and the Early Church.* pp.19–25, 35.
11   Towner, *Commentary*, p.894.
12   Quinn and Wacker, *First and Second Letters*, p.226.
13   Cf. 1 Cor. 14:34-35, 2 Cor. 11:3, Eph 5:22.
14   See also Rom 5:12-14, 1 Cor. 15:22, 45 (Ἀδάμ) and 2 Cor. 11:3 (Εὕα).
15   Cf. also 2:19 where the same word is used of the creatures of the land.
16   Towner, *Commentary*, p.894.

So it is not surprising that the writer of 1 Timothy would use this verb in connection with Adam but by implication with Eve as well, even when not explicitly quoting the text, for the verb had probably come to be used not only for the creation of Adam but implicitly for Eve as well.

The idea in 2:13 that being formed first according to the Genesis account (Gen. 2:7, 22) gave Adam special status rests on the principle that that which comes first in the literary sequence has priority.[17] The author provides no direct defence of the principle, which suggests he thought it needed none, though the argument in 2:14 elaborates the basic point still further. We might also assume that the created order found in the Genesis narrative linked with the larger Greco-Roman concept of a structured social order, represented most clearly in the letter's use of household imagery, to which both men and women in the church were expected to conform.[18] To that extent, both Scripture and Greco-Roman social practice are thought to be consistent. This begs the question why the Genesis references were thought necessary in the first place. The most plausible explanation is that the Genesis allusions reinforce, now with the authority of Scripture, the expectation that a structured sense of church order supports the instructions given to Timothy. In this case, it relates directly to the behaviour expected for the church's gatherings, where it might be assumed people prayed and read Scripture. Now remember what Scripture says, the author reminds Timothy and the audience. The community in worship reads and hears Scripture, but Scripture now arcs back to support the writer's view of a woman's place and behaviour in the community, at least as this relates to the specific circumstances of church gatherings. Hence, the Genesis material is more than merely illustrative, it has instructive force.

The second stage of the allusion continues in 2:14 with the distinction between Adam who was not deceived and Eve who was and became a transgressor. Again, a verbal connection in 2:14 (ἠπατήθη) and Gen. 3:13 (ἠπάτησεν) links the pastoral argument to the Genesis text, but here the entire temptation and transgression of Eve in Gen. 3:1-7 comes to the fore. It is her activity in Gen. 3:6 that supposedly determines the woman's role in church assemblies, although Adam, too, eats of the fruit. Here the priority of the woman's deception, or so goes the interpretation, is identified negatively to reinforce yet again her position relative to Adam and to direct her proper behaviour in the community's gatherings. She does not have priority in the order of creation, but she does have priority in terms of deception and transgression.[19] At the very least, this type of social and behavioural

---

17   Bassler, *1 Timothy, 2 Timothy, and Titus*, p.60; Raymond F. Collins, *1 & 2 Timothy and Titus* (NTLS; Louisville and London: Westminster/John Knox, 2002), p.70; Quinn and Wacker, *First and Second Letters*, p.226. A similar principle appears in Rom. 4:9-11.

18   Aageson, *Paul, the Pastoral Epistles, and the Early Church*, pp.19–25.

19   Towner, *Commentary*, p.894. Note also the argument by Ben Witherington III (*Letters and Homilies*, pp.217–30) regarding the social, rhetorical, and status implica-

ordering is consistent with the hierarchical structure of things represented in the household of God in 1 Timothy. Immediately following this text in 3:1-13, the instruction concerns the appropriate behaviour and qualities for overseers and deacons. Throughout the letter, the pastoral instruction presumes a particular way of thinking about roles and behaviours and how they are to be determined. The author's instruction and use of Scripture in 2:8-14 is consistent with that broader concern for order and structure, perhaps seen most especially in the face of community controversy.

First Tim. 2:15 has long perplexed interpreters,[20] but given its context in the current discussion it is hard to imagine the instructions (2:9-12) and the scriptural references (2:13-14) not shaping the reception of these words. To be sure, saviour language and by implication the notion of salvation are important in the Pastoral Epistles,[21] but the use of the term τεκνογονία also seems to echo τέξῃ τέκνα in Gen. 3:16. The bearing of children figures prominently in the punishment narrative of Gen. 3:15-16 and in the life of women in the Greco-Roman household, two domains that stand close at hand in 2:15.[22] As these domains interface, the punishment of pain in childbirth, evidence of the fall, serves in the background as the prelude to salvation which is expected through childbirth, if they remain in faith and love and holiness, with modesty. The punishment of pain in childbirth, echoing in the background of the text, is juxtaposed with salvation and child-bearing. This complex of echoes and images might reasonably be thought to reinforce the instruction to women in 2:9-12 and their proper role in local community gatherings, while at the same time holding out the expectation of salvation for those who exhibit the proper behaviour.[23] But once again, it is difficult to make the case that the author is also endorsing a more general principle regarding the proper roles and behaviours that should apply at all times and in all places to women in church assemblies. This claim, however, became easier to make once the original circumstances receded into the background and the letter moved towards canonization.

tions of the controversy he claims provides the context for the discussion. If he is correct, this makes the specific circumstances for the instructions and the allusions to the Genesis material in 2:12-15 highly determinative for the meaning of the text and guards against the inclination to universalize its message.

20   For a discussion of some of the various interpretations, see Stanley E. Porter, 'What Does it Mean to be "Saved by Childbirth" (1 Timothy 2:15)?', *JSNT* 49 (1993), pp.87–102.

21   For a discussion of saviour language, see Aageson, *Paul, the Pastoral Epistles, and the Early Church*, pp.58–9, 97–8.

22   Towner leaves open the possibility that the allusion does not extend to 2:15, *Commentary*, pp.894–6.

23   There are some peculiarities in the text such as the person represented by the two verbs σωθήσεται and μείνωσιν and the possibility as some have argued that the giving birth is to Christ who is the saviour. The latter point seems rather unlikely given the context of the argument.

Gen. 1:27, 1:29, 1:31, 2:18, 2:20-25, 3:6-7, 9:3 in 1 Tim. 4:3-4

These verses in 1 Timothy clearly reflect some type of ascetic opposition
to which the author feels compelled to respond, and he distinguishes the
opponents from those who believe and know the truth. Unlike those who
know the truth,[24] the opponents, here described in unflattering terms (4:1-2),
forbid marriage and abstain from certain foods.[25] Whether the opponents
are motivated by a type of proto-Gnostic theology or by a particular interpretation of the Jewish law,[26] the author responds with a strong affirmation
of the goodness of creation, from which nothing is to be rejected if it is
received in thanksgiving.[27] The theological opposition in 4:3-4 is clear and
may in fact portend later Christian debates with the Gnostics, but here it is
confined to a few brief comments in which the goodness of God's creation
and marriage are defended. It might be the case that the use of Genesis in
4:3-4 is tailored to refute the actual interpretation of Genesis put forward
by the opponents in support of their views and practice.[28] In that case, we
might assume their emphasis was not on the goodness of creation but the
fallen character of creation and human relationships. Abstinence from these
things, or so the argument would go, ought to be observed in order to attain
or preserve a state of purity and righteousness.

Into his refutation of these opponents and their misguided ways, the
author introduces the imagery from Genesis, especially the repeated references to the goodness of creation culminating in Gen. 1:31 with the claim
that everything that was created is good (καλόν) and in Gen. 1:29 and 9:3
with the claim that all plants and fruit and living things shall be food for the
humans whom God also created. Likewise, echoing in the background is the
imagery that the male and the female are paired with each other in creation
(1:27, 2:18, 20-25, 3:6-7). Hence, neither food nor marriage ought to be
rejected outright, as the opponents apparently claim. As indicated above,
the author writing for those who understand the truth sees the biblical
story as presenting a view of creation that provides instructive value for the
present controversy. In this case, the value of Scripture pertains directly to
the refutation of the opponents and their renunciation of certain foods and
marriage.

Unlike the scriptural allusions in 2:13-14 where the imagery pertains
to temptation, deception, and transgression, the allusions in 4:3-4 refer to
the goodness of creation, eating what God instructs, and marriage. Taken
together, the writer of 1 Timothy refers to various sections of the first three
chapters of Genesis, and at the same time alludes to the two narrative centres
of this part of the text, creation and disobedience. The author in both cases,

---

24   See Aageson, *Paul, the Pastoral Epistles, and the Early Church*, pp.28–31, 63,
65.

25   Cf. the discussion in 1 Cor. 8:1–11:1.

26   Aageson, *Paul, the Pastoral Epistles, and the Early Church*, p.65.

27   Cf. Rom. 14:2-6, 14, 1 Cor. 7:8-9, 10.25-30, Col. 2:16.

28   Towner, *Commentary*, p.899.

however, shapes the Genesis material to support the argument at hand and does not seemingly use it simply to generate abstract principles separated from specific circumstances.

Ephesians

Gen. 1:26 in Eph. 4:24

In 4:17, the writer of Ephesians, building on the discussion of unity and diversity in 4:1-16, appeals to his readers to turn their ways from darkness, ignorance, licentiousness, and futility. Put away your former lives and be renewed in the spirit of your minds, exhorts the writer. It is in this context that the author writes: '... and to put on the new person who was created in the likeness of God (τὸν κατὰ Θεὸν κτισθέντα) in righteousness and holiness of the truth' (4:24).[29] This unmistakable allusion to humans being created in the likeness or image of God in Gen. 1:26-27 conveys a sense of the new person that is put on through life in Christ. The implication is that in Christ and in obedience to him the likeness of God, realized in the creation of humanity, is restored in a new way and the blot of human ignorance and transgression is put away.[30] The new person, now fulfilled in Christ, reflects the image of God in the first creation, and it is the imagery of the Genesis narrative that conjures up for the reader a connection between life in Christ and the goodness of humankind as the handiwork of God. This is not a mechanistic restoration of creation, but rather the followers of Christ are called to reflect the image of God through obedience to divine will.[31] Through Christ who joins together the body, the church, and through individual lives patterned on the truth of Christ and God's will, the true righteousness and holiness of human beings prevail.[32] The imagery of the first creation echoes through the author's appeal to his readers to reflect the new person in Christ.

Gen. 2:24 in Eph. 5:31 (quotation)

Although a virtual quotation of Gen. 2:24 appears in 5:31, the literary context for the reference includes 5:21-33, and echoes of the quotation are heard at least as early as 5:28. The quotation only varies from the LXX with the omission of αὐτοῦ following πατέρα and μητέρα and with the substitution of ἀντὶ τούτου for ἕνεκεν τούτου. The omissions do not substantially change the sense of the reference, and the meaning of the substitution is virtually interchangeable with the original reading. Both can mean 'for this reason' or 'on account of this', but if Thielman is correct the change signals

---

29   See also Col. 3:10.
30   Andrew T. Lincoln, *Ephesians* (WBC, 42; Dallas: Word Books, 1990), p.287.
31   Cf. 2 Cor. 5:17, Gal. 6:15, and also 1 Cor. 15:42-45, 47-48.
32   Lincoln, *Ephesians*, p.288.

that the author intended the phrase to carry meaning in light of his own argument about the members of the body of Christ and the two persons becoming one flesh.[33]

What is most striking about 5:21-33 is the interweaving of the author's claims about the relationship between husbands and wives in marriage and the relationship between Christ and the church. In 5:21, the author launches into his discourse, which includes marital relationships, ecclesio-logical claims, and Christological analogies, with the actual citation of Gen 2:24 appearing late in the discussion. The text begins with an appeal to be subject to one another in reverence for Christ (5:21), followed immediately by the provocative claim that wives are to be subject to their husbands for the husband is the head of the wife, just as Christ is the head of the church. As the church is subject to Christ so by analogy the wife is to be subject to her husband (5:22-24). The author asserts further that as the husband loves his wife so Christ has loved the church and gave himself for her (5:25). For this reason, the husband should love his wife as his own body for he who loves his wife loves his own body. No one hates his own flesh but cares for it as Christ cares for the church, because we are members of his body (5:28-30). At this point, the writer cites the text from Genesis (5:31) and follows it with the claim that this mystery is great and that he speaks about the relationship between Christ and the church (5:32). One final time, he returns to the marital relationship claiming that each husband ought to love his wife and each wife ought to respect her husband (5:33).[34] A text from Gen. 2:24 about husbands leaving their fathers and mothers and becoming one flesh with their wives contributes by analogy to an image of Christ with his church, and at the same time the Christological and ecclesiological context of the discussion shades the author's use of the Genesis text. The specific Christological emphasis is on Christ and the church being in union, being one.

While σάρξ appears in the Genesis citation and in 5:29, the author uses σῶμα in 5:23, 28, and 30. Though the two terms are largely equivalent in the text,[35] the use of σῶμα in 5:30 reflects the distinctively Pauline notion of the church being a body with many members. Whether Christ is the head of the church or the church is the body of Christ, the Christological interplay with the Genesis text is unmistakable. Following the quotation, the author makes the distinctive claim that this is a great mystery. The term μυστήριον in all likelihood refers to the deep mystery of the union of Christ and the church rather than some special hermeneutic of Scripture.[36] As Caragounis

---

33   Frank S. Thielman, '*Ephesians*', in G. K. Beale and D. A. Carson (eds), *Commentary on the New Testament Use of the Old Testament* (Grand Rapids, Michigan: Baker Academic, 2007), p.827.

34   Cf. outline of the argument by Andrew T. Lincoln, 'The Use of the OT in Ephesians', *JSNT* 14 (1982), p.16.

35   Ibid., p.31.

36   J. Paul Sampley, '*And the Two Shall Become One Flesh': A Study of Traditions*

describes μυστήριον: '... the author here no doubt refers it primarily to the union of Christ and the Church. But this union is not a great *secret* for it has been openly proclaimed; it is a deep mystery, unsearchable and inexplicable, for it involves, in some sense, the union of God and man (sic).'[37] To leave no doubt, the author makes explicit that he is speaking about Christ and the church (ἐγὼ δὲ λέγω, 5:32b), and in so doing echoes the rather common Pauline practice of verbally signalling an interpretation or clarification of Scripture following an actual quotation.[38]

Whether the author of Ephesians is Paul or someone else writing in his name, the discussion in 5:21-33 seems to echo various images from 1 Cor. 6:12-20; 11:2-6, and 2 Cor. 11:2: marital union, the relationship between husbands and wives, and the believers' bodies as members of Christ.[39] This suggests that there is a Pauline tradition that precedes the writing of Ephesians and that perhaps even influences the character of the discussion in the Deutero-Pauline text. If Sampley is correct, there is in fact an identifiable complex of terms and ideas regarding marriage in the undisputed Pauline letters that draw on the *hieros gamos* of Christ and the church and that relate to one another and to Eph. 5:21-33. Hence, the language of the head, body, and members quite naturally connects to the language of Gen. 2:24 and to the interplay between the relationship of husbands and wives and the relationship of Christ with his church.[40]

Whether we side with Sampley, who argues that Gen. 2:24 is critical to the whole of the discussion in 5:21-33, or with Lincoln, who claims that Gen. 2:24 relates to both marriage and Christ's relationship with the church but only in verses 28-33, the important point is that the Old Testament text informs the Ephesians argument before it is actually quoted.[41] It is not uncommon in Paul's use of Scripture for a direct quotation to inform or echo through the discussion before or after its actual appearance in the epistolary text.[42] Moreover, as appears to be the case in this text, the citation is instrumental in the formulation of the argument. Regardless of whether the scriptural text comes to the author directly or in connection with some emerging complex of prior traditions, it brings to the epistolary discussion

in Ephesians 5.21-33 (SNTSMS 16; Cambridge: Cambridge University Press, 1971), pp.95–6 and Lincoln, 'OT,' p.32.

37   Chrys C. Caragounis, *The Ephesian Mysterion: Meaning and Content* (ConBNT, 8; Lund: CWK Gleerup, 1977), p.30.

38   See the discussion by Sampley, *'And the Two shall become One Flesh'*, p.89. Cf. e.g. Rom. 9:6-7, 11:4, 15:3, 1 Cor. 9:9-10, 14:21, Gal. 3:16.

39   Sampley, *'And the Two shall become One Flesh,'* pp.77–85, 97–100. Cf. also 1 Tim. 2:8-15 and Col. 3:18-19.

40   Ibid., p.84.

41   Ibid., pp.90, 146–7 and Lincoln, 'OT', p.35.

42   See the discussion of this in my dissertation, *Paul's Use of Scripture: A Comparative Study of Biblical Interpretation in Early Palestinian Judaism and the New Testament with Special Reference to Romans 9-11*, Oxford University, Oxford, 1983, pp.86–96.

both authority and conceptual value. In this case, both the marital union and the claims about the relationship between Christ and the church are elaborated in light of the assertion that the 'two shall become one flesh'. But it is also the case that the discussion reflects aspects of the Haustafel and the hierarchical structure of the Greco-Roman household with their emphases on proper order and relationships.[43] In short, there is a fascinating interplay between Gen. 2:24 and certain Greco-Roman social structures in the formulation of the argument in Eph. 5:21-33, but there are clear echoes in the text from Romans and the Corinthian correspondence as well. Still it is the relationship of Christ with his church here linked to Gen. 2:24 that provides the most striking feature of the writer's use of Scripture in this text.

Colossians

Gen. 1:26-27 in Col. 3:10

Similar to the reference in Eph. 4:24,[44] Col. 3:10 (κατ' εἰκόνα τοῦ κτίσαντος αὐτόν) clearly reflects the image of God language from Gen. 1:26-27 (καὶ ἐποίησεν ὁ θεὸς τὸν ἄνθρωπον κατ' εἰκόνα θεοῦ ἐποίησεν αὐτόν ...LXX). This follows immediately the statement in 3:9 about having taken off the old self with its practices and behaviours. The contrast is made with the new self that is being renewed in knowledge according to the image of the one who created it.[45] The old self and the new self each relate to different ways of living with the former being spelt out in 3:5-9 and the latter in 3:12-17.[46] Through baptism in Christ, the life of the new self is received and renewed; and, at the same time, the writer exhorts the readers to conform their pattern of life to that befitting those who live in the knowledge of Christ and bear the image of the creator.[47] Implicit in the Christological argument of this text is the eschatological tension between the 'now' where exhortation is necessary and the 'not yet' where in Christ the distinctions between Greek and Jew, circumcised and uncircumcised, Barbarian, Scythian, slave and free disappear.[48]

Perhaps most importantly for our purposes is the question of how pronounced the Adam/Christ imagery is in this text. While the allusion to

---

43   Lincoln, *Ephesians*, pp.364–5.

44   In addition to Eph. 4:24, cf. also 2 Cor. 5:17, Gal. 6:15, and perhaps also Rom. 8:19-23 for new creation language and imagery.

45   Jerry L. Sumney, *Colossians: A Commentary* (NTL; Louisville and London: Westminster/John Knox Press, 2008), pp.202.

46   It is unclear if the author intends the statements about husbands, wives, children, and slaves in 3:18-25 to be included in the pattern of life associated with putting on the new self.

47   See Sumney, *Colossians*, pp.201–2.

48   Gal 3:28.

Gen. 1:26-27 is unmistakable,[49] a developed Adam/Christ Christology is not and at most may be only implicit.[50] However, this question is not simply a matter of the author's intention or the character of the text itself, it also raises the question of what any given reader or audience member might have heard in the text. It is probably safe to say that the author did not see the new self imprinted with the image of God in Christ to be a mere restoration of the original creation. Clearly there is a connection to the creation recounted in Genesis 1, but putting on the new self is more than a mere repetition of it. In that regard, this text seems to echo the other examples of new creation in the Pauline corpus and links it to the early church's tradition of connecting creation and redemption.

Conclusion

Among the Deutero-Pauline letters, the use of scriptural material, especially the frequency of explicit citations, is certainly more limited than in, for example, Romans or Galatians. In fact, much of the Genesis material in the Deutero-Paulines, limited as it is, clearly falls into the realm of allusion or echo. This should not suggest that these letters necessarily place less authority on Scripture than the Pauline corpus as a whole. Outside the Hauptbriefe, the character and quantity of direct quotations in the other undisputed Paulines diminishes substantially, just as in the case of the Deutero-Pauline letters.[51] Moreover, in 2 Timothy, we have the most forthright statement about Scripture in the entire body of Pauline letters. The sacred writings are God breathed, able to instruct for salvation, and they are useful for teaching, reproof, correction, and training in righteousness (2 Tim. 3:15-16). Regardless of whether these sacred writings refer just to the Jewish Scriptures or also more broadly to the emerging apostolic tradition, it is evident in this case that these writings have clear functional authority.[52] This is not to deny, however, that in the case of the Pastoral letters we can begin to see already an emerging Pauline tradition that is coming to function authoritatively alongside Scripture.[53] Even here, however, it should not be concluded that Scripture and Pauline tradition were somehow set against each other

---

49   James D. G. Dunn, *The Epistle to the Colossians and to Philemon: A Commentary on the Greek Text* (NIGTC; Grand Rapids: Eerdmans/Carlisle: Paternoster, 1996), p.221.

50   Sumney, *Colossians*, p.203. Cf. Rom. 5:12-21, 1 Cor. 15:21-23, 45-49.

51   As we see in Romans and Galatians, much of the explicit use of scriptural material relates to questions of righteousness, faith, and more generally to matters of Gentile inclusion in the community of faith.

52   It is difficult to sustain the view in light of this text that the Pastoral letters represent a depreciation of Scripture or foreshadow a type of Marcionism. For a refutation of this view, see B. Paul Wolfe, 'Scripture in the Pastoral Epistles: PreMarcion Marcionism,' *PRS* 16, 1 (1989), 5–16.

53   Aageson, *Paul, the Pastoral Epistles, and the Early Church*, pp.90–102.

or inconsistent in the Deutero-Pauline epistles.[54] The authority of Paul as apostle of Christ and teacher carries the authority of Scripture properly understood, in this case Genesis, into its new context.

54   Ibid., pp.138–9. The point made here about the Apostolic Fathers may be germane in this context as well.

Chapter 8

GENESIS IN HEBREWS

Susan Docherty

Introduction

Texts from Genesis are presented and used in Hebrews in a number of different and interesting ways. There are three definite citations (Heb. 4:4; 6:14; 11:18), one probable citation (Heb. 11:21), and a further two passages (Heb. 7:1-2; 11:5) which, although close to a citation, are usually classified as extended verbal allusions or 'virtual' citations. At least nineteen allusions to Genesis also occur, echoing both individual verses and longer narratives. In all cases, the author follows a text identical or very close to the standard Septuagint reading. The references to Genesis are often introduced in support of texts drawn from elsewhere in Scripture rather than functioning as primary quotations, but they still play an important part in establishing some of the letter's central theological arguments and in shaping its exhortatory sections. This investigation will give particular attention to the author's exegetical methods, which locate him very firmly within a first-century Jewish context.

Genesis 1–2 in Heb. 1:2-3 (cf. Heb. 11:3)

One of the first statements made in Hebrews about the son is that it was through him that God created the world, a view reflected also elsewhere in the New Testament (e.g. Jn 1:3, 10; 1 Cor. 8:6; Col. 1:16). There are no definite echoes of the Genesis creation narratives in the prologue, though, and it is probable that Heb. 1:2-3 owes more to the wisdom tradition than to direct allusion to Genesis: the book of Wisdom states that wisdom was present with God at creation (Wis. 9:9; cf. Prov. 8:22-31), and praises wisdom in language very similar to that used of the son here, describing it as an emanation of God's glory and a reflection of eternal light (Wis. 7:25-6; cf. Heb. 1:3). Contemporary Jewish interest in the role in creation of an intermediary is attested by Philo, who develops the idea of the logos as God's creative principle, and even writes of the involvement of God's son in creation (*Conf. Ling.* 63).[1] This kind of speculation arises directly from a

---

1   For further references, see: P. Ellingworth, *The Epistle to the Hebrews* (NIGCT; Grand Rapids, Michigan: Eerdmans/Carlisle: Paternoster Press, 1993), p.96; M. E. Isaacs,

close reading of the scriptural text, with the plural pronouns and verb forms of Gen. 1:26 suggesting the presence of two creators. The significance of the theme of creation within Hebrews should not be overlooked: in addition to the citation of Gen. 2:2 in Heb. 4:4, there is an allusion to creation by God's word in Heb. 11:3 and a further possible allusion to the creation narrative in Heb. 6:7. Creation imagery also features in several of the psalms cited in chapter 1 (Pss. 102 [LXX 101] and 104 [LXX 103]).

Gen. 2:2 in Heb. 4:4

In this first direct citation from Genesis in Hebrews, the author follows the standard Septuagint text exactly, but reproduces only part of the verse. Selective citation is an exegetical technique widely employed in Hebrews, allowing the author to focus attention on the particular word or phrase which is central to his argument, in this case the concept of God's 'rest'. The vague introductory formula used: 'For he has spoken somewhere of the seventh day in this way...' is also characteristic of Hebrews (cf. Heb. 2:6; 3:7), perhaps suggesting that detail about the human authors of the scriptures is insignificant since they are regarded as being spoken ultimately by God (cf. Heb. 1:1).

Gen. 2:2 is introduced at this point in order to support the author's interpretation of Psalm 95 (LXX 94). Ellingworth has noted that the citations from Genesis in Hebrews rarely stand alone, but are almost all used as secondary texts in connection with other scriptural passages.[2] These two texts can be linked because in the Septuagint (although not in the Hebrew original) both include a common word for 'rest', the verb κατέπαυσεν in Gen. 2:2, and the related noun κατάπαυσις in Psalm 95 (94):11. This technique of catchword linking or *gezera shawa* is a feature of contemporary Jewish scriptural exegesis and is employed elsewhere in Hebrews (see the discussion of Melchizedek below; cf. the juxtaposition of citations concerning the words 'son' and 'angels' in 1:5-7). It depends on both a very close reading of every word of the biblical texts and an understanding of Scripture as a coherent whole, allowing for the use of originally separate passages to interpret one another. In this case, the fact that Psalm 95 (94):11 speaks of '*my* rest' means the author has to search for another text about *God* resting. Both the Genesis text and the psalm (v.9) also refer to God's works, thus providing a further catchword link between them, one which is picked up in the interpretative comment that '...whoever enters God's rest also ceases from his *works* just as God rested from his...' (Heb. 4:10). The references to God as creator in Ps. 95 (94):5, just before the verses actually cited in Hebrews, may also have contributed to the establishment of a connection between these two passages.

Sacred Space: An Approach to the Theology of the Epistle to the Hebrews (JSNTSup, 73; Sheffield: JSOT Press, 1992), pp.188ff.
    2   Ellingworth, *Epistle*, p.39.

The author of Hebrews is able to apply Psalm 95 (94) directly to his audience because he interprets verse 11 as meaning that *they* (i.e. the disobedient Israelites of the wilderness generation, Heb. 3:18) will not enter God's rest, but some other people (i.e. his community) *will* enter it (see Heb. 4:6). The psalm therefore becomes a word of promise for his hearers as well as a warning: '...there remains a sabbath rest for the people of God...' (Heb. 4:9). Gen. 2:2 is critical for this part of the author's exegesis, because it enables him to give a specific new meaning to this term 'rest'. He argues that, when it occurs in Psalm 95 (94):11, it cannot be referring to possession of the land of Canaan, its most natural reading, because that had already been achieved by the time the psalm was written (Heb. 4:7-8), and yet the text still holds out the promise of rest to some. It is therefore linked by analogy to God's original act of rest on the seventh day, and interpreted precisely as σαββατισμός or 'sabbath rest'. This word seems to have been coined by the author himself, to refer to '...a heavenly reality, which God entered upon the completion of creation'.[3] This exegesis depends also on a chronological argument (Heb. 4:8–9; cf. Heb. 10:5-10), a method not widely attested in other forms of Jewish exegesis, which on the whole display little interest in the historical background of scriptural passages.[4]

Gen. 1:11 and 3:17-18 in Heb. 6:7-8

These verses offer an agricultural metaphor for divine blessing and judgement. This is a fairly stock image, occurring several times in the Old Testament (e.g. Isa. 5:6; Hos. 10:8), and familiar from both classical Greek[5] and Jewish sources, such as the parables of Jesus, the writings of Philo[6] and rabbinic texts.[7] However, it is probable that Heb. 6:8 contains an intentional allusion to the punishment laid on Adam after he ate the fruit of the forbidden tree, in the reference to the earth being 'cursed' (Gen. 3:17), and in the phrase 'thorns and thistles' (see Gen. 3:18). There may also be an echo of the first creation narrative in the description at Heb. 6:7 of the 'land' bearing 'vegetation' (cf. Gen. 1:11). The author of Hebrews does not use exactly the

3   H. W. Attridge, *The Epistle to the Hebrews* (Hermeneia; Philadelphia: Fortress Press, 1989), pp.123–8.

4   See A. Goldberg, 'The Rabbinic View of Scripture', in P. R. Davies and R. T. White (eds), *A Tribute to Geza Vermes: Essays on Jewish and Christian Literature and History* (Sheffield: Sheffield Academic Press, 1990), pp.153–66.

5   J. Moffatt, *A Critical and Exegetical Commentary on the Epistle to the Hebrews* (ICC; Edinburgh: T&T Clark, 1924), p.81, notes particularly Euripides, *Hecuba* 592 and Quintilian, *Institutio Oratoria* 5.11.24.

6   See especially *Her.* 204; cf. *Spec.* 1:246; *Leg.* 3:248; and *Agr.* 17.

7   A. Vanhoye has drawn together some relevant examples in 'Heb. 6.7-8 et le mashal rabbinique', in W.C. Weinrich (ed.), *The New Testament Age: Essays in Honour of Bo Reicke* (Macon, GA: Mercer University Press, 1984), Vol.2, pp.527–32.

same Greek words as the Septuagint in describing the land as 'cursed' or as 'bringing forth' vegetation or thorns and thistles, so the allusion to Genesis is fairly fleeting. It is nevertheless an example of his use of Scripture to reinforce the exhortatory as well as doctrinal sections of the letter.

Gen. 22:16-17 in Heb. 6:13-14

This is the first of several discussions of Abraham in Hebrews (see also chapters 7 and 11; cf. 2:16), indicating his great significance to the author. The focus is particularly on the promise made to Abraham of numerous descendants, which is not only cited here, but also alluded to in Heb. 11:12, 17-18. This is of more concern to the author than the promise of entry into the land of Canaan, with which it is usually associated in Genesis, because he has already transferred the hope of this inheritance to the expectation of future 'rest' in the heavenly Jerusalem (Heb. 4:9-10; cf. 12:22). These verses include both a direct citation of part of Gen. 22:17 and an allusion to God 'swearing by himself' when he made that promise (Gen. 22:16), taken from the narrative of the binding of Isaac, referred to again later in Heb. 11:17. Parallels to this explanation of why God needed to swear an oath are to be found in Philo (e.g. *Leg.* 3:203-7; *Sacr.* 91; *Abr.* 273; *Somn.* 1:12).

Gen. 14:17-20 in Heb. 7:1-3

Hebrews chapter 7 has attracted considerable scholarly interest because of its use of Melchizedek in a way unparalleled in the New Testament, as a figure of Jesus' priesthood (Heb. 5:6, 10; 6:20; 7:11, 15, 17). Melchizedek was probably an early Canaanite king-priest, and is a very minor scriptural character, appearing only in Gen. 14:17-20 and Ps. 110 (109):4, but these brief references generated extensive later speculation about him. The writings of Philo and Josephus,[8] for example, show the development of a variety of post-biblical Melchizedek traditions which are reflected also in later rabbinic and early Christian literature.[9] The possibility that Hebrews may be drawing on some of these traditions, or even be an attempt to refute them, was further strengthened when a text discovered at Qumran, *11QMelchizedek*, was found to present Melchizedek as a heavenly being with an eschatological role which includes freeing people from their iniquities (II.6).[10] He is not explicitly

---

8   Philo interprets Melchizedek as an allegory of reason in *Leg.* 3:79-82; for Josephus' treatment of him, see *War* 6:438 and *Ant.* 1:180.

9   A full survey of these sources was undertaken by F. L. Horton, *The Melchizedek Tradition: A Critical Examination of the Sources to the Fifth Century A.D. and in the Epistle to the Hebrews* (SNTSMS, 30; Cambridge: Cambridge University Press, 1976).

10   Extensive discussion of *11QMelchizedek* is to be found in: M. de Jonge and A. S. van der Woude, '*11QMelchizedek* and the New Testament', *NTS* 12 (1966), pp.301–26; J. A. Fitzmyer, 'Further Light on Melchizedek From Qumran Cave 11', *JBL* 86 (1967), pp.25–41; and P. J. Kobelski, *Melchizedek and Melchiresaʿ* (CBQMS, 10; Washington: Catholic Biblical Association of America Press, 1981).

called a priest in this work, however, and the emphasis is on his judgemental functions rather than his self-sacrifice, so most scholars conclude that Qumran does not provide the direct source for the author's christology. The letter, does, however, clearly reflect these contemporary Jewish interpretative currents, including the expectation by some groups of a priestly messiah (see e.g. *1QS* 9:11; cf. *1QSa* 2:12-15; *CD* 5:17-6.1; *4QTest* 9-13; *T.Levi* 18).[11]

The figure of Melchizedek appears very abruptly in Genesis, without introduction or explanation of his role, and then after just three verses disappears, never to be mentioned again in the Pentateuch. This leads most modern commentators to regard Gen. 14:18-20 as a later interpolation into the original narrative, perhaps aimed at legitimating the right of David to collect tribute from the other tribes of Israel.[12] The author of Hebrews finds his answer to the exegetical issues surfaced by this passage through connecting it with another text, Ps. 110 (109):4, which has been previously cited (at Heb. 5:6; cf. the allusions in Heb. 5:10; 6:20), and which is really the main text under discussion in this section of Hebrews.[13] Rabbinic interpretation commonly introduces a second or enriching verse to support the exegesis of a base text, and the use of one scriptural text to interpret another in Hebrews has already been noted. As in chapter 4, a passage from Genesis is again linked to a psalm. It is also a particularly characteristic feature of this author's exegetical method to cite or allude to the same text more than once (e.g. the double citation of the 'new covenant' passage from Jeremiah in Hebrews 8 and 10; cf. the allusion in Heb. 1:14 to Psalm 104 (103):4 cited at Heb. 1:7). There is nothing surprising about the author bringing together the only two scriptural passages which mention Melchizedek, but he is not simply juxtaposing two verses which feature a single word in common on the basis of *gezera shawa*: rather he reads the Genesis passage in the light of the Psalm. So the fact that Ps. 110 (109):4 attributes an eternal priesthood to the order of Melchizedek leads him to make the same assumption of the Melchizedek of the Genesis text (Heb. 7:3). He further claims that this Melchizedek is '...without father or mother or genealogy, and has neither beginning of days nor end of life...' (Heb. 7:3). An argument from silence seems to be at work here, with the lack of expected reference in Genesis to Melchizedek's origins or ancestors, a matter of great importance for the establishment of priestly credentials, bringing about the interpretation in

11   A useful overview of this subject is provided by A. J. B. Higgins, 'The Priestly Messiah', *NTS* 13 (1966–7), pp.211–39; see also Attridge, *Hebrews*, pp.97–103.

12   See e.g. G. von Rad, *Genesis: A Commentary* (London: SCM, 1963), pp.174–6.

13   Most commentators take the view that Ps. 109.4 LXX is the base text: see e.g. Attridge, *Hebrews*, p.187; Ellingworth, *Epistle*, p.350; C. R. Koester, *Hebrews* (AB; New York: Doubleday, 2001), p.335; W. L. Lane, *Hebrews* (2 vols; WBC; Dallas: Word, 2000), Vol.1 p.159. For the alternative position, that Gen. 14:17-20 is the base text, see e.g. F. Schröger, *Der Verfasser des Hebräerbriefes als Schriftausleger* (BU, 4. Regensburg: Pustet, 1968).

Hebrews.[14] The author may also have been influenced by the text of Ps. 110 (109):3, in which God declares to the Davidic king: 'From the womb, before Morning-star *I* brought you forth...' If mysterious birth is true of the one who is a 'priest after the order of Melchizedek', then such origins could be attributed by analogy also to the original Melchizedek. Although it has often been suggested that a traditional hymn may underlie all or part of Heb. 7:1-3, there seems, therefore, no convincing reason to suppose that the author's interpretation could not have been derived directly from a close reading of Gen. 14:17-20 and Psalm 110 (109), or from traditional exegesis of these texts.[15]

This is the first of several examples in Hebrews where a text from Genesis is reproduced by means of an extended allusion rather than as a direct citation.[16] Although the Genesis text is not formally quoted, these verses clearly offer more than a brief echo of it, thereby illustrating the fluidity of the categories 'citation' and 'allusion'. The figure of Melchizedek is described here using a combination of the author's own words, phrases taken directly from the scriptural text, and information drawn from the Genesis narrative but not reproduced exactly. The author does, however, remain very close to the wording and sequence of the biblical source, a characteristic of other contemporary Jewish interpreters.[17] Summarising the passage in this way enables him to include only those elements of it which are directly relevant to his argument, whilst still retaining scriptural authority for his interpretation. Notable selective omissions are the lack of reference to Melchizedek bringing out bread and wine (Gen. 14:18) and to the content of his blessing of Abraham (Gen. 14:19-20). This leads to a foregrounding of the person of Melchizedek in Hebrews, and a corresponding diminution of the significance and honour of Abraham.[18] In Hebrews, for example, it is as if Melchizedek alone made a purposeful decision to come out and meet Abraham after the battle. In the Genesis account, however, the King of Sodom, accompanied by Melchizedek, comes out to meet and offer hospitality to the conquering hero Abraham, and the words of Melchizedek's blessing exalt Abraham. The fact that these details are largely omitted in Hebrews helps to reverse this picture and emphasises the role of Melchizedek, as do the author's interpretative comments, which focus on Melchizedek's greatness, on his resemblance

14   See e.g. R. P. Gordon, *Hebrews* (Sheffield: Sheffield Academic Press, 2000), p.81.

15   Ellingworth (*Epistle*, pp.352–4) offers a useful summary and evaluation of the main scholarly proposals regarding the possible *Vorlage* of Heb. 7:1-3.

16   Most commentators (e.g. Attridge, *Hebrews*, p.188) agree that this is an allusion or paraphrase, but some classify it as a citation, e.g. C. Spicq, *L'Épître aux Hébreux* (2 vols; Paris: Libraire Lecoffre, 1952–3), Vol.1, p.331.

17   See e.g. A. Samely, *The Interpretation of Speech in the Pentateuch Targums: A Study of Method and Presentation in Targumic Exegesis* (Tübingen: Mohr Siebeck, 1992), pp.179–84.

18   This point is noted by some commentators; see particularly Koester, *Hebrews*, p.347.

to the son of God, and on his receiving a tithe of the spoils from Abraham (Heb. 7:3-4).

This section of Hebrews provides a really interesting example of the numerous exegetical methods which can be applied to a scriptural text to subtly shift its meaning. So, the idea of Melchizedek's priesthood is singled out for special stress here, and attention drawn to it immediately, because the designation 'priest of God most high' is used earlier in Hebrews than in Genesis. The term 'the patriarch' is then applied to Abraham in Heb. 7:4; this is a perfectly apt description of Abraham, but it is not drawn from this Genesis text. It is introduced here because the author wishes to argue that the descendants of that patriarch are included in his action of paying tithes to Melchizedek (Heb. 7:5-10). Making apparently minor changes in wording can also be employed as an exegetical technique. Significantly, the language of Genesis about the division of the spoils after the battle is made more formal in Hebrews, which reads that 'Abraham apportioned (ἐμέρισεν) a tenth of everything...' to Melchizedek (Heb. 7:2); contrast the Septuagint version: 'And he gave (ἔδωκεν) to him a tenth of everything' (Gen. 14:20). The use of the verb ἐμέρισεν allows the author of Hebrews to link this narrative more effectively to the ensuing interpretation about the system of priestly tithing. When this part of the text is repeated in Heb. 7:4, he uses ἔδωκεν; this suggests that he was familiar with the standard Septuagint reading, and indeed concerned to render it accurately, but deliberately chose to add the formal connotation of 'apportioning' in his initial reference to the incident.

A further exegetical method at work here is the precise specification of words in the scriptural source which may appear ambiguous, especially when they are removed from their original context.[19] The final sentence of the Septuagint version of Gen. 14:20, for example, could appear indeterminate: 'And he gave him a tenth of everything.' The author of Hebrews specifies both the subject and object of this sentence, as Abraham and Melchizedek respectively, and also defines 'everything' as 'the spoils' of the battle with the kings (Heb. 7:4). These interpretations all make good sense of the Genesis text, and are to be found also in some contemporary Jewish sources such as Josephus (*Ant.* 1:181; cf. *1QapGen.* 22:17).[20] The meaning of the word δέκατος (tenth) is similarly narrowed down to mean 'tithe' in a formal, religious sense, so that this point can be developed in what follows (Heb. 7:4-10). This is certainly a legitimate meaning of the noun δέκατος, which is the word used throughout the Septuagint of Leviticus for tithe, but it does not have to bear this ritual connotation; Josephus, for instance, writes of Melchizedek accepting Abraham's *gift* (*Ant.* 1:181), an interpretation

---

19   This explanation of the hermeneutical methods at work in Hebrews is influenced by the work of Alexander Samely, especially his *Rabbinic Interpretation of Scripture in the Mishnah* (Oxford: Oxford University Press, 2002).

20   As noted by e.g. Koester, *Hebrews*, p.341; the targums, however, do not specify Abraham as the subject of the tithing.

which is perhaps designed to stress Abraham's generosity. This may, then, be a New Testament example of an exegetical technique which Samely argues is widespread in rabbinic interpretation, involving: 'Explication of a biblical word form by choosing a meaning from the full range of...semantic possibilities for that word-form.'[21] Further exegesis of the text follows, as the author selects key words or phrases in turn for particular emphasis. Firstly, the name Melchizedek is broken down into two constituent parts, read in the light of their Hebrew meaning, king (Hebrew *melek*) of righteousness (Hebrew *zedeq*). Secondly, the place name Salem is interpreted as meaning peace, because of its similarity in sound and root consonants to the Hebrew word *shalom*. These etymologies are paralleled in Philo (*Leg.* 3:79) and in some of the writings of Josephus (*Ant.* 1:180), although Salem is also identified with Jerusalem, following Ps. 76:2, in other Jewish sources such as most of the targums (cf. Josephus, *War* 6.438). The exegetical technique of giving a new meaning to a proper name by breaking it down into semantic components is also employed by the rabbis.[22] An impressively wide range of interpretative methods are, then, brought to bear on this Genesis text, many of which are applied also elsewhere in Hebrews, to both direct citations and to extended allusions of this kind.

Hebrews chapter 11

Hebrews chapter 11 has always occasioned particular interest because of both its literary form and its theological content, especially its understanding of 'faith'. Numerous scriptural exemplars are presented of the kind of faith the author advocates, which is not explicitly linked to belief in Jesus, but involves looking forward with hope and confidence to a better future (Heb. 11:1, 40).[23] Formal parallels can be drawn firstly with the catalogues of virtues or heroes lists used in Graeco-Roman rhetorical literature to recommend a particular virtue. In his treatise *On Rewards and Punishments*, for instance, Philo includes a discussion of hope which has some similarities in form to Hebrews 11, although it is briefer and lacks specific scriptural exemplars (*Praem.* 11-14; cf. *Virt.* 198-227). Secondly, this chapter is part of the Jewish literary and exegetical tradition of reviewing Israel's history (see e.g. Neh. 9:6-31; Psalms 78, 105, 106, 135, 136; Ezek. 20:5-38; Judith 5; 1 Macc. 2:49-64; 4 Macc. 16:16-23; 18:11-13; Sirach 44-50; Wisdom 10; *CD* cols. II-III; cf. Acts 7). These retellings of the biblical narrative differ in their purposes and emphases, and select a variety of characters and events for inclusion. Hebrews mentions some unexpected figures like Rahab (Heb. 11:31), but omits others who feature prominently in related texts, Phinehas (see e.g. Sir. 44:23-24), for instance, and highly regarded kings such as

---

21   Samely, *Rabbinic Interpretation*, p.401.
22   Samely, *Rabbinic Interpretation*, pp.375-6, 402.
23   The complexities of Heb. 11:1 are fully treated in all major commentaries; see e.g. Attridge, *Hebrews*, pp.307-14, and Ellingworth, *Epistle*, pp.564-7.

Josiah. The relationship between Hebrews 11 and these comparable Jewish sources has been thoroughly investigated by Eisenbaum,[24] who argues that the author is seeking to present significant biblical characters as having lived on the margins of Israel's national history in order to create space for all the members of his audience to identify with salvation history, even those who are gentiles or stand outside Israel in some other way. On any reading of Hebrews 11, however, it is significant that the author wishes to demonstrate that the origins and hopes of his community are in direct continuity with the scriptures.

There have been suggestions that an already extant source may underlie this historical review.[25] Whether or not this is the case, the author's own hand is clearly in evidence in the overall shaping of the chapter and in the exegetical methods employed. As in earlier sections of the letter, texts from Genesis are reproduced by means of selective extended allusion and interpreted in the light of another passage of Scripture, in this case the citation from Hab. 2:3-4 in Heb. 10:37-38. The figures presented in chapter 11 can therefore be taken as exemplars of 'faith' even when this characteristic is not claimed for them in Scripture if another term drawn from Hab. 2:3-4 *is* applied to them – if they are said to be 'righteous', for example, or to 'live'. Associations which a word has in one verse are thus transferred to another biblical location where the same term occurs, demonstrating again the underlying exegetical presupposition of scriptural coherence. The episodes included here are selected to fit the particular understanding of faith given in the introduction. Thus the term 'faith' within the Habakkuk citation could be understood in different ways, but the author of Hebrews excerpts it from its original context and surrounds it with new words so that it can take on a particular meaning: 'Now faith is the assurance of things hoped for, the proof of things not seen...' (Heb. 11:1). This same hermeneutical technique was observed at work also in the exegesis of the term 'rest' in chapters 3–4.

Two further themes in addition to faith appear to be significant within this section of Hebrews: firstly the idea that key biblical characters have been 'testified to' by God. This claim is made specifically of Abel and Enoch (Heb. 11:4-5), but also appears in a more general sense in the introduction and conclusion (Heb. 11:2, 39; cf. 2:6; 3:5; 10:15). Secondly, the choice of exemplars indicates that the author is influenced by the word 'live' from the Habakkuk citation, and may have been prompted by the exegetical question: in what sense can the righteous be said to *live* when in fact everybody dies? He therefore directs attention to righteous scriptural characters who either

---

24   P. M. Eisenbaum, *The Jewish Heroes of Christian History: Hebrews 11 in Literary Context* (SBLDS, 156; Atlanta: Scholars Press, 1997).

25   German commentators are particularly associated with this view; see e.g. O. Michel, *Der Brief an die Hebräer* (KEK, 13; 6th edn; Göttingen: Vandenhoeck & Ruprecht, 1966). The various positions are reviewed by Ellingworth (*Epistle*, pp.558–9), who does not find in favour of a source; Attridge (*Hebrews*, p.307), however, is more persuaded.

do not die, or seem to live on after death in some way. This is reminiscent of a rabbinic exegetical method first identified by Samely, in which a scriptural word is taken as deliberately ruling out its opposite, so that if the text says that the righteous 'live', this is taken literally to exclude the possibility of their dying.[26]

Gen. 4:1-10 in Heb. 11:4

The first biblical character presented in this catalogue is Abel. The author alludes to the narrative of Gen. 4:1-10 without directly citing it, which enables him to highlight only certain parts of the passage, and to interweave his own words with those of Scripture in order to bring about a particular interpretation. There is, for example, no discussion here of what gifts were offered, or of why Abel's sacrifice should have been considered more acceptable than Cain's, questions which were important to other Jewish exegetes. Although he closely follows the structure and wording of the scriptural source, his selective omissions and emphases result in a greater focus on the person of Abel when compared to the Genesis account, which is mainly about Cain. A similar result was noted above in the retelling of the Melchizedek passage. Abel is declared to be 'righteous', a word not present in Genesis 4, but transferred from the Habakkuk citation to him as one who still speaks even though he has died. This presentation of Abel as righteous is in line with other Jewish sources (e.g. *1 En.* 22:7; *T.Abr.* 12:2-3; cf. Mt. 23:35; 1 Jn 3:12),[27] and is a reasonable inference from the scriptural narrative, assuming that God looks with favour upon the offerings of the righteous.[28] The claim that Abel is still speaking after his death is drawn from Gen. 4:10: 'The voice of your brother's blood is crying out to me from the earth...', a text which will be alluded to again later (Heb. 12:24).[29]

Gen. 5:24 in Heb. 11:5

The author next turns his attention to Enoch, and specifically to the scriptural phrase that 'Enoch was not found because God translated him' (Gen. 5:24). Such a mysterious claim, and the fact that it is made only of Enoch amongst Israel's ancestors, has generated considerable exegetical interest.[30]

---

26   Samely, *Rabbinic Interpretation*, pp.278–302. Gordon in particular (*Hebrews*, pp.16–18) notes the importance of this theme, arguing that Hebrews is partly concerned to address the fear of death within the community; cf. J. Swetnam, *Jesus and Isaac: A Study of the Epistle to the Hebrews in the Light of the Aqedah* (AnBib, 94; Rome: Biblical Institute Press 1981), pp.89, 128.

27   On this point see further Eisenbaum, *Jewish Heroes*, p.149.

28   E.g. Prov. 15:8-9.

29   Some commentators, e.g. Eisenbaum (*Jewish Heroes*, p.149) and Lane (*Hebrews*, Vol.2, p.474), interpret this verse to mean that Abel lives because the record of Scripture still 'testifies' to God's approval of his sacrifice.

30   For some of the key references to early Jewish and Christian texts dealing with Enoch, see Attridge, *Hebrews*, p.317.

Again the author reproduces his text with a mixture of citation, allusion, and the interweaving of his own words to link Enoch's 'translation' to his 'faith'. Here he makes his reasoning clear, and once more brings information drawn from one scriptural passage to the interpretation of another: Genesis does not say that Enoch had faith, but it does say that Enoch pleased God (Gen. 5:22); since Scripture has said elsewhere, at Hab. 2:4, that God does not take pleasure in those who do not live by faith, it can be inferred that those with whom God is pleased do have faith (Heb. 11:6). There is, then, something like a catchword link between these texts, but it is made on the basis of words with a similar meaning rather than deriving from an exact verbal correspondence, because Genesis uses the verb εὐαρεστέω and Habakkuk εὐδοκέω. There is also a kind of chronological argument at work in this verse, similar to that discussed above in relation to Heb. 4:7-8, in that it is significant for the interpretation in Hebrews that Genesis states that Enoch pleased God *before* it says that he was translated.

Gen. 6:8-7:1 in Heb. 11:7

The third exemplar, Noah, is also presented through an allusive summary of a Genesis narrative, the account of the building of the ark (Gen. 6:13-22). Gen. 6:9 provides the key to the author's interpretation of this passage, as it reads: 'Noah was a righteous man, being perfect in his generation; Noah was pleasing to God...' (cf. Gen. 7:1). This theme of Noah's righteousness is further developed in early post-biblical Jewish exegesis,[31] and provides a catchword link to the citation from Hab. 2:3-4. Since Noah is explicitly stated in Scripture to be *righteous*, and since he and his household are allowed to *live* when the rest of creation is destroyed by the flood, the attribute of *faith* can also be ascribed to him. The use of the term εὐαρεστέω ('be pleased') also connects Noah with Enoch, clearly demonstrating the textual basis for the author's selection of examples. Unlike Abel and Enoch, Noah is not said to have received divine attestation; in an allusion back to Heb. 11:1, however, there is reference to God informing him about 'things as yet unseen'.

Abraham

Abraham appears to be a particularly significant character for the author of Hebrews. Having already featured in an earlier discussion (Hebrews 6–7), he is now subject to lengthy treatment in the central section of the historical review. The particular prominence of Abraham is illustrated by a comparison with Sirach 44–50 and other early post-biblical texts retelling Israel's history, which, whilst naturally paying due attention to Abraham, usually put more

---

31   See e.g. R. L. Bailey, *Noah, The Person and the Story in History and Tradition* (Columbia: University of South Carolina Press, 1989).

emphasis on the climactic event of the exodus.[32] Hebrews focuses on three key moments in Abraham's life which will be examined in turn below.

Gen. 12:1-8 in Heb. 11:8-9

Hebrews' account of Abraham's call to leave Haran for Canaan paraphrases the Genesis narrative, but includes two words taken directly from Scripture, ἐξῆλθεν ('to go out'), which occurs twice in Heb. 11:8 (cf. Gen. 12:1, 4) and σκηναῖς ('in tents') (Heb. 11:9; cf. 12:9). The introduction also of the verb παρῴκησεν ('he sojourned'), echoing the wider narrative of Abraham's journey to Canaan (e.g. Gen. 17:8; 20:1; 26:3) enables the author to draw out the interpretation that Abraham was not settled in the promised land, but was looking forward to a better homeland (Heb. 11:9-10). As already observed then, he is selective in his paraphrasing of scriptural episodes, and surrounds key scriptural terms with his own words in order to provide a new meaning for them. He also claims insight into Abraham's thinking or motivation (Heb. 11:10), a technique employed widely in various forms of Jewish exegesis, including rewritten Bible and targum and by Josephus.

Gen. 21:1-7 in Heb. 11:11-12

Hebrews next links the birth of Isaac to the theme of faith, and, rather unusually, refers to the role of *Sarah* in his conception. Heb. 11:11 is a difficult verse to translate, as it is not entirely clear whether Sarah or Abraham should be taken as the subject of the sentence, because the phrase εἰς καταβολὴν σπέρματος ('for the sowing of seed') more naturally refers to the male role in conception. The attribution of faith to Sarah also seems problematic, since the Genesis narrative states that she laughed at the idea she would bear a child in her old age (Gen. 18:12). Given, then, that the figure of Abraham is at the centre of this section of chapter 11, many commentators take the verse to mean that he 'together with Sarah' received power to conceive.[33] Attridge suggests that Sarah has been deliberately introduced here to emphasise the communal dimension of faith (cf. Heb. 12:1), so that the audience would realize that they, too, need to be actively involved in responding to God's promises.[34] The important point is that this miraculous conception of Isaac brought about the fulfilment of the key scriptural promise to Abraham of many descendants (Gen. 15:5; 22:17; cf. Heb. 6:14).

Gen. 21:12 and Gen. 22:1-18 in Heb. 11:17-19

The final episode from the life of Abraham recalled in Hebrews is his willingness to offer his son Isaac in sacrifice, retold through both an allusive

32   See Eisenbaum, *Jewish Heroes*, pp.17–60.
33   Detailed discussions of this verse are to be found in all of the major commentaries; see e.g. Ellingworth, *Epistle*, pp.586–9.
34   Attridge, *Hebrews*, p.326.

summary of that narrative (Gen. 22:1-18) and a direct citation of a text spoken on a different occasion, at the banishment of Hagar and Ishmael (Gen. 21:12 in Heb. 11:18). It is perhaps significant that it is a verse containing direct divine speech which is formally cited, as often in Hebrews, whereas narrative events are retold indirectly.[35] The linking of scriptural passages has already been identified as a major exegetical technique of the author. He again employs the technique of surrounding scriptural terms with new co-text to direct their meaning, describing Isaac as Abraham's *only* son (μονογενῆ, Heb. 11:17), when the standard Septuagint version refers to him as Abraham's *beloved* son (ἀγαπητόν, Gen. 22:2).[36] The word μονογενῆ is used at this point in some Jewish sources, such as Josephus (*Ant.* 1:222) and the translations of Aquila and Symmachus, and this interpretation fits with the original context of Genesis, which highlights the significance of Isaac as the only son of Sarah and Abraham, and the one through whom the promises were to be fulfilled. A belief in resurrection seems to be attributed to Abraham in Heb. 11:19, and serves to illustrate the message of the citation from Hab. 2:3-4 that the righteous 'will live'. As noted above, it is not an uncommon move in early Jewish exegesis to ascribe motives or emotions to scriptural characters, and in writings such as *Jubilees* the patriarchs are, for instance, shown following laws which were actually inaugurated only after their death.

Gen. 27:27-40 in Heb. 11:20

This reference to Isaac's blessing of Jacob and Esau is extremely truncated, reminiscent of the abbreviated treatment of some biblical episodes in rewritten Bible texts. The author of Hebrews makes no mention of the trickery which led to Jacob's usurpation of his brother's blessing, for example, and seems to ignore the fact that, according to Genesis, Esau did not receive a paternal blessing anything like equal to that bestowed on his brother. He, does, however, develop that part of the narrative later (Heb. 12:16-17), demonstrating his ability to use the same scriptural text to make different points. This is the first in a series of three brief statements about Israel's patriarchs (Heb. 11:20-22), focusing only on the final blessings or instructions they gave to their descendants.

---

35   This point is noted by Eisenbaum, *Jewish Heroes*, pp.90–3, 104–8. On the interpretation in Hebrews of scriptural texts including first person direct speech, see further: S. E. Docherty, *The Use of the Old Testament in Hebrews* (WUNT, 2/260; Tübingen: Mohr Siebeck, 2009), pp.143–79.

36   The development of Christological interpretations of the binding of Isaac is discussed by several commentators; see e.g. M. Bockmuehl, 'Abraham's Faith in Hebrews 11', in R. Bauckham et. al. (eds), *The Epistle to the Hebrews and Christian Theology* (Grand Rapids, Michigan/Cambridge: Eerdmans, 2009), pp.364–73.

Gen. 47:31 and 48:1-20 in Heb. 11:21

Two scriptural passages have been conflated here, because the blessing of Joseph's sons by Jacob as he lay dying is a separate incident in Scripture (see Gen. 48:1-20) from the occasion when he is said to have 'bowed down on the head of his staff' (Gen. 47:31), after making Joseph swear that he would bury him not in Egypt but in Canaan. The two episodes are close together in the Genesis narrative, however, and share the same general context of Jacob's death-bed instructions and blessings on his descendants. In the first half of this verse, Hebrews provides only a brief allusive summary of Gen. 48:1-20. The second half of the verse reproduces exactly the Septuagint version of the latter part of Gen. 47:31, so is usually regarded as a direct citation,[37] although the setting of the 'bowing down in worship' has been transferred from Jacob's conversation with Joseph to the blessing of his grandsons. This new context enables the author to emphasise the theme of future blessing which is central to this section of the letter (see e.g. Heb. 11:20). The blessing of the patriarchs is passed on through the generations, from Isaac to Jacob and then on to Ephraim and Manasseh (Heb. 11:20-21), so that *all* their future descendants can share in it, including the recipients of Hebrews. Jacob thus 'lives' on through his descendants. The phrase 'bowing in worship over the head of his staff' has attracted a great deal of attention throughout the centuries, partly because of the differences between the Greek version and the Hebrew text, which points the consonants to read 'bed' rather than 'staff'. It has been subject to a range of interpretations by Jewish and Christian exegetes, with particular concern evident to establish the *object* of Jacob's worship, often understood messianically by the fathers.[38] It is, however, probable that the phrase originally indicated simply that, due to his age, Jacob could not prostrate himself on the ground in worship as was the custom (see e.g. Gen. 48:12).[39]

Gen. 50:24-25 in Heb. 11:22

The last exemplar drawn from Genesis is Joseph, specifically his mention on his death-bed of the future exodus and his desire to be buried in Canaan. These final instructions of Joseph about his bones tend to feature in later accounts of his story (see e.g. Sir. 49:15; *Jub.* 46:5; Jos. *Ant.* 2:200; *T. Sim.* 8:3-4; *T. Jos.* 20:6).[40] Both this example and the previous reference to Jacob

---

37   See e.g. Ellingworth, *Epistle*, p.606; L. T. Johnson, *Hebrews: A Commentary* (NTL; Louisville: Westminster John Knox, 2000), p.24; J. C. McCullough, 'The Old Testament Quotations in Hebrews', *NTS* 26 (1980), pp.363–79, see pp.374–5.

38   See e.g. Attridge, *Hebrews*, p.336.

39   This is the view of e.g. Ellingworth, *Epistle*, pp.606–7.

40   M. Wilcox argues that Joseph's reference to God's 'visitation' was interpreted messianically in Jewish tradition in 'The Bones of Joseph: Hebrews 11:22', in B. P. Thompson (ed.), *Scripture: Meaning and Method. Essays Presented to Anthony Tyrell Hanson for His 70th Birthday* (Hull, Hull University Press, 1987).

serve to reinforce the author's argument that the patriarchs were looking to something promised but not yet realized. The use of the phrase 'sons of Israel' in this verse illustrates an interesting exegetical technique. This term occurs in the underlying Genesis text (at Gen. 50:25), where Joseph makes the 'sons of Israel' to whom he was speaking swear that they would make sure his bones were taken up from Egypt to Canaan. In context, these Israelites are his brothers and their households (Gen. 50:22, 24). In Hebrews, however, the term refers to those who would later take part in the exodus. A scriptural phrase is thus receiving a new referent, but one related to the original context, in which the future exodus is mentioned. Samely provides several examples of this method in operation within the targums, where the wording of Scripture is reproduced exactly, but the text is reinterpreted by specifying different speakers or addressees.[41] This section of the review of Israel's history ends, then, where Genesis does, with the death of Joseph.

Gen. 25:29-34 and 27:1-40 in Heb. 12:16-17

Here the author holds out a scriptural character as a negative example, in contrast to the positive exemplars of chapter 11, to urge his community not to reject their opportunity to inherit what is promised to them. Two scriptural narratives are being alluded to and partially conflated, Esau's selling of his birthright to his brother for a bowl of pottage (Gen. 25:29-34), and his loss of his father's blessing (Gen. 27:30-40). The Genesis account is directly critical of Esau in the first of these episodes: 'Thus Esau despised his birthright.' (Gen. 25:34), but not in the second, where he is tricked by Jacob and Rebekah, rather to the distress of his father (Gen. 27:33). The details that Esau was 'rejected' and 'found no opportunity for repentance' are, therefore, the author's own emphases, serving to reinforce the warning of Heb. 6:4-6 that repentance is not possible after apostasy. He follows Jewish exegetical tradition in presenting Esau negatively (e.g. Philo, *Leg.* 3:2, 139-40; *Virt.* 208). Esau's marriage to two non-Israelite women (Gen. 26:34) may be the basis for the charge that he is 'immoral' (Heb. 12:16; cf. *Jub.* 25:1).

Gen. 4:10 in Heb. 12:24

This verse provides a further example of the author's characteristic use of the same scriptural text more than once. The allusion to Gen. 4:10 here is closer than in Heb. 11:4 because it refers to Abel's blood. The way in which Jesus' sprinkled blood speaks 'better' than the blood of Abel is not explained. A number of commentators argue that there is a distinction between Abel's cry of vengeance and the forgiveness brought about by the death of Jesus.[42]

---

41   In one example, Gen. 31:46, Jacob's 'brothers' are redesignated by Targum Pseudo-Jonathan as 'his sons whom he called his brothers' (Samely, *Interpretation of Speech*, pp.9-19).

42   See e.g. B. F. Westcott, *The Epistle to the Hebrews* (London: MacMillan and co., 1889), p.417.

This aspect of Abel's cry is not, however, brought out either here or in the earlier reference to this passage, and this section of Hebrews stresses the voice of divine judgement rather than forgiveness (Heb. 12:18-29; see especially 12:26). Attridge, therefore, suggests that the author may have regarded Abel as a martyr whose death had some atoning significance, but less than the sacrificial death of Jesus.[43]

Gen. 18:1-15 in Heb. 13:2

The author urges his audience to show hospitality to strangers, grounding this exhortation in what is probably an allusion to Abraham's welcome of three men who turn out to be divine messengers (Gen. 18:1-15). Alternatively, the reference may be to Lot providing shelter to two angels (apparently the same ones who visited Abraham) in his home on the evening before the city of Sodom is destroyed (Genesis 19). There are also other scriptural examples of Israelites offering hospitality to angels in human form, including Gideon and Manoah (Judg. 6:11-24; 13:2-20). It is not clear, therefore, which one of these incidents the author has specifically in mind, but he may well have wished to remind his readers of all of them by his reference to 'some', rather than just one person, having entertained angels without knowing it. The virtues which he recommends in this chapter (Heb. 13:1-6) would have found favour amongst many gentiles as well as Jews: hospitality, marital fidelity and avoidance of avarice. The fact that he provides scriptural warrant for them, however, demonstrates his commitment to the ongoing authority of Scripture as a source of moral instruction.

Conclusion

The influence of Old Testament texts and themes on the theology of Hebrews is widely recognized. This opportunity to focus specifically on the author's use of the book of Genesis produces some interesting particular results, however. Firstly, it is important simply to note the number and distribution of references to Genesis throughout the letter. Although not as prominent as the Psalms or prophetic books, texts from Genesis are used several times to ground ethical injunctions and exhortation. Above all, the interpretation of Genesis is essential to the development of the author's most significant and innovative theological arguments, such as the concepts of Jesus' Melchizedekian priesthood and heavenly 'rest'. Secondly, Genesis is the source of some of the minor themes of Hebrews which can be overlooked: the widespread use of creation imagery and the significance of the figure of Abraham as the recipient of divine promise have been highlighted here, for instance. Thirdly, this study has sought to direct attention

43   Attridge, *Hebrews*, p.377.

particularly to the author's exegetical methods and their relationship to those employed more widely within early Jewish exegesis. His most characteristic techniques include repeated allusion to the same text, an understanding of Scripture as 'testimony', and the use of passages from different parts of the Bible to interpret one another. Another noteworthy feature of his use of Genesis is the tendency to reproduce it by means of extended allusion and paraphrase rather than in the form of a direct citation, and in some cases (e.g. Heb. 7:1-2; 11:5) the distinction between the categories 'citation' and 'allusion' appears very blurred. A difference has, however, emerged in the author's attitude to narrative passages and those containing direct speech, which are usually formally cited. The same techniques can be applied to both citations and allusions, though, including selective omission and stress on key words which are then surrounded with new co-text to precisely specify their meaning. Finally, the author's exegesis of Genesis provides an important insight into his presuppositions about Scripture, many of which are shared by other early Jewish interpreters, notably that Scripture is to be read as a coherent whole as well as a collection of individual verses or phrases, and that its every single word has significance. It is, then, abundantly clear that the author of Hebrews regards Genesis as having ongoing validity and direct relevance for his community, who are in continuity with its narrative of salvation history (Hebrews 11), and have before them the possibility of inheriting the scriptural promises made to Abraham (Heb. 6:13-18) and achieving entry into God's rest (Heb. 4:9-11).

Chapter 9

GENESIS IN JAMES, 1 AND 2 PETER AND JUDE

David M. Allen

Introduction

Although commonly grouped together (with the Johannine letters) as the Catholic Epistles because of their more 'general' disposition and genre, the shared characteristics of James, 1 and 2 Peter and Jude are less numerous than their points of dissimilarity or individual distinctiveness. One has, for example, only to make a cursory comparison of James and 1 Peter to discover a dearth of Christological interest in the former epistle and a central focus within the latter one; likewise the familiar synoptic similarities of Jude and 2 Peter become less notable when one considers their usage of common material, especially in terms of their respective appropriation of Jewish 'scriptural' imagery.[1] The task of this chapter is to consider how the four epistolary texts utilize Genesis material, and to ascertain the degree to which they exhibit any common approach to the canonical text or to identify any particularity of method in the individual letters. Key areas of concern will be the extent to which the NT author is interested specifically in the *text* of Genesis (i.e. to exploit it in terms of quotation or lexical allusion), or whether his focus is more attuned to Genesis' (familiar) narratives (i.e. that the 'story' is more significant than any precise verbal affinity). Likewise, it will consider whether the respective authors are using Genesis itself (what one might term the 'canonical' text) or whether they are working with (familiar) Jewish traditions that secondarily reflect it. Bearing in mind the capacity for Genesis narratives to be adapted or expanded within 'Rewritten Bible' or pseudepigraphical texts, of what source material are the NT authors availing themselves? Or to put the matter another way, for these four epistolary texts, when does Genesis become Genesis, and when does it stop being so?

---

1   T. Callan, 'The Use of the Letter of Jude by the Second Letter of Peter', *Bib* 85 (2004), pp.42–64.

Genesis in James

Abraham in Jas 2:18-26

James' interest in Genesis derives primarily from the exemplary figure of Abraham, located within the (in)famous discussion of the merits of justification by works, much of which has been filtered through the comparative lens of Paul's treatment of similar, or related, issues. James' faith-works discourse begins in 2:14, but its first undisputed appeal to Genesis imagery emerges in 2:21, the allusion to Abraham's offering of Isaac utilized by James as a paradigm of works and faith functioning synergistically. Jas 2:23 quotes Gen. 15:6 in this regard, enabling the conclusion that Abraham was justified by works, and not by faith alone (2:24). James claims faith without deeds is 'dead' (2:26), literally the same outcome if Abraham had actually fulfilled the command to sacrifice Isaac, and there may therefore be a narrative echo even at this point. At the very least, James' engagement with Genesis functions at two levels, both narrative allusion and formal quotation.

Although 2:21 begins the interaction with Genesis in earnest, James perhaps prepares the way for it in the previous verse, by portraying faith without works as ἀργός (2:20). Although his choice of phrase is likely a rhetorical pun on ἔργον (2:20), thereby creating a deepening sense of emptiness when compared to the empty hearer (ἄνθρωπε κενέ), it may also render an echo of Sarah's barrenness, particularly in view of the subsequent context. The case is not persuasive purely on a lexical basis – the more customary term, στεῖρα, is used of Sarah in Genesis itself (11:30; cf. Heb. 11:11) – but it has a thematic resonance, especially bearing in mind the comparative 'emptiness' within Genesis' narratival trajectory. The Sarah-Abraham situation is 'empty' so long as Sarah remains στεῖρα, and much of their shared narrative relates their efforts to rectify such 'emptiness' through the exercise of both faith and action.[2] There may likewise be a further Genesis narratival allusion in the previous verse. The commended belief that God is 'one' (Jas 2:19) possibly relates back to Abraham's standing as one who believed in the one God. Abraham is elsewhere described as the first monotheist (Philo, *Virt.* 214-216), and whilst Genesis itself is not explicit in such a designation, its narrative does affirm his faithful embrace of the one God (Gen. 12:1-5).

James identifies Abraham as 'our father' (2:21), likely reflecting the Jewish nature of the epistle's authorship[3] or audience. It may well also echo Gen. 12:1-3 (cf. the similar use in Heb. 2:16) or Gen. 17:4,[4] where, in both

---

2   The NRSV translation of ἀργός (2:20) as 'barren' may be further recognition of the imagery.

3   P. H. Davids, *The Epistle of James: A Commentary on the Greek Text* (NIGTC; Grand Rapids: Eerdmans, 1982), p.126.

4   So L. T. Johnson, *The Letter of James: A New Translation with Introduction and Commentary* (AB 37A; New York: Doubleday, 1995), p.242.

instances, Abraham's ancestral heritage is foretold. But as a widespread contemporary designation, its origins are likely to be within a general Jewish milieu rather than the formal text of Genesis itself (cf. Isa. 51:2, Sir. 44:19, Mt. 3:9). The particular event to which James alludes is the sacrifice of Isaac (the so called *Aqedah*), the narrative of Gen. 22:1-19 and its supposed testing of Abraham by God (Gen. 22:1). James is notably unconcerned with Isaac's role in the proceedings, but rather focuses in on Abraham's particular actions. The story is a familiar one, with substantial precedent for the type of faith-reckoning association James draws. First Maccabees 2:51-52 is perhaps the closest parallel, associating the testing of Abraham with the reckoning to him of righteousness, whilst Sir. 44:20 similarly associates Abraham's exercise of faith with his testing (presumably the offering of Isaac).[5] It is entirely possible, therefore, that James is working with traditions – oral or written – beyond the 'text' of Genesis itself.

The language used in Jas 2:21 draws predominantly from Genesis 22, though remains a conflation of terminology from the chapter. Abraham offers up (ἀναφέρω – Jas 2:21; cf. Gen. 22:2, 13) Isaac on an altar, but, within Genesis itself, reference to such an altar is found only within 22:9; Isaac is there *laid* on this altar, but is not offered up. In the instances where ἀναφέρω is used, it is with the relatively unusual term ὁλοκάρπωσις (Gen. 22:2, 3, 6-8, 13). Furthermore, the difficulty with James' analysis is that Abraham does not actually perform the action ascribed to him by the epistolary text. The very action that supposedly manifests his justification, for Genesis at least, he does not 'do'. Davids may overstate the case in saying that 'it is…obvious that James knows a different story of Abraham from that of Genesis,'[6] but it remains the case that James' reading of the Genesis narrative technically goes beyond the canonical testimony. Although Abraham is said not to have spared his son (Gen. 22:16), lexically at least, he does not offer up Isaac on an altar in the manner James suggests; he merely lays him on it (22:9), and only the ram is 'offered' (22:13), albeit in Isaac's place.

One might, however, also argue the contrary, namely that James actually offers a sophisticated interpretation or retelling of the *Aqedah*. God's reply that Abraham had not withheld Isaac (22:12) may mean that James understands the sacrifice as having *de facto* taken place – the *intent* was what mattered. Philo arrives at a similar conclusion, describing Abraham's action as a 'complete and perfect sacrifice' (*Abr.* 177), and as his most significant and greatest deed (*Abr.* 167). Alternatively, by combining the language of the command (22:2; cf. 22:13) with that of the sacrificial act (22:9), along with the altar language of 22:9, James may be concluding (however erroneously) that Abraham did sacrifice Isaac, or rather rhetorically did so. A 'sacrifice' had conceptually taken place, even if – narratively, at least, for Genesis – it

---

5   Sirach 44:19 shares, with Jas 2:21, the reference to Abraham as 'father'.

6   P. H. Davids, 'The Pseudepigrapha in the Catholic Epistles', in J. H. Charlesworth and C. A. Evans (eds), *The Pseudepigrapha and Early Biblical Interpretation* (JSPSup, 14; Sheffield: JSOT Press, 1993), p.228.

had *not* done so. Or third, it may be that James recognizes an oddity in the Genesis text; the fact that ἀναφέρω never accompanies θυσιαστήριον is an intriguing non-combination, and it is possible that James identifies the significance of their non-association in the Genesis account.

The matter is further complicated by the plural noun ἔργοις (2:21, 22). James argues that Abraham was justified by works (plural), rather than by *a* work (singular). This 'synergistic' aspect of faith and works seems to be in tension with the singular sacrificial act that 2:21 sets forth,[7] however climactic or symbolic that work might be. Abraham is elsewhere described as experiencing ten trials (*Jub.* 19:8), and ἔργοις may therefore allude to other parts of the Abraham narrative, other deeds previously performed, without necessarily incorporating the *Aqedah* event. Taking seriously the immediate Jacobean context of mercy and works of hospitality (2:14-17), Ward opines that sacrifice is hardly a 'merciful' act and therefore forms an unlikely illustration for 2:14-17. He ventures instead that James has in mind Abraham's acts of hospitality, specifically the entertaining of three visitors (Gen. 18:1-8), an interesting possibility bearing in mind that Philo elsewhere associates the appellation 'friend of God' (cf. Jas 2:23) with subsequent events in that chapter (18:17-18. cf. *de Sob.* 56).[8] Ward also appeals to the association of Abraham and Rahab in 1 Clement 10 and 12, their respective offers of hospitality matching Jas 2:21-26.[9]

There is, however, no pressing requirement to treat Abraham and Rahab as equivalents; Rahab, for example, is not commended for any exercise of faith, nor does she receive the significant Jacobean 'friend of God' designation, so key to James' epistolary purposes (2:23; cf. 4:4). If Gen. 18:1-8 were indeed the backdrop for 2:14-26, then one might expect a more explicit reference to those events.[10] Instead, it is more likely that the plurality of ἔργοις alludes to the full gamut of Abraham's tests,[11] with the sacrifice of Isaac the most significant or demonstrable one. Not only does this correlate with the completion language James ascribes to the event (2:22), but it would also locate the *Aqedah* as the climax of Abraham's testing, the point at which his faithfulness is most substantively (but not exclusively) demonstrated.

---

7   Though James never uses 'work' in the singular – cf. J. S. Siker, *Disinheriting the Jews: Abraham in Early Christian Controversy* (Louisville: Westminster/John Knox, 1991), p.99.

8   R. B. Ward, 'The Works of Abraham: James 2:14-26', *HTR* 61 (1968), pp.283–90.

9   R. W. Wall, *Community of the Wise: The Letter of James* (Valley Forge, PA: Trinity Press International, 1997), p.147, observes that, for James, Rahab entertains 'messengers' rather than 'spies', a sense akin to those welcomed by Abraham in Genesis 18.

10   James may see Genesis 18 and 22 as inextricably intertwined, both narratives exhibiting the same promise (Gen. 18:18, 22:18). See S. McKnight, *The Letter of James* (NICNT; Grand Rapids: Eerdmans, 2011), pp.250–1.

11   See also S. Laws, *A Commentary on the Epistle of James* (London: A. & C. Black, 1980), p.135.

The quotation of Gen. 15:6 forms the culmination of James' argument at this point (2:23). Rather than using the lemma as a text by which subsequently to exegete or unpack the Aqedah narrative, James instead 'proves' his case first, and then cites the verse as the evidential or confirmatory datum. The choice of the particular verse also invites the contrast with Paul, Popkes going as far to suggest that 'the decisive source of scripture in Jas 2 was Pauline tradition'.[12]

The citation is the LXX form of the text.[13] The Hebrew version has YHWH as the subject of an active reckoning of righteousness to Abraham, whereas such reckoning assumes a passive aspect in the LXX form. Aside from the replacement of καὶ by the adversative δὲ, and the alteration of the name from Abram to Abraham, the quotation of Gen. 15:6 is effectively that of the LXX (cf. the same form in Rom. 4:3). James characterizes the lemma as a single 'scripture' rather than part of the Scriptures,[14] but it remains unclear where his listeners might think the quotation is supposed to end. The final clause of 2:23 – 'and he was called a friend of God' – is appended to the Gen. 15:6 citation and 'for someone inexperienced in scripture, it would read as being a part of the scripture quote'.[15] The source for the 'friend of God' ascription, however, is neither Genesis 15 or 22; it is perhaps more reminiscent of Isa. 41:8 or 2 Chron. 20:7, but the precise origin of the reference remains debated.[16] Whilst it may be merely a familiar, contemporary phrase,[17] and whilst Philo can also describe Abraham in such terms (*Abr.* 273), the closest analogy is probably *Jub.* 19:9, especially considering the latter's juxtaposition of faithfulness and friendship with God. Indeed, Watson proposes that '(t)he statement in James reads almost like an abbreviation of the longer statement in *Jubilees*', and that it offers further evidence of James reading Gen. 15:6 in similar fashion to his contemporaries (but with the notable exception of Paul).[18] The friendship language may not be drawn from Genesis, but remains essentially 'in spirit' with it.

Cast in such terms, the Jacobean Abraham becomes the embodiment of Jas 1:3-4, one whose faith is tested such that he becomes complete (1:4), who embodies divine friendship (2:23) rather than friendship with the world (4:4). He is not so much 'on trial' in James (cf. 1:2-3), but rather becomes a paradigm case of someone who, at the climactic point of the trial, is found

12   W. Popkes, 'James and Scripture: An Exercise in Intertextuality', *NTS* 45 (1999), p.224.

13   D. A. Carson, 'James', in G. K. Beale and D. A. Carson (eds), *Commentary on the New Testament Use of the Old Testament* (Grand Rapids: Apollos, 2007), p.997, notes that James' quotations and allusions are almost always to the LXX.

14   Popkes, 'James', p.215.

15   W. Popkes, 'Two Interpretations of "Justification" in the New Testament: Reflections on Galatians 2:15-21 and James 2:21-25', *ST* 59 (2005), p.135.

16   On the 'friend of God' designation, see Johnson, *Letter*, pp.243–4.

17   Carson, 'James', p.1005.

18   F. Watson, *Paul and the Hermeneutics of Faith* (London: T&T Clark, 2004), p.235, n.20.

to be faithful through action (2:21-24). The *Aqedah* narrative begins with God's explicit decision to put Abraham to the test (Gen. 22:1), and therefore provides an appropriate example of the kind of testing through endurance to which the opening verses of James allude (cf. 1:2-4). The influence of the Abraham motif (and of Genesis material) thereby extends beyond the immediate confines of 2:21-24.

At the same time, James does declare that God tests no one (1:13), and this would be in some tension with the divine decision to put Abraham to the test (Gen. 22:1). This causes some to suggest that James is working with extra-canonical accounts of Genesis 22, potentially that of *Jubilees*, whereby the mysterious Mastema figure assumes responsibility for inaugurating the Abrahamic testing (*Jub.* 17:16-18, 18:12).[19] Alternatively, it is possible that James has in mind Abraham's lack of complaint in regard of being 'tested' by God, particularly as temptation can result in death (1:15), the very outcome *not* engendered by Abraham's (faithful) action. On such a construal, Jas 1:13 attests to Abraham's perspective on the *Aqedah* experience (i.e. that God was not actually 'testing' him) rather than forming a programmatic statement on theodicy.

James' hermeneutical strategy vis-à-vis Genesis also warrants further comment. He expects his argument to be straightforward, self-evident even – cf. the double use of 'you see' (2:22, 24) – and as the *Aqedah* narrative is not recounted in any detail, one surmises that James assumes his readers will be familiar with it. Yet some commentators also find in 2:23 the framework of a prophecy-fulfilment discourse. Johnson, for example, proposes that James identifies 'a prophecy/fulfilment pattern within Torah itself', and further that, for James: 'the *graphe* declaring Abraham righteous in Gen. 15.6 was fulfilled by the *deed* that Abraham performed by offering his son Isaac'.[20] Whilst others have demurred from this, viewing the πληρόω language of 2:23 as having something more akin to a confirmatory aspect,[21] it is hard to ignore the conclusion that James specifically makes Gen. 22:9-12 the fulfilment of Gen. 15:6. Other texts do similarly juxtapose the two events (cf. 1 Macc. 2:51-52; Sir. 44:20; also Neh. 9:7-8), but James seemingly takes it one stage further by casting the relationship in 'fulfilment' terms. The action of the sacrifice completes the process begun in 15:6.

Furthermore, the 'completion' phraseology (τελειόω) in 2:22 closely parallels the fulfilment language (πληρόω) of 2:23. Although the precise terminology is not the same, there is a parallel teleological action between the 'completion' manifest by the *Aqedah* (2:22), and the 'fulfilment' of the prophecy (2:23). The close location of the verbs gives suggestive parallels such that we see two corresponding processes of completion. Narrative-wise, the 'emptiness', or barrenness, of Sarah (cf. 2:20) is coupled with the 'as yet

19   Davids, 'Pseudepigrapha', pp.229-30.
20   Johnson, *Letter*, p.243.
21   Cf. R. P. Martin, *James* (WBC, 48; Waco: Word, 1988), p.93: 2:23 is 'confirmation of what James has been saying'.

unfulfilled' nature of the 'text' promise to Abraham in 15:6. The fulfilment of this promise, or the recovery of the emptiness, both climax not with the birth of Isaac, but with the (faithful) offering of the promised son on the altar. Narrative (the promise to Abraham/Sarah) and text (the *graphe* of 15:6) are inextricably intertwined, and for James, both find their culmination, or fulfilment, in the Genesis 22 account.

Genesis 1–3 in Jas 3:5-9

James' elaboration on the dangerous capacity of the tongue (3:5-9) provides its next interaction with Genesis imagery. The odd turn of phrase in 3:6 – 'the world of unrighteousness' – may be an allusion back to the Fall narrative of Gen. 3:1-19, particularly as the created order is disordered by words uttered by the serpent, famed for its duplicitous tongue. The grounds for the allusion are even stronger when one considers the rest of Jas 3:6, namely that the tongue sets on fire the whole cycle of creation, or literally its γένεσις. Such terminology seems to be deliberately loaded. On the one hand, the (serpent's) tongue has transgressed the good ordering of creation outlined in Gen. 1:1–2:3; on the other hand, the specific use of γένεσις invokes the narrative of the eponymous text,[22] and solidifies the expectation that James has Genesis narratives specifically in view.

The subsequent verses sustain this expectation. James 3:7 appeals to imagery drawn from Gen. 1:26 (cf. also Gen. 9:2), recalling the imagery of naming and taming (1:26, 28, 2:18-20). More specifically, the fourfold division of 'beast and bird, of reptile and sea creature' evokes the similar ascription in Gen. 1:26 (the words are not the same, but the separation remains consistent).[23] The Genesis call to have dominion over the animals is commensurate with James' double mention of taming (especially the second, perfect tense form), and it seems likely that a formal allusion is in place here.[24] Likewise, the double mention of φύσις ('species' – cf. 3:7) links humanity with the fourfold animal kingdom, and if the latter invokes the Genesis narrative, presumably the 'species' of humanity – the creation of that species – similarly picks up Genesis 1 imagery.[25]

The serpent portrayal returns in Jas 3:8, and in more suggestive fashion, its description of the tongue as both poisonous and death-bearing transporting the intertextual reader back to Gen. 3:1-19 and the catastrophic effects of the serpent's tongue.[26] The word for poison (ἰός) occurs only three

---

22   Philo knows of the name of 'Genesis' (*Post.* 127, *Abr.* 1, *Aet.* 19).

23   Wall, *Community*, p.172.

24   That 3:9 similarly alludes to Gen. 1:26 strengthens the case for 3:7.

25   θηρίον (3.7) can carry the specific meaning of 'snake', and seems to acquire that dimension in Acts 28:4-5.

26   Cf. C. J. Blomberg and M. J. Kamell, *James* (Grand Rapids: Zondervan, 2008), p.160: 'The metaphor suggests the image of a serpent, poised to strike, much like the destructive, deceptive words of the snake to Eve in the garden of Eden, which poisoned paradise.'

times in the NT, and, aside from James, only within Paul, who links the word specifically with anguine activity. He quotes Ps. 139:4 LXX (Rom. 3:13), itself a denunciation of those 'vipers' seeking to trick David, and (re)places it within the catena of quotations in Rom. 3:10-18. In such a context, to speak with a deceptive tongue or venomous lips becomes a primary paradigm of sinfulness. The tongue's 'death-bearing' mantle is also evocative of Gen. 3:1-19; bearing in mind the accompanying 'poison' designation, it is hard to ignore the mortal implications of the serpent's speech (cf. Gen. 3:19), particularly as the serpent's discussion with the woman relates to whether or not death is the outcome of eating from the fruit of the tree (Gen. 3:1-5).

James concludes that the tongue can be both blessing and curse (3:9-10; cf. Rom. 3:14), and, once more, such terminology seems to reflect the broader narratives of Genesis 1–3, the blessing of a good creation, or the cursing of the duplicitous serpent. Moreover, the verse alludes once again to Gen. 1:26, and the language of the divine image;[27] as that same verse is already echoed in 3:7, 'the reference to Gen. 1:26 is surely intentional',[28] and sustains, or even climaxes, the broad creation-fall backdrop. The parallels are not exact, of course; humanity is not so much 'cursed' by the events of Genesis 3 (though death does come), and interpreters will debate as to exactly what fate 3:16-19 entails. But it remains the case that the serpent *is* cursed, or perhaps that cursing is the fate laid upon the effects of the serpent's speech. Just as the serpent's tongue – apparently affirming (or blessing?) in tone – tarnished the blessing upon humanity, so the divine voice utters a curse upon that which has tarnished the one bearing the divine image.

Genesis 6 in Jas 4:5

Whilst seeming to promise some scriptural warrant or quotation, Jas 4:5 infamously offers 'no transparently obvious OT reference',[29] and it remains ambiguous as to whether a quotation or summary allusion is intended. Full exploration of the exegetical possibilities are beyond the scope of this chapter, but it seems possible at least that the NRSV rendering ('God yearns jealously for the spirit (πνεῦμα) that he has made to dwell in us') opens up the possibility that πνεῦμα alludes to the indwelling human spirit of creation (Gen. 1:27, 2.7), even if the LXX does not render πνεῦμα here. Perhaps because Gen. 6:3 *does* speak of the removal of the divine spirit from the rebellious 'sons of god', Wall instead conjectures that 4:5 echoes the Noah narrative of Genesis 6. He notes the designation of Noah as both righteous and blameless (Gen. 6:9), and thus that Noah personifies 'a wise person in a wicked world',[30] effectively one in whom the spirit of God properly dwells. Like Abraham, he becomes a prototype or paradigm of the kind of friend of

27   Johnson, *Letter*, p.262: 'The allusion anticipated by 3:7 is here made explicit.'
28   M. J. Townsend, *The Epistle of James* (London: Epworth, 1994), p.65.
29   Carson, 'James', p.1006.
30   Wall, *Community*, pp.203–4

God James yearns for (4:4-5), and effectively assumes, for Wall, the role of a fifth exemplar within the Jacobean epistle. There is, however, no compelling textual invitation to make such an association; there is no mention of a divine 'spirit' present within Noah in the Genesis narrative, and the interpretative challenges of 4:5 notwithstanding, one would expect a clearer form of exemplary link if it were the case. Prockter's suggestion that Gen. 8:21 LXX is the source of the quotation in Jas 4:5[31] is likewise hard to justify. Whilst the source of the allusion or quotation is notoriously disputed within Jacobean scholarship, to find it in the Noah account is to push beyond the text.

Gen. 4:10 in Jas 5:4

Compared to the strong narratival and citational parallels found in Jas 2:19-26 and 3:6-12, the supposed echo of Gen. 4:10 in Jas 5:4 is somewhat faint. There is no obvious narratival connection, and any association is implicit, the primary common motif being the shared 'cry of the oppressed'.[32] Genesis 4:10 LXX renders the verbal form βοάω, whereas Jas 5:4 uses κράζω, saving the nominal form βοαί for 5:4b. There is the thematic association of labourers in the field crying out for wages, akin to the blood of Abel crying out from the ground, but the imagery is perhaps more obviously that of the exodus and Israelite slavery, or the imagery of the defrauded worker is merely a familiar contemporary image.

At the same time, it is possible that Jas 5:1-6 has in mind the broad narrative of Cain and Abel,[33] Abel potentially the anonymous righteous one (5:6), killed by his brother such that his blood cries out from the ground (Gen. 4:10). Byron argues that Jewish tradition construed Abel as an archetype of unjust suffering (*1 En.* 22:6-7) or righteous action (Mt. 23:35; cf. Heb. 11:4), whilst Cain becomes an exemplar of exploitative profiteering (Josephus, *Ant.* 1:53, 61; cf. 1 Jn 3:12), one who benefits from his brother's demise.[34] Together, they form a potential comparative template for the type of comparison James is making, and the fact that James has adopted a similar narratival echo strategy in 3:6-12 makes the case for one operating in 5:1-6 more compelling. In the same way that one can profitably engage with Jas 3:6-12 by juxtaposing it with the narrative of Genesis 3, so the severity of the defrauding of the poor is enhanced by hearing the Cain and Abel story set against Jas 5:1-6.

31   L. J. Prockter, 'James 4:4-6: Midrash on Noah', *NTS* 35 (1989), pp.625–7.
32   McKnight, *James*, p.392.
33   J. Byron, 'Living in the Shadow of Cain: Echoes of a Developing Tradition in James 5:1-6', *NovT* 48 (2006), pp.261–74.
34   Byron, 'Living', pp.263–8.

Genesis in 1 Peter

References to Genesis in 1 Peter are less numerous than those in both James and the second Petrine text. There may be some thematic association between the 'semi-nomadic existence of the Patriarchs' of Genesis and the 'elect foreigners' designation of 1 Peter's audience,[35] but the Petrine author does not explicitly exploit such parallels. What the references lack in number, however, they more than make up for in terms of complexity and ambiguity, particularly in terms of their original source.

Gen. 23:4 in 1 Pet. 2:11

Although not classified as such within UBS[4], there is good reason to view 1 Pet. 2:11 as an echo of Gen. 23:4. The verses share the common pattern of 'stranger and alien' (with 2:11 in the plural); although the exilic context to 1 Peter is well attested elsewhere (1:1, 1:17), and whereas there is a similar use of the doublet in Ps. 38:13 LXX,[36] the association between 2:11 and Gen. 23:4 seems particularly close. Abraham uses the designation in conversation with the Hittites, and there may be a narratival allusion in that his dealings with them involve mutual respect and interchange (i.e. he receives a place to bury Sarah), akin to the broad mode of engagement with external society that Peter seeks from his audience (2:11-17). As noted above, however, Peter does not explicitly exploit such a context, and it may be that the terminology merely provides a convenient framework for his readers' milieu.

Gen. 18:12 in 1 Pet. 3:6

Within the discourse of wives submitting to husbands (1 Pet. 3:1-6), Sarah is affirmed as a primary exemplar of such uxorial obedience, specifically that she called Abraham κύριός (3:6). The reference seemingly recalls the events of Gen. 18:12;[37] Sarah here uses the given κύριός address, and in the context of discussions over her (non-)childbearing. Where the Genesis narrative anticipates the promise to Sarah that will ultimately come forth in Isaac, Peter ascribes a *female* line to her, namely those women who honour their husbands in the manner Sarah modelled.

The basis for the allusion, however, is problematic. Sarah is presented elsewhere as a model of faith (cf. Heb 11:11), but Hebrews, for example, offers no suggestion as to how this relates to her role as Abraham's wife. Whilst Gen. 18:12 is the only time – in the canonical text at least – that

---

35   R. Feldmeier, *The First Letter of Peter: A Commentary on the Greek Text* (Waco: Baylor University Press, 2008), p.53. He cites Gen. 17:8, 23:4, 28:4, 35:27, 36:7, 37:1 in this regard.

36   J. R. Michaels, *1 Peter* (WBC, 49; Waco: Word, 1988), p.116 limits the scope of the echo to the psalm.

37   UBS[4]; so also, among others, P. J. Achtemeier, *1 Peter: A Commentary on First Peter* (Minneapolis: Fortress, 1996), p.215.

Sarah addresses Abraham as κύριός, it remains *all* that she acknowledges, and the word's broad reference as either 'husband' or 'lord/master' enables potentially different interpretations. Furthermore, Genesis 18 itself offers little evidence of Sarah acknowledging her husband's authority; her comment is made in relation to Abraham's aged seniority, and reads more as a term of *disrespect* than of demure obedience. Her laughter (18:12) is barely that of an exemplary submissive wife, particularly bearing in mind her subsequent denial of so doing (18:15). LXX Genesis has no record of Sarah obeying Abraham in terms of the ὑπακούω language Peter utilizes, and, instead, the reverse applies – it is Abraham who is said to attend to (ὑπακούω) his wife's voice (Gen. 16:2).[38] Finally, Peter stresses the fearless capacity of Sarah's 'daughters', but she is specifically said to be *afraid* (18:15), and is hardly the embodiment of that to which Peter thinks her daughters should aspire.

It may be that the source for the allusion comes from elsewhere in Genesis, specifically chapters 12 and/or 20. Here Sarah shows respect to her husband by either departing her homeland (12:5) or by her supplication when being passed off as Abraham's sister (20:1-18). The 'foreign land' context to both narratives would also sit well with 1 Peter's broader milieu of alien or exilic experience (cf. 1 Pet. 2:11).[39] Kiley suggests that the way in which Abraham treats Sarah – passing her off as his sister in somewhat servile fashion – also befits the slavery context that Peter alludes to in the previous unit (2:18-25), and which forms the apparently hierarchical backdrop to the discourse.[40] However, whilst the slave context makes for an interesting parallel, it has its limitations, if only because the women of 3:1-6 exhibit more power than Sarah; they are not asked to empty themselves in quite the way Sarah, bidden by her husband, effectively had to do. It may therefore be that the source for the allusion is not Genesis itself, but rather associated texts within Jewish tradition. Within the *Testament of Abraham*, for example, Sarah calls Abraham 'Lord', and is identified as the mother of the Elect, commensurate with the model role Peter seemingly accords her.[41] It may equally be that Peter follows the tendencies of both Philo and Josephus and 'molded Sarah to the image of the ideal Hellenistic wife, even at the price of reversing the biblical record'.[42] In sum, even if Gen. 18:12 is the source of the allusion, Peter has given it a very particular nuance and reworking that

---

38   D. I. Sly, '1 Peter 3:6b in the Light of Philo and Josephus', *JBL* 110 (1991), p.127.

39   M. C. Kiley, 'Like Sara: The Tale of Terror Behind 1 Peter 3:6', *JBL* 106 (1987), pp.689–92. A. Besancon Spencer, 'Peter's Pedagogical Method in 1 Peter 3:6', *BBR* 10, (2000), pp.107–19 conceives of the Petrine Sarah as a "proactive" model of vicarious suffering.

40   Kiley, 'Like Sara', pp.690–1. He avers that 1 Pet 3:6 conveys the '*Gestalt*' of Genesis 12 and 20.

41   T. W. Martin, 'The TestAbr and the Background of 1 Pet 3.6', *ZNW* 90 (1999), pp.139–46.

42   Sly, '1 Peter 3:6b', p.129.

effectively removes it from the original Genesis context.[43]

Genesis 6-7 in 1 Pet. 3:18-21[44]

Few passages of the New Testament have proved as complex as this short, but infamous, pericope. Whilst the Genesis allusion formally occurs in 1 Pet. 3:20-21, with the reference to Noah's soteriological experience, debate invariably focuses around 3:19 and how it informs the argument of the subsequent verses. The contentious or debated aspect is not so much the use of Genesis narrative *per se*, but rather the particular scenario it is used to support. Likewise, debates over 3:19 also commonly refer to 1 Pet. 4:6, and whether the respective verses address the same event, and whether the νεκροί (4:6) and the πνεύματα (3:19) depict equivalent beings. Since 4:6 lacks any explicit reference to Genesis 6 imagery, and since such absence may be reason to think that they are actually different events,[45] in terms of intertextual reference at least, discussion of 3:18-21 is best located on its own.

The context of 3:19-21 is demonstrably that of the flood narrative (Genesis 6), and Peter's reference to God's patient forbearance is likely an allusion to Gen. 6:3, or at least to the limits of such forbearance. Likewise the eight saved through water (1 Pet. 3:20b) is a narrative allusion to Gen. 7:13 (cf. 7:23) and the preservation of Noah's extended family. But Peter's reworking of the narrative beyond this is complex. Debates tend to focus on the identity of the πνεύματα of 3:19,[46] with three perspectives customarily discerned. Some have speculated that, for Peter, these were the contemporaries of Noah in the lower world, visited during the period between Christ's death and resurrection. Such a visit has been construed in three different scenarios: offering salvation to the unconverted, bringing good news to those who had been previously faithful, or proclaiming condemnation upon the disobedient. Alternatively, Peter understands the spirits still as Noah's contemporaries, but with Christ having made witness to them via and through the person of Noah, who potentially assumes some form of Christ prototype figure; the spirits are in prison, *now*, because they have rejected the message.[47] On this perspective, Peter is engaging with Genesis 6, but going

---

43   M. Misset-van de Weg, 'Sarah Imagery in 1 Peter', in A.-J. Levine (ed.), *A Feminist Companion to the Catholic Epistles and Hebrews* (London: T&T Clark, 2004), pp.50–62.

44   On the paragraph generally, see W. J. Dalton, *Christ's Proclamation to the Spirits: A Study of 1 Peter 3:18-4:6* (AnBib 23; Rome: Pontifical Biblical Institute, 1965), passim; R. T. France, 'Exegesis in Practice: Two Samples', in I. H. Marshall (ed.), *New Testament Interpretation* (Carlisle: Paternoster, 1997); C. L. Westfall, 'The Relationship between the Resurrection, the Proclamation to the Spirits in Prison and Baptismal Regeneration: 1 Peter 3.19-22', in S. E. Porter (ed.), *Resurrection* (JSNTSup, 186; Sheffield: Sheffield Academic, 1999), pp.106–35.

45   See D. Horrell, 'Who Are "the Dead" and When Was the Gospel Preached to Them? The Interpretation of 1 Pet 4.6', *NTS* 49 (2003), pp.70–89.

46   See R. Bauckham, 'Spirits in Prison', *ABD* 6, pp.177–8.

47   See, for example, J. H. Skilton, 'A Glance at Some Old Problems in First Peter',

beyond it, inserting Christological explanation for which Genesis itself gives no basis.

A third option,[48] and that most favoured by recent commentators, is to view the πνεύματα as fallen angels, and specifically the disobedient angels of Gen. 6:2-3, but viewed through the lens of the Enoch tradition. Within such tradition, it is observed, πνεύματα is the customary term for supernatural beings (cf. *1 En.* 15:4, 6-8); Christ's encounter with these fallen angels or Watchers may have been a downward Triduum visitation between crucifixion and resurrection, or, more likely, an 'encounter from above', the meeting part of Christ's heavenly ascension.[49] Specifically, the portrayal of Christ's action is akin to the task given to Enoch in respect of the disobedient Watchers, namely to proclaim condemnation to them as part of his heavenly journey (*1 En.* 12:4, 13:1, 3), and their consequent, eternal imprisonment (*1 En.* 14:5). Enoch is also taken to their place of imprisonment (*1 En.* 21:7-10) and, bearing in mind such parallels, it is no surprise that France surmises: 'To try to understand 1 Peter 3.19-20 without a copy of the Book of Enoch at your elbow is to condemn yourself to failure.'[50] Indeed, the lack of explanation or elucidation Peter gives to his argument suggests he thought his audience would be familiar enough with the Enoch material not to require any further elucidation.

The second part of 1 Pet. 3:20 maintains the broad Genesis backdrop, but extends it to the narrative of the flood, and does not therefore *necessitate* recourse to Enochic literature. The flood narrative is construed salvifically, but Genesis 6 (and therefore Genesis 6-9) is read as a whole, with the sons of God and the Nephilim apparently responsible for the diluvian trauma. However, such reading seems driven by baptismal concerns, rather than any exploration of the flood narrative. For Genesis, it is the ark – not water – that 'saves' Noah and his family, yet Peter, wishing to make the baptismal connection (3:21), attributes the salvific capacity to water instead (3:20b). Dalton therefore proposes that 3:18, 22 are a baptismal liturgy, with some catechesis placed in the middle (3:19-21) as help. 'As Noah was delivered by water from the evil instigated by these fallen angels, so also will the Christian be saved by the waters of baptism.'[51]

WTJ 58 (1996), pp.1–9.

48   Alternatively see Michaels, *1 Peter*, pp.206–9, who concludes that the spirits are the offspring of the Watchers. This perspective struggles, however, to justify the language of imprisonment.

49   So Dalton, *Proclamation*, passim; Davids, 'Pseudepigrapha', pp.234–6.

50   France, 'Exegesis', p.265.

51   Dalton, *Proclamation*, p.188.

Genesis in Jude

Jude's use of Old Testament and Pseudepigraphical imagery exhibits a characteristic interest in triadic constructions, with appeal made to three motifs or personages (Jude 5-7, 11), followed by some form of contemporary explication or application (8, 12-13). When appealing to Genesis characters, Jude notably focuses solely upon negative incidences; contrary to James and 1 Peter, it lacks any mention of more praiseworthy characters such as Sarah or Abraham, instead appealing to Sodom/Gomorrah and Cain as negative exemplars.

The first potential Genesis reference is found in Jude 6, its description of the descent of the angels reminiscent of Gen. 6:1-4. Although Gen. 6:2 LXX renders the phrase 'sons of god' to describe the rebellious beings, and whereas that terminology may pertain to creatures other than angels,[52] Jude is surely identifying the Gen. 6:2 figures in angelic terms. As with 1 Peter, however, the broader narrative of *1 Enoch*, especially chapters 6-19, is more likely the source for Jude's exemplar[53] (though cf. similarly *Jub.* 7:20-25); Genesis does not speculate on the fate of the angels, divine judgment or otherwise, nor does it place the angels in chains for the actions (cf. *1 En.* 10:4-6, 15-17). Moreover, the subsequent quotation of *1 En.* 1:9 (Jude 14-15) suggests the author is well versed in Enochic material, and perhaps that it was a textual tradition well known to Jude's readers.[54] Jude does not expand on the Enochic narrative, though, and the reason for the angels' fatal demise is left unspecified, at least explicitly so.

The third aspect of the Jude 5-7 triad is the first genuine Genesis allusion (v.7). It draws more evidently from the canonical text, appealing to the familiar imagery of Sodom and Gomorrah's demise (Gen. 19:24-29), but, even here, one seemingly encounters some midrashic, or creative, exposition. Sodom's paradigmatic function as a place of disobedience is widespread within both biblical and extrabiblical sources,[55] but Jude's appropriation of the material remains somewhat distinctive. As with vv.5-6, it emphasizes the punitive destiny of the immoral inhabitants of Sodom and Gomorrah, but the *eternal* nature of the fiery punishment is an addition to the canonical record (cf. Gen. 19:24). Likewise, the inclusion of the 'surrounding cities' is

---

52   See D. A. Carson, 'Jude', in G. K. Beale and D. A. Carson (eds), *Commentary on the New Testament Use of the Old Testament* (Grand Rapids: Apollos, 2007), pp.1070–1 for discussion of the various possibilities.

53   R. Bauckham, *Jude and the Relatives of Jesus in the Early Church* (Edinburgh: T&T Clark, 1990), pp.182–3 lays out several textual affinities between Jude 6 and *1 Enoch*.

54   So J. D. Charles, '"Those" and "these": the use of the Old Testament in the Epistle of Jude', *JSNT* 38 (1990), pp.109–24.

55   Deut. 32:32; Isa. 1:9; 13:19; Jer. 23:14; Amos 4:11; 3 Macc. 2:5; *Sacr.* 122; Mt. 11:24; Lk. 10:12, amongst others. On the Sodom and Gomorrah tradition, see W. J. Lyons, *Canon and Exegesis: Canonical Praxis and the Sodom Narrative* (JSOTSup 352, London: Sheffield Academic Press, 2002).

an expansion of the canonical plot (though cf. Gen. 19:28-29); the inhabitants of such cities are not viewed as 'active' sinners in the narrative of Gen. 19:4-11, but Jude infers they become culpable through geographical association. His depiction of the city dwellers' sin is also a contested point; whereas the Genesis account seems to relate it more to (in)hospitality to strangers (19:2-11),[56] a theme retained within later material (Wis. 19:14; *Ant.* 1:194-195), Jude casts it in terms of sexual immorality, and specifically as seeking after 'other flesh' (cf. also *Jub.* 16:5, 20:5). Webb suggests that the lust is for the angel visitors (19:1) – i.e. it is the wrong sort of flesh that they lust after, human to angelic,[57] with Bauckham similarly arguing that the sinful aspect is the crossing of species.[58] Davids, however, avers that Jude has in mind homosexual practice, and that whilst 'crossing of the species' is indeed in view, the context is a 'different type of [human] flesh'.[59] Jude is not absolutely clear either way, but the former option remains more persuasive, if only because it inverts the trajectory of Jude 6; angel to human becomes human to angel. That said, Jude's focus remains the inevitability of the angels' fate; the emphasis is on the consequences of sinfulness, and less on the sin *per se.*[60]

Jude returns to Genesis imagery in v.11, Cain cited as the first of a triad alongside Balaam and Korah. The reference is limited to an exhortation not to follow after the 'way of Cain', and Jude's lack of commentary on each figure limits the capacity to explore further the source of his material. Davids consequently argues that, for the woe list of v.11, the canonical text provides the source for Jude's speculation, as there is no reason *not* to make it the authoritative one.[61] However, the comparative force of other contemporary sources suggests that all three images 'are refracted through haggadic tradition';[62] indeed, the allusion to the *way* of Cain suggests a compendium of activity that goes beyond just Cain's fratricidal activity of Genesis 4.[63] As noted above, Cain emerges as a quintessentially negative figure within a variety of traditions (1 Jn 3:12; Wis. 10:3; *1 En.* 22:5-7), and may be summarily viewed as a paradigm negative character or 'the epitome of wickedness'.[64] Webb thus suggests two possible sources for the Cain tradition,

---

56   Lyons, *Canon*, p.235, argues that the Sodomites' sin is more ambiguous. 'The actions of the men of Sodom are – to the canonical reader – a blank space that nevertheless includes the sin of Gen. 19.4-11, however defined, and which merits judgment. The required response therefore is to look on "wondering what they did there".'

57   R. L. Webb, 'The Use of "Story" in the Letter of Jude: Rhetorical Strategies of Jude's Narrative Episodes', *JSNT* 31 (2008), p.58 n. 11, citing *T. Ash.* 7:1 as a parallel.

58   Bauckham, *Relatives of Jesus*, p.187.

59   P. H. Davids, *The Letters of 2 Peter and Jude* (London: Apollos, 2006), p.53.

60   Carson, 'Jude', p.1072.

61   Davids, 'Pseudepigrapha', p.241, n.32.

62   Bauckham, *Relatives*, p.189.

63   Though Carson, 'Jude', p.1072, suggests that the 'way of Cain' implies that the murder of Abel 'stands as the primal example of hatred'.

64   Charles, 'Those', p.116.

either his portrayal as one who overindulged in pleasure (cf. *Ant.* 1:61), or as one depicted as a heretic and false teacher.[65] Either option seems possible bearing in mind both the judgment context of the allusion, and the broader situational context of outsiders promoting some form of heresy

Beyond the specific reference to the Genesis characters, one might comment more generally on Jude's hermeneutical approach. The Old Testament imagery is utilized as a source for contemporary application, an exegetical approach Bauckham characterizes as akin to Qumran pesher;[66] more generally, Charles notes how the 'the midrashic treatment of Jewish tradition in Jude…applies lessons of the past to present needs of the Christian community'.[67] Hence Jude is not so much offering an extended retelling or reworking of the Genesis narratives so much as marshalling a series of evidential exemplars whose characters typify the actions and destiny of the contemporary opponents. Jude seemingly assumes the audience will be familiar with the respective traditions;[68] the appeal to the 'way of Cain', for example, presupposes knowledge of a broader context beyond merely the nominal mention. Thus, several themes undergird Jude's appropriation of Genesis. There is emphasis on the fatal consequences of the episode; there is appeal to a broader story (of content and consequence), what Webb calls 'narrative episodes';[69] and there is interpretative usage beyond the canonical record. In short, whilst Jude's cast list may be drawn from the Genesis retinue, its usage of such motifs likely derives from other sources within the pseudepigraphical tradition – it is both *at least*, but certainly *more than*, Genesis retelling.

Genesis in 2 Peter

2 Peter lacks any direct quotation from Genesis, but contains several allusions to narratives drawn from the canonical text. Its relationship to Jude is well established, and the use of Genesis material comprises part of that similarity; 2 Peter appropriates the material, but reworks it, partly by correcting Jude's narrative ordering, partly by supplementing the account with extra descriptive detail, and partly by omitting material where fitting. Its references to Genesis are consequently more extended and expanded than those in Jude, and thus the variation between the two texts in terms of Genesis appropriation should not be underestimated. In respect of Sodom

---

65   Webb, 'Story', p.61.
66   R. Bauckham, 'James, 1 and 2 Peter, Jude', in D. A. Carson and H. G. M. Williamson (eds), *It Is Written: Scripture Citing Scripture: Essays in Honour of Barnabas Lindars, SSF* (Cambridge: Cambridge University Press, 1988), pp.303–4.
67   J. D. Charles, 'Jude's Use of Pseudepigraphical Source-Material as Part of a Literary Strategy', *NTS* 37 (1991), p.131.
68   Davids, 'Pseudepigrapha', p.240.
69   Webb, 'Story', p.54.

and Gomorrah, 2 Peter omits the other cities on the plain (2 Pet. 2:6-10; cf. Jude 7), but emphasizes the way in which God is the agent of the condemnatory judgement. Likewise Peter lacks any reference to Cain (cf. Jude 11), but introduces the figure of Lot into its retelling of the Sodom incident (2 Pet. 2:7), thereby providing an example of a righteous figure rescued from the cities' demise. Noah is similarly added (2 Pet. 2:5), depicted as the righteous one saved from diluvian demise; he functions as a parallel to Lot, both being upright figures saved from the destruction caused by their ungodly counterparts. Callan thus avers that the Petrine alterations to Jude 5–7 are not inconsiderable – they comprise a 'thorough revision' – and that 2 Peter is a 'free paraphrase' of its Judan predecessor.[70]

Second Peter 2:4-10 sets forth a compendium of allusions to early Genesis material, the first of which is, akin to Jude 6, a play on the imagery of Gen. 6:1-4 and *1 Enoch* 6–10. Elsewhere in the letter, Peter's imagery is less obviously Enochic than that of Jude, and it may be that 2 Pet. 2:4 is therefore dependent on Jude as its primary source rather than specifically *1 Enoch*.[71] At the same time, Peter's articulation of the angels' situation remains beyond the Genesis testimony – the chained bondage, for example – and the imagery is likely still drawn from Enochian tradition, even if filtered through Judan spectacles. Like Jude, Peter does not explicitly name the sin of the angels, though is clear that they have sinned (2:4). Instead the emphasis is on the impending judgment that is to come, and the parallel salvation of the Noah family that will come as a result. The flow of the Genesis narrative continues into 2:5 with the fatal demise of the angels compared with the diluvian destiny of the world, and contrasted with the fate of Noah and his family as the righteous ones who are saved. Reference to the Flood may reflect its mention in 1 Peter, and the correlation there of the Watchers and Flood imagery (1 Pet. 3:19-20), but it remains a common motif within other Second Temple sources[72] and a convenient hortatory example. That said, Peter's retelling is generally commensurate with the Genesis record;[73] the reference to Noah as the 'herald of righteousness' may be absent from Genesis, but is not inimical to it, and likely reflects contemporary portrayal of him (cf. Josephus, *Ant.* 1:74-75 which affirms both Noah's missional zeal and his righteous character).

The salvation/destruction motif is reiterated in 2:6-10, once again by recourse to a Genesis-sourced comparison.[74] The sin of Sodom and

---

70   Callan, 'Jude', p.52.

71   Davids, *Letters*, p.225, though he notes that Peter knows Enoch material sufficiently well to remove the quotation of Jude 14-15.

72   *Jub.* 5:21-32; 3 Macc. 2:3; *L.A.B.* 3:4-11.

73   Davids, 'Pseudepigrapha', p.242, avers that 2 Peter's audience were likely more sceptical of pseudepigraphical traditions than were that of Jude, and Peter therefore keeps closer to the Genesis record.

74   Noah and the Sodom and Gomorrah narrative are similarly linked in *T. Naph.* 3:4-5.

Gomorrah is not specified in vv.6-7, but is implicitly explicated in v.10 in sexual terms. Peter follows Jude by expanding the Genesis narrative, but does so in different fashion, with its portrayal of Lot (2:7-9) perhaps the most significant departure from the canonical text. Bearing in mind Genesis' seemingly negative portrayal of him as one who offers the sacrifice of his daughters (19:8), Peter's choice of *him* as a positive exemplar, rather than the characteristically righteous Abraham, is somewhat notable. Further additions to the Genesis record include the reference to Lot's internal troubling (2:7-8), and the way in which, for Peter, Lot's salvation is not from the city dwellers, but only from the destruction that befell the city (though that aspect is, of course, partially found in the Genesis account – 19:14ff). The choice of Lot may be tied to Peter inheriting the Sodom paradigm from the Jude source, or may perhaps reflect a more positive reading of Lot as one who shows commendable hospitality akin to that of Abraham in Genesis 18.[75] Other possibilities include an allusion back to Abraham's prayer to save the righteous in Sodom (therefore including Lot – Gen. 18:23-32)[76] or the view that Genesis 19 actually portrays Lot in a positive light.[77] None of these explanations, though, obviously account for the emphatic, triple attribution of righteousness to Lot (2 Pet. 2:7-8), and it is likely that Peter is drawing on a tradition that already attributed righteousness to Lot (Wis. 10:6).[78] Peter's emphasis is not so much on retelling the familiar stories (Genesis or otherwise), but rather in demonstrating the salvation of a righteous one (Noah/Lot) from among the destruction of their contemporaries. Narrative 'accuracy' is subsumed by paraenetic or rhetorical interest.

The Genesis allusions in 2 Pet. 3:5-6 are more general, and less paraenetic than the earlier manifestations, and amount merely to thematic reference. Peter shows awareness of creation and flood imagery, potentially drawn from Genesis accounts, but there is not the exegetical punch that comes forth from the earlier references. The destructive water-fire sequence also alludes back to the Genesis imagery of 2 Pet. 2:5-6, the respective Flood/Sodom judgment episodes mapping onto the destruction outlined in 3:5-6. Where the Flood was the first world-destroying act of judgment, so a (new Sodom) fire-initiated action will be the next judgment of the godless (3:6).

75   So T. D. Alexander, 'Lot's Hospitality: A Clue to His Righteousness', *JBL* 104 (1985), pp.289–91.

76   So Bauckham, *Jude*, p.252.

77   S. Morschauser, '"Hospitality", Hostiles and Hostages: On the Legal Background to Genesis 19.1-9', *JSOT* 27 (2003), pp.461–85.

78   Related ideas are found in Philo (*Mos.* 2:58) and 1 Clement (11:1), but neither explicitly label Lot as righteous.

Conclusion

If there is, then, any overarching theme or focus to the use of Genesis in the Catholic Epistles, it is at a narratival level, rather than one premised upon formal quotation. Only James can be said to 'quote' Genesis. Familiar narratives are alluded to, or exemplary figures held up as role models, but the appropriation of them is 'very much the OT figures as interpreted in current Jewish haggadah'.[79] In all of the four epistles, one finds that the emphasis is on the interpretative tradition of the figure/image, rather than a precise exegetical exploration of the Genesis narrative. Where James reads Abraham as actually sacrificing Isaac, 1 Peter reads fallen angels Enochically transposed into the flood narrative of Genesis 6. Likewise, Jude and 2 Peter utilize imagery that is broadly drawn from the Genesis record, but shape it in directions found both in and beyond the canonical record; the depiction of the Genesis narratives is subsumed under the particular requirements of each NT author. Such a conclusion raises the question as to exactly what NT authors understood by 'Genesis' as *text* anyway, and whether Rewritten Bible text functioned in equivalent fashion to what has been subsequently identified as canonical Genesis.

79   Bauckham, 'James, 1 and 2 Peter, Jude', 306.

Chapter 10

GENESIS IN REVELATION

Steve Moyise

Introduction

The book of Revelation has been referred to as *The Climax of Prophecy* and various monographs have considered its use of such prophets as Isaiah, Ezekiel, Daniel and Zechariah.[1] However, the epithet is also an allusion to the fact that Revelation is the last book of the Bible, although it took many centuries for this to be recognized. Most of the early canon lists or manuscripts either omit the book altogether[2] or end with something else.[3] In the Eastern Church, it was not until the 11th century that it was established as the final book of the canon and it is still not recognized in the lectionary. For the Western Church, it was the festal letter of Athanasius in 367 CE and later endorsed by Augustine that secured its position and most people today would recognize the correctness of that judgement. In particular, the destruction of the serpent (Rev. 20:2, 10), the end of death (Rev. 21:4) and access to the tree of life (Rev. 22:2) form an *inclusio* with the disruption of Paradise in Genesis 3. Less prominent themes from Genesis are the imagery of Sodom and Gomorrah in Rev. 9:2, 14:10 and 18:5 and the important juxtaposition of the 'Lion of the tribe of Judah' (Gen. 49:9) with the slain Lamb in Rev. 5:5-6.

---

1   R. Bauckham, *The Climax of Prophecy: Studies on the Book of Revelation* (Edinburgh: T&T Clark, 1993); J. Fekkes, *Isaiah and Prophetic Traditions in the Book of Revelation: Visionary Antecedents and their Development* (JSNTSup, 93; Sheffield: JSOT Press, 1994); B. Kowalski, *Die Rezeption des Propheten Ezechiel in der Offenbarung des Johannes* (Stuttgarter Biblische Beiträge, 52; Stuttgart: Verlag Katholisches Bibelwerk, 2004); G. K. Beale, *The Use of Daniel in Jewish Apocalyptic Literature and in the Revelation of St. John* (Lanham: University Press of America, 1984); M. Jauhiainen, *The Use of Zechariah in Revelation* (WUNT, 2.199; Tübingen: Mohr Siebeck, 2006).
2   Marcion, Cyril, Synod of Laodicea, Apostolic Constitutions, Gregory of Nazianzus, Peshitta.
3   *Revelation to Peter* in the Muratorian Canon and Codex Claromontanus and *Sirach* in Epiphanius. See L. M. McDonald, The *Biblical Canon: Its Origins, Transmission, and Authority* (Peabody: Hendrickson, 2007), pp.445–51.

Tree of life, serpent and death (Genesis 2–3)

Tree of Life

After the introductory greetings and a description of the risen Christ, John records a series of messages or oracles to the churches at Ephesus, Smyrna, Pergamum, Thyatira, Sardis, Philadelphia and Laodicea. Each of these messages ends with a promise to the one who overcomes (ὁ νικῶν) and the first of these promises is to 'eat from the tree of life that is in the paradise of God' (Rev. 2:7). We are immediately reminded of Adam and Eve's expulsion from the Garden of Eden lest Adam 'reach out his hand and take also from the tree of life, and eat, and live for ever' (Gen. 3:22).[4] The text does not say why this would be a bad thing. It is clearly related to the couple's act of disobedience, which has led to הָאָדָם ('the man' or 'the human') knowing good and evil, but then that is also a characteristic of the heavenly beings: 'See הָאָדָם has become *like one of us*, knowing good and evil' (Gen. 3:22). Osborne says: 'In Gen. 3.22 the tree of life is the source of eternal life, so Adam and Eve must be banished from the garden lest they find immortality in the midst of their sin.'[5] However, Westermann cautions against such explanations. In his view, it is quite clear that the reference to the 'tree of life' in Gen. 2:9 is artificial ('Out of the ground the LORD God made to grow every tree that is pleasant to the sight and good for food, the tree of life *also* in the midst of the garden, and the tree of the knowledge of good and evil'). The conversations that follow in Gen. 3:3, 5 and 11 assume a single tree in the midst of the garden and the couple are banished for partaking of it. Gen. 3:22 tries to make sense of Gen. 2:9 but cannot alter the fact that the story has been about a single forbidden tree, in contrast to all the other trees. Had there been a special tree that bestows eternal life, it would surely have figured in the conversations.[6] Von Rad agrees but nevertheless tries to offer an explanation from the standpoint of the final form of the text. He says that the 'severe denial of eternal life also has a merciful reverse

---

4   The origins of a 'tree of life' are obscure. In the *Epic of Gilgamesh*, we hear of a 'plant held in secret by the gods that grants life to the one who grasps hold of its fruit' but this is referring to rejuvenation rather than immortality. Trees with magical powers are sometimes mentioned in Akkadian literature and appear on monuments, stelae and cylinder seals. And in a Mari wall-painting from the 18th century BCE, four streams with fish are depicted as emerging from a tree or plant held by two goddesses. See G. Luttikhuizen (ed.), *Paradise Interpreted* (Leiden: Brill, 1999); P. T. Lanfer, 'Allusion to and Expansion of the Tree of Life and Garden of Eden in Biblical and Pseudepigraphical Literature' in C. A. Evans and H. D. Zacharias (eds), *Early Christian Literature and Intertextuality* (JSNTSup, 391; London and New York: T&T Clark, 2009), p.96–108.

5   G. R. Osborne, *Revelation* (BECNT; Grand Rapids: Baker Academic, 2002), p.771.

6   C. Westermann, *Genesis 1–11: A Commentary* (London: SPCK, 1984), pp.271–8. He also challenges the translation 'eternal life', which suggests the Greek idea of immortality as a different mode of existence. The text simply means 'living on'.

side, namely, the withholding of a good which for man would have been unbearable in his present condition'.[7]

This is perhaps why the 'tree of life' is largely absent from the rest of the Old Testament. Four verses in Proverbs (3:18; 11:30; 13:12; 15:4) state that various aspects of the wise or righteous are like *a* tree of life, but the indefinite reference appears to mean 'like a living tree' rather than a specific allusion to the Genesis story. The same can be said for the Hebrew text of Isa. 65:22, where God's people are given the promise that they will be able to build houses and plant vineyards because their days will be 'like a tree', a reference to longevity. However, the LXX has made the comparison more definite: 'according to the days of *the* tree *of life* shall the days of my people be' (NETS). It is not difficult to see how this came about, for the context is of God creating a new heaven and earth (Isa. 65:19), where the 'wolf and the lamb shall feed together, the lion shall eat straw like the ox; but the serpent – its food shall be dust!' (Isa. 65:25). The latter is clearly an allusion to Gen. 3:14, which appears to have led the Septuagint translator to think of 'the tree of life' instead of the general reference.

There are significant references to the Garden of Eden in Ezekiel 28 and 31 and the Temple vision in Ezekiel 40–48 contains a miraculous river that waters a multitude of super-abundant trees (Ezek. 47:12). In Ezekiel 28, a lament is directed against the king of Tyre and draws on Eden imagery to highlight the extent of his fall:

> You were the signet of perfection, full of wisdom and perfect in beauty. You were in Eden, the garden of God; every precious stone was your covering, carnelian, chrysolite, and moonstone, beryl, onyx, and jasper, sapphire, turquoise, and emerald; and worked in gold were your settings and your engravings. On the day that you were created they were prepared. With an anointed cherub as guardian [or 'You were anointed as a guardian cherub' – NIV] I placed you; you were on the holy mountain of God; you walked among the stones of fire.
> (Ezek. 28:12-14)

There is nothing eschatological about this, but in the light of later developments it is interesting that Ezekiel connects the garden of Eden with priestly imagery. Thus the Genesis story mentions gold, bdellium and onyx (Gen. 2:12) but in Ezekiel, the occupant of Eden is adorned/covered with nine precious stones, which substantially coincide with Aaron's breastplate (Exod. 28:17-20). The connection was not missed by the LXX translator, who not only restored the original order of the stones but also supplied the missing three items. There is some debate as to whether the king is thought to be wearing such a garment or whether מְסֻכָה/ἐνδέω is to be taken figuratively.

---

7   G. Von Rad, *Genesis* (OTL; London: SCM, 1972), p.97. More positive still are the comments of B. C. Birch *et al.* in *A Theological Introduction to the Old Testament* (Nashville: Abingdon, 1999): 'The humans leave the garden with integrity, and are not described in degrading terms; they are still charged with caring for the earth' (p.57).

Either way, Eden's occupant is pictured as having some sort of priestly role. Furthermore, the precious stones are said to have been prepared or established (כוּן) on the day that he was created, so that priestly ministry was not an innovation in Moses' time but was present from the very beginning.[8]

The mention of a 'guarding cherub' is also reminiscent of the Genesis story, though Ezekiel's meaning is difficult to determine. The MT begins the clause with a feminine pronoun (אַתְּ), which is either an orthographic error for the masculine (אַתָּה :'you are...a guardian cherub') or should be re-pointed (אֵת) to agree with the LXX's μετά ('with'), so that the cherub is envisaged as a companion for the king. If the latter, it is possible that Ezekiel (or his source) envisages the cherub as remaining in Eden when the man was expelled, thus providing an explanation for the presence of the guarding cherubim in the Genesis story. Block mentions this as a possibility but he himself prefers to follow the MT's pronoun and identify the cherub with the king.

Lastly, Ezekiel speaks of the king being 'on the holy mountain of God'. This could mean that the garden of Eden is located on the mountain or that the two are being equated. If we take this as an allusion to Sinai and/or Zion, then cultic traditions are being associated with God's presence in Eden (graphically described in Gen. 3:8 as an evening walk in the garden). However, Block suggests that the reference is more general (as in Isa. 14:13) and refers to the assembly of the gods.[9] If so, then it is not specifically a priestly reference (in the Israelite tradition), although it is to do with the presence/location of the gods.

It is surely significant that while this lament mentions creation, perfection, Eden, garden, precious stones and a cherub, it makes no mention of the 'tree of life'. Indeed, the many differences suggest that Ezekiel is not simply interpreting the Genesis account but drawing on other traditions. This is supported by the reference to the 'cosmic tree' tradition in chapter 31. Pharoah is invited to consider the rise and fall of Assyria under the image of a great cedar tree.[10] Assyria's fame was such that 'no tree in the garden of God was like it in beauty' (Ezek. 31:8); it was the 'envy of all the trees of Eden that were in the garden of God' (Ezek. 31:9); and it will share the same fate as befell them (Ezek. 31:18). Allen thinks that Ezekiel is blending the well known 'cosmic tree' tradition (cf. Dan. 4:10-12; 1QH 6:14-18) with

---

8   That is not to say that Ezekiel is identifying the king of Tyre with Israel's High Priest. It is more that priestly associations are being read back into the Eden narrative. Indeed, many scholars now think that priestly ideas are present in the Genesis narrative. Referring to the garden, rivers, gold and precious stones, Gordon Wenham (*Genesis 1–15* [WBC; Dallas: Word Books, 1987]) says: 'These features all combine to suggest that the garden of Eden was a type of archetypal sanctuary, where God was uniquely present in all his life-giving power' (p.86). See also D. I. Block, *The Book of Ezekiel: Chapters 25–48* (Grand Rapids: Eerdmans, 1998), pp.99–121.

9   Block, *Book of Ezekiel*, p.114.

10   MT reads אַשּׁוּר ('Assyria') and is followed by all the versions. However, many commentators find this an impossible reading and believe an initial ת had dropped out from the noun 'cypress' (תְּאַשּׁוּר). Block (*Book of Ezekiel*, pp.184–5) supports the MT.

the 'tree of life' from Genesis but this seems unlikely.[11] It is hard to imagine Ezekiel including the 'tree of life' in his references to the envy and fate of the trees in the Garden of Eden. Block is nearer the mark when he concludes that Ezekiel's 'appeal to the garden of God/Eden carries little if any mythological baggage'.[12] It simply provides him with an example of a fruitful place or region, which is nevertheless surpassed by the reputation of Assyria.

The most significant reference to the Eden/Tree of life tradition is found in Ezekiel's New Temple section (Ezekiel 40–48). In chapter 47, Ezekiel is shown a vision of a river emerging from the Temple and flowing east, where it makes the stagnant waters (presumably the Dead Sea) fresh and full of 'every living creature that swarms' (Ezek. 47:9), an obvious reference to the first creation story. Then we read:

> On the banks, on both sides of the river, there will grow all kinds of trees for food. Their leaves will not wither nor their fruit fail, but they will bear fresh fruit every month, because the water for them flows from the sanctuary. Their fruit will be for food, and their leaves for healing.
>
> (Ezek. 47:12)

The relationship of this passage with the Genesis story is complex. Parallels include the wonderful fruit-bearing trees, a special river that waters them, and a particular reference to their fruit acting as food. On the other hand, there are many differences: Ezekiel does not refer to a particular 'tree of life', the river flows from the sanctuary, the fruit appears every month, and a particular role is given to the leaves. Nothing in the promise to the church at Ephesus suggests that John has this plurality of fruit-bearing trees in mind but when we turn to his vision of the New Jerusalem, we read:

> Then the angel showed me the river of the water of life, bright as crystal, flowing from the throne of God and of the Lamb through the middle of the street of the city.[13] On either side of the river is the tree of life with its twelve kinds of fruit, producing its fruit each month; and the leaves of the tree are for the healing of the nations.
>
> (Rev. 22:1-2)

The reference to a tree bearing fruit every month and the special healing property of its leaves confirms that he has Ezekiel 47 in mind. Indeed, many commentators suggest that John's singular reference to 'the tree of life' must be intended as a collective, since its location is said to be on 'either side of the river'. As Beale says: 'The one tree of life in the first garden has become

---

11   L. C. Allen, *Ezekiel 20–48* (Texas: Word Books), p.126.
12   Block, *Book of Ezekiel*, p.188
13   This is the most straightforward punctuation and followed by most modern translations. The alternative is to take the clause 'through the middle of the street of the city' as the start of the next sentence (so KJV).

many trees of life in the escalated paradisal state of the second garden...
But since these trees are all of the same kind as the original tree, they can
be referred to from the perspective of their corporate unity as "the tree of
life".'[14] On the other hand, it is noteworthy that the singular is used here, as
in the promise to the church at Ephesus, and also in its two further occurrences in Rev. 22:14 and 19:

> Blessed are those who wash their robes, so that they will have the right to *the
> tree of life* and may enter the city by the gates.
>
> (Rev. 22:14)

> I warn everyone who hears the words of the prophecy of this book...if any-
> one takes away from the words of the book of this prophecy, God will take
> away that person's share in *the tree of life* and in the holy city, which are
> described in this book.
>
> (Rev. 22:18-19)

It would seem that although John draws much of his imagery from Ezekiel
47, he does not want to lose the allusion to the singular 'tree of life' from
the Genesis account. It is not that Ezekiel transformed the singular tree of
life into a multitude of trees and John follows suit. All the evidence suggests
that Ezekiel only knew Eden traditions that spoke of a multitude of trees. His
contribution was to highlight their fruitfulness by stating that they bear fruit
every month and assigning a healing role to the leaves. He did not transform
the singular tree of life into a multitude of trees and nor does John. Rather,
John stands in the tradition where the elect will once again be granted access
to the tree of life in the (new) paradise of God:

> And I saw seven magnificent mountains...three of the mountains towards
> the east...three towards the south. And there was a seventh mountain in the
> middle of these, and in their height they were all like the seat of a throne, and
> fragrant trees surrounded it. And there was among them a tree such as I have
> never smelt...and its leaves and its flowers and its wood never wither; its fruit
> is good...very delightful in appearance...no creature of flesh has authority to
> touch it until the great judgement when he will take vengeance on all and
> will bring everything to a consummation for ever – this will be given to the
> righteous and humble. From its fruit life will be given to the chosen.
>
> (*1 En.* 24:3-12; 25:9-12)

> But think of your own case, and inquire concerning the glory of those who
> are like yourself, because it is for you that paradise is opened, the tree of
> life is planted, the age to come is prepared, plenty is provided, a city is built,
> rest is appointed, goodness is established and wisdom perfected beforehand.
>
> (*4 Ezra* 8:51-52)

---

14   G. K. Beale, *The Book of Revelation* (NIGTC; Grand Rapids: Eerdmans/
Carlisle: Paternoster, 1999), p.1106.

And he will open the gates of Paradise,
And destroy the power of the sword that threatened Adam.
And he will give the saints the right to eat from the tree of life,
And the spirit of holiness will be on them.

(*T. Lev.* 18:10-11)[15]

Thus it would seem that John is dependent on two different traditions that stem from the Genesis narrative.[16] The first is found in Ezekiel, where the trees in the garden of Eden have become so fertile that they produce fruit every month, are watered by a river that flows from the sanctuary, and whose leaves have special healing properties. The second envisages the elect feeding on the tree of life in the eschatological garden of God. Other trees are mentioned (*1 Enoch*) or assumed (*4 Ezra, T. Levi*) but it is only the tree of life that has the special life-giving properties. There is a third tradition, found in Proverbs and Psalm 1, where the characteristics of the wise or righteous are said to be like 'well-watered' or 'living' trees. This is developed in *Ps. Sol.* 14:3-4, where the holy ones are identified as the 'trees of life' (ξύλα τῆς ζωῆς ὅσιοι αὐτοῦ).[17] This could suggest a vision of a transformed Eden where the multitude of trees are the followers of Jesus who partake of the (singular) tree of life. However, there is no evidence that John took this step. What we can say is that John focuses on the tree of life, awkwardly mentioned in the Genesis account, and develops it by means of Ezekiel 47 and traditions about the elect feeding on it in the eschatological paradise of God.

The Serpent

Chapter 12 marks a new section of Revelation where attention turns to the cosmic battle that underlies events on earth. Drawing on a range of biblical and non-biblical sources,[18] John sees a woman about to give birth to a son whose destiny is to 'rule all the nations with a rod of iron' (Ps. 2:9). Opposing this stands a 'great red dragon, with seven heads and ten horns', poised to

---

15   D. Aune (*Revelation 1–5* [WBC, 52a; Dallas: Word Books, 1997], p.152) thinks this text is dependent on Revelation because the wording (καὶ δώσει τοῖς ἁγίοις φαγεῖν ἐκ τοῦ ξύλου τῆς ζωῆς) is very close to Rev. 2:7 (τῷ νικῶντι δώσω αὐτῷ φαγεῖν ἐκ τοῦ ξύλου τῆς ζωῆς).

16   So H. Wallace, 'Tree of Life', *ABD* 6:656-60.

17   The idea of a cosmic tree that unites heaven, the earth and the underworld (cf. Ezekiel 17, 31; Dan 4:10-12) takes a particular form in 1QH 6:14-18, where it is a metaphor for the community: 'They shall send out a bud [for ever] like a flower [of the fields], and shall cause a shoot to grow into the boughs of an everlasting Plant. It shall cover the whole [earth] with its shadow [and its crown] (shall reach) to the [clouds]; its roots (shall go down) to the Abyss [and all the rivers of Eden shall water its branches]' (trans. Vermes).

18   Biblical sources include God's battles with Leviathan in Job 26:13, Ps. 74:14 and Isa. 27:1. NA[27] also suggests Joseph's dream in Gen. 37:9 ('Look, I have had another dream: the sun, the moon, and eleven stars were bowing down to me'). The non-biblical parallels are discussed in A. Y. Collins' classic study, *The Combat Myth in the Book of Revelation* (HDR, 9; Missoula: Scholars Press, 1976). She concludes that the Leto/Apollo myth is the closest.

devour the child the moment it is born. When it is thwarted in this (the child is snatched away to God's throne), it turns its attentions first to the woman, who it seeks to kill by means of a flood, and then to her offspring (σπέρμα). Somewhat awkwardly, another story is told within this one: war breaks out in heaven and the dragon is thrown down to the earth. That is why it pursues the woman and her offspring with such venom; it knows that its time is short (Rev. 12:12).

Although an attack on a woman and her offspring might bring a faint recollection of Gen. 3:15 ('I shall put enmity between you and the woman, and between your offspring and hers'), it is the specific identification in Rev. 12:9 that is significant: 'The great dragon was thrown down, *that ancient serpent*, who is called the Devil and Satan, the deceiver of the whole world – he was thrown down to the earth, and his angels were thrown down with him.' Since the identification is repeated in Rev. 20:2,[19] just before its final destruction in the lake of fire is narrated, it is clear that John wishes to form something of an *inclusio* with the Garden of Eden story. The serpent in that story deceived Eve, has become the 'deceiver of the whole world' (Rev. 12:9), but will finally be destroyed in the lake of fire, bringing the whole sorry story of disobedience and rebellion to a close.

However, it is difficult to determine *how* John understood the relationship between the ancient serpent that deceived Eve and the dragon that is cast out of heaven. One solution, popularized in Milton's *Paradise Lost*, is that John is speaking of a primordial fall from heaven, as known in such texts as *1 En.*1–6, *2 En.* 29:4-5 (recension J), *Sib. Or.* 5:528-9 and *Adam and Eve* 13:1-2. Such an explanation is somewhat out of favour today but it has an advocate in Osborne. He notes its occurrence in the texts just cited and how the description of the dragon as a 'deceiver' who goes after the woman and her offspring closely parallels the language of the Genesis account. Furthermore, some sort of primordial fall seems to be presupposed in those texts where God is said to have fought Leviathan (Ps. 74:14), which in Isa. 27:1 is described as 'Leviathan the fleeing serpent, Leviathan the twisting serpent'. He also suggests that Jesus' saying recorded in Lk. 10:18 ('I watched Satan fall from heaven like a flash of lightning') is a reference to a past event (ἐθεώρουν) and is plausibly interpreted in the light of this tradition. On this view, John's contribution is to state that 'the accuser' (שׂטן, διάβολος) in texts like Job 1–2 (cf. Zech. 3:1-2) is also connected with the fall of the dragon and the work of the serpent.[20]

19   Rev. 12:9: ὁ ὄφις ὁ ἀρχαῖος ὁ καλούμενος Διάβολος καὶ ὁ Σατανᾶς;
       Rev. 20:2: ὁ ὄφις ὁ ἀρχαῖος ὅς ἐστιν Διάβολος καὶ ὁ Σατανᾶς.
20   Osborne, *Revelation*, p.472.

On the other hand, Caird insists that it is Christ's death and resurrection that triggers the dragon's expulsion from heaven and so John cannot be referring to a primordial fall. On this view, Michael's battle with the dragon is 'simply the heavenly and symbolic counterpart of the earthly reality of the Cross'.[21] This is supported by the song from heaven which declares, '*Now* have come the salvation and the power and the kingdom of our God and the authority of his Messiah' (Rev. 12:10). This is extended to include the martyrs who conquer the dragon 'by the blood of the Lamb' and the reference to the woman's offspring as 'those who keep the commandments of God and hold the testimony of Jesus' (Rev. 12:17) is clearly a reference to the church. A difficulty with this view is that the vision began by saying that the dragon 'stood before the woman who was about to bear a child' (Rev. 12:4), which appears to locate it on earth prior to the crucifixion. However, Caird believes that this objection is based on a fundamental misunderstanding of the imagery. The so-called 'birth' has nothing to do with Jesus' nativity but is a symbol of the cross. The woman is not Mary[22] giving birth to Jesus but the 'messianic community' ('the loyal people of God as they waited for their anointed king'[23]) 'giving birth' to the messianic victory. The dragon (in heaven) is seeking to destroy Jesus before he can take up his messianic reign and is thus a reference to Jesus' earthly trials and, in particular, his crucifixion. When it is defeated, it is thrown down to the earth and seeks to destroy the 'woman and her offspring', namely, the church.

In terms of geographical and chronological consistency, both views run into difficulties. If the primordial view is correct, then what is Satan (identified as the ancient serpent) doing in the heavenly council in Job 1–2? On the other hand, if the Christological view is correct, what is the serpent doing in the Garden of Eden when he is only thrown down to earth as a result of the cross? Osborne recognizes the difficulty and says that the 'telescoping of time in chapters 11–12 continues here, and all three "bindings" of Satan (in the primordial past, at the ministry and death of Jesus, and at the eschaton) are intertwined in chapter 12'.[24] What is certain is that John's identification of the serpent with the fallen dragon aims to bring the rebellion begun in Genesis 3 to a close: 'And the devil who had deceived them was thrown into

---

21   G. B. Caird, *The Revelation of St. John the Divine* (BNTC; 2nd edn; A. & C. Black, 1984), p.154.

22   In favour of the 'corporate' interpretation are the following: (1) The imagery of sun, moon and stars alludes to Jacob's dreams (Genesis 37) and is applied to the faithful in Num. 2:4; 9:14; Isa. 60:19-20; *Exod. Rab.* 15:6; (2) the unusual wording of 'she gave birth to a son, a male child' (ἔτεκεν υἱὸν ἄρσεν) in Rev. 12:5 points to Isa. 66:7 (ἔτεκεν ἄρσεν) and the following verse (ἔτεκεν Σιων τὰ παιδία αὐτῆς) is corporate; (3) the word used for her agony is βασανίζω, which is frequently used for the persecution of the faithful (60 times in 4 Maccabees) but never of birth pains; (4) protection in the wilderness evokes the people of Israel; and (5) the 'rest of her children' (Rev. 12:17) clearly refers to Christians ('hold the testimony of Jesus') and not to siblings of Jesus.

23   Caird, *Revelation*, p.149.

24   Osborne, *Revelation*, p.469.

the lake of fire and sulphur, where the beast and the false prophet were, and they will be tormented day and night for ever and ever' (Rev. 20:10).

Death

After the devil is thrown into the lake of fire, all the dead stand before the throne of God and are 'judged according to their works, as recorded in the books' (Rev. 20:12). That this includes all who have ever died is emphasized by the reference to 'small and great' and further by the sea and 'Death and Hades' both giving up their dead. This personification of death first occurred in the inaugural vision where Christ says, 'I was dead, and see, I am alive for ever and ever; and I have the keys of Death and of Hades' (Rev. 1:18). It then occurs as the name of the fourth rider in the opening of the seals, accompanied by Hades, the abode of the dead (Rev. 6:8). But the climax is that Death and Hades are thrown into the lake of fire, so that the heavenly voice can say of the New Jerusalem:

> See, the home of God is among mortals. He will dwell with them; they will be his peoples, and God himself will be with them; he will wipe every tear from their eyes. *Death will be no more*; mourning and crying and pain will be no more, for the first things have passed away.
>
> (Rev. 21:3-4)

This passage contains a number of allusions, most obviously to Ezek. 37:27 and Isa. 25:8.[25] But given the references to the tree of life and the ancient serpent, it is possible – probable even – that John also has Gen. 2:17; 3:3 in mind. The Genesis story is obscure since Adam and Eve do not immediately die upon eating the fruit, though the murder of Abel in Genesis 4 is perhaps intended as the beginning of its fulfilment. However, Paul can state that sin and death came into the world through Adam, without any need to justify it (Rom. 5:12-14), and John probably knows of such a tradition. Now that the ancient serpent has been thrown into the lake of fire, God will dwell with his people as in Eden, they will partake of the tree of life and death will be no more. The curse pronounced on creation in Gen. 3:14-19 has finally been lifted (Rev. 22:3). Revelation not only pictures a 'Paradise restored' but also a 'Paradise transformed'.

---

25   Ezek. 37:27: 'My dwelling place shall be with them; and I will be their God, and they shall be my people'; Isa. 25:8: 'he will swallow up death for ever. Then the Lord GOD will wipe away the tears from all faces, and the disgrace of his people he will take away from all the earth, for the LORD has spoken.'

Sodom and Gomorrah (Genesis 19)

The destruction of Sodom and Gomorrah in Genesis 19 became a byword
for judgement in the Prophets (Isa. 1:9; Jer. 23:14; Ezek. 16:46; Amos 4:11;
Zeph. 2:9) and was used by Jesus (Matt. 10:15) and Paul (Rom. 9:29), as
well as other Christian writers (2 Pet. 2:6/Jude 7). Sodom is named in Rev.
11:8 and alluded to in Rev. 9:2 ('and from the shaft rose smoke like the
smoke of a great furnace') and in those texts that speak of 'fire and sulphur'
(Rev. 9:17-18; 14:10; 19:20; 20:10; 21:8). The former has caused great
debate since its interpretation has a dramatic effect on the rhetorical function
of the book. In the vision of the two witnesses in Revelation 11, their
prophetic ministry is brought to an end by the beast, and their bodies are said
to lie in the 'great city that is prophetically called Sodom and Egypt, where
also their Lord was crucified' (Rev. 11:8). Although the use of 'prophetically'
(πνευματικῶς) suggests that the reference to where Jesus was crucified is not
'literal', it could be argued that the association of Jerusalem with Sodom in
such texts as Jer. 23:14 and Isa. 1:9 supports it. Ford adds that Jerusalem is
referred to as the 'great city' in the Sibylline Oracles (5:154), Josephus (*Ag.
Ap.*, 1:197) and Pliny (*Nat.* 5:14) and so John's reference 'cannot be other
than Jerusalem'.[26]

On the other hand, all the other references to the 'great city' in Revelation
16-18 appear to point to Rome or Roman power[27] and so Sweet is probably
correct that the reference is not geographical but refers to the 'social and
political embodiment of human self-sufficiency and rebellion against God',
which surfaced in Sodom, Egypt and Babylon in the Old Testament, and
Jerusalem and Rome in the present.[28]

The expression 'fire and sulphur' (cf. Ps. 11:6; Isa. 30:33; Ezek. 38:22;
Lk. 17:29) is used in a variety of ways in Revelation: it destroys a third of
humanity as it emerges from the horses' mouths (Rev. 9:17-18); it torments
the worshippers of the beast (Rev. 14:10); and finally it destroys the beast,
false prophet and devil in the lake of fire (Rev. 19:20; 20:10), along with
those loyal to them (Rev. 21:8). One might conclude from this that John is
simply using a stock phrase for judgement but Rev. 9:2 ('he opened the shaft
of the bottomless pit, and from the shaft *rose smoke like the smoke of a* great
furnace') seems to be a deliberate allusion to Gen. 19:28 ('he looked down
towards Sodom and Gomorrah and towards all the land of the Plain, and
saw the *smoke* of the land *going up like the smoke of a furnace*'). If 'Paradise
transformed' is an appropriate description of salvation in Revelation, then
'Sodom magnified' describes the destruction of all that would thwart it.

---

26   J. M. Ford, *Revelation: Introduction, Translation and Commentary* (AB, 38;
New York: Doubleday, 1975), p.180.
27   Particularly the reference to 'Babylon' in Rev. 16:19 (cf. 1 Pet. 5:13), sitting on
'seven mountains' in Rev. 17:9 and the luxurious list of imports in Rev. 18:11-13.
28   J. P. M. Sweet, *Revelation* (London: SCM/Philadelphia: Trinity Press, 1990),
p.187.

The Lion of Judah (Gen. 49:9)

A lion is a universal symbol for power and strength. It occurs over 150 times in the Old Testament, sometimes for the actual animal[29] but mostly as a metaphor for devouring enemies: 'Look, a people rising up like a lioness; and rousing itself like a lion! It does not lie down until it has eaten the prey and drunk the blood of the slain.' (Num. 23:24). Of particular interest are those passages that portray God as a lion, either fighting on behalf of Israel (Isa. 31:4; Jer. 50:44) or against her, as in Hos. 5:14: 'For I will be like a lion to Ephraim, and like a young lion to the house of Judah. I myself will tear and go away; I will carry off, and no one shall rescue.' However, it is the particular connection with Judah in Rev. 5:5 ('See, the Lion of the tribe of Judah, the Root of David, has conquered, so that he can open the scroll and its seven seals') that suggests a specific reference to Gen. 49:9:

> *Judah*, your brothers shall praise you; your hand shall be on the neck of your enemies; your father's sons shall bow down before you. *Judah* is a lion's whelp; from the prey, my son... he stretches out like a lion, like a lioness – who dares rouse him up? The scepter shall not depart from *Judah*, nor the ruler's staff from between his feet, until tribute comes to him; and the obedience of the peoples is his...he washes his garments in wine and his robe in the blood of grapes.
>
> (Gen. 49:8-11)

The text was widely understood as messianic[30] and John appears to draw on such traditions: Jesus is the messiah from the tribe of Judah who defeats his enemies in bloody battle and rules over them as Lord and King (Rev. 19:13-15; cf. 14:14-20). However, it is the juxtaposition of what John heard ('Lion of Judah') with what he saw ('a Lamb standing as if it had been slaughtered') that has been the focus of discussion. Resseguie puts it like this: 'The traditional expectation of messianic conquest by military deliverance (the Lion of Judah) is reinterpreted so that messianic conquest occurs through sacrificial death (the Lamb).'[31] This works well for Rev. 5:5-6[32] but is less convincing for the other 'battle' passages, for why does John include so much violence and bloodshed if his intention was to emphasise the non-violent nature of Christ's victory? For Bauckham, the answer is that the Book of Revelation has the form of a Christian war scroll:

---

29   Judg. 14:5; 1 Sam. 17:34; 1Kgs 13:24.

30   Targum (*Neofiti*; *Pseudo-Jonathan*); Midrash (*Gen. Rab.* 98); Qumran (1QSb 5:29).

31   J. L. Resseguie, *Revelation Unsealed: A Narrative Critical Approach to John's Apocalypse* (Leiden: Brill, 1998), p.34.

32   Although it is to be noted that the slaughtered lamb in Rev. 5:6 has 'seven horns and seven eyes, which are the seven spirits of God sent out into all the earth'. These would appear to be symbols of power and omniscience, respectively.

By reinterpreting the militant Messiah and his army John does not mean simply to set aside Israel's hopes for eschatological triumph: in the Lamb and his followers these hopes are both fulfilled and transformed. The Lamb really does conquer, though not by force of arms, and his followers really do share his victory, though not by violence.[33]

On the other hand, the parallel with John's use of 'Sodom' could suggest that John does wish to emphasise the bloody nature of the final victory. For Murphy, the spiritual victory was won on the cross but when Christ returns, he will 'exercise force against the partisans of evil (chapter 19) and will punish them as they deserve'.[34] Thus there is considerable debate as to whether readers are to understand Gen. 49:9 as fulfilled, reinterpreted or replaced.

Conclusion

Although it was many centuries before it was recognized, John's vision of the destruction of the ancient serpent and the saints partaking of the tree of life in an eschatological paradise where there is no more death or curse make Revelation a fitting conclusion to the biblical story. However, it is John's transformation of these stories that stands out. The actual details that he takes from Genesis are minimal compared with the sources that he uses to transform them. Thus what we learn about the tree of life or the serpent comes mainly from traditions such as Ezekiel and *1 Enoch*, although it is clear from John's use of *the* tree of life and *the* ancient serpent that it is intended as an interpretation of Genesis. But it would be difficult to argue that the serpent/dragon's battle with Michael or the tree's healing leaves are somehow 'inherent' in the Genesis stories. Rather, John is drawing on diverse traditions – including non-biblical sources – to offer his own vision of how the story begun in Genesis is to end.

There is perhaps more continuity in his use of the 'Sodom' and 'Lion of Judah' traditions. The former is used in a variety of ways but always to emphasise judgement and destruction; we might call it a 'heightened' or 'magnified' use of the imagery. The same could be said of the 'Lion of Judah', where Christ is not just superior to the other tribes of Israel but conqueror of the nations. However, most scholars think that the juxtaposition with 'Lamb' in Rev. 5:5-6 is intended as a major reinterpretation (Sweet) or even replacement (Caird) of such military hopes. If this is the case, then it belongs with John's interpretation of Genesis 2–3 rather than his use of the Sodom story. Again, it would be difficult to argue that the Lion's victory through voluntary self-sacrifice is somehow 'inherent' in Genesis 49. It is what has

33   Bauckham, *The Climax of Prophecy*, p.230.
34   F. J. Murphy, *Fallen is Babylon: The Revelation to John* (Harrisburg: Trinity Press International, 1998), p.193.

happened since that dominates John's visionary interpretations, although its starting point in Genesis is not forgotten. One might say that he is more influenced by the trajectory of interpretation than the actual texts. He is, after all, a visionary rather than a scribal exegete.[35]

---

35 A point particularly associated with C. Rowland, *Revelation* (London: Epworth Press, 1993). For the idea that John is more interested in 'trajectory' than 'originating source', see S. Moyise, 'Does the Author of Revelation Misappropriate the Scriptures?', *AUSS* 40 (2002), pp.3–21.

Index of Quotations and Allusions –
New Testament Order

Index of Quotations and Allusions – Genesis Order

INDEX OF MODERN AUTHORS